and nanny makes three

and
nanny
makes three

MOTHERS AND NANNIES
TELL THE TRUTH ABOUT
WORK, LOVE, MONEY,
AND EACH OTHER

jessika auerbach

ST. MARTIN'S PRESS
NEW YORK

www.stmartins.com

Library of Congress Cataloging-in-Publication Data

Auerbach, Jessika.
    And nanny makes three : mothers and nannies tell the truth about work, love, money, and each other / Jessika Auerbach—1st ed.
        p. cm.
    ISBN-13: 978-0-312-35598-2
    ISBN-10: 0-312-35598-X
    1. Working mothers—Psychology. 2. Working mothers—Attitudes. 3. Nannies—Psychology. 4. Nannies—Attitudes. 5. Child care—Psychological aspects.

HQ759.48 .A84 2007
306.874/3—dc22   2007008635

First Edition: May 2007

10   9   8   7   6   5   4   3   2   1

*a*LL OF THE NAMES have been changed. Internet Web sites may have changed or disappeared between when this book was written and when it is read. Further, the fact that an organization or Web site is referred to as a citation and/or a potential source of further information does not mean that the author or the publisher endorses the information the organization or Web site may provide or recommendations it may make.

To Jonathan

CONTENTS

I CANNOT DECIDE WHETHER writing this book was mostly sheer pleasure, above all a cathartic and deeply humbling learning experience, or principally an opportunity to probe, ask questions, and have profoundly personal, moving, and eye-opening conversations with countless wonderful and fascinating women. It was, I believe, in equal measure all of the above, and for this I owe thanks to many people: First and foremost my husband, Jonathan, who has been my unflagging supporter and coconspirator at every turn, and without whom my life would be empty, sad, and dull. My long-suffering children, who have patiently endured my many absences as I went away to explore my relationship with the women who have helped me look after them. My agent, Theresa Park, who has never allowed me to believe that this book would be anything less than brilliant. My editor, Sheila Curry Oakes, who has always understood what I was getting at even when I myself temporarily lost the plot, and whose patience and skill enabled her to extract coherence and meaning where there was none. All the nannies, au pairs, and babysitters who have ever worked for me, for—simply—doing what you do so I could do this. Shirley, for your extraordinary intelligence, tact, and wit, as well as your ability to make me not only a more organized person but also a better mother. And finally, all the women who so generously, honestly, openly, and unreservedly shared your thoughts and feelings about this pivotal relationship that we all share. This book could not have been written without any of you.

and nanny makes three

one mother
of a relationship

*t*HE RELATIONSHIP BETWEEN any working mother and the caretaker of her child involves some of the most intense, important, conflicted, and complicated interactions a woman is ever likely to have. Once a mother returns to work—full-time, part-time, anytime and anywhere—it's the one relationship that almost more than any other will keep her awake at night, make her furious, desperate, grateful, and guilty.

For a mother who both loves her children and needs her job, it's also often a relationship she wishes she would never have to have. Yet from the moment it begins, it becomes hopelessly and forever entangled with her view of herself, her love of her family, and her need to support them. In this way it becomes instantly and inextricably folded into the dialogue every mother carries on within herself, and with her partner, her colleagues, and her friends: If playground, cocktail-party, and book-group conversation is anything to go by, the topic of nannies, what they do to us and what we do to them, is right up there with talk about love, sex, and school waiting lists.

Many employers are blissfully unaware of this relationship, and contrary to what they might wish for, a new mother never returns to her job alone. She comes back changed in some fundamental way, having had to rearrange her priorities and her life, though hopefully not in a way that will affect her performance on the job. She brings a little of the homefront to the office—not only her child, but also the woman who does her other job with the kids at home, at school, or in day care. That other woman is her companion every day, and she has citizenship in her computer, briefcase, and cell phone, not to mention her head and heart.

Ironically, often the women acting as de facto mommy substitutes to the children of other working women have children of their own to love and raise. Nannies by any other name, they are also the children's caretakers and their mothers' alter egos, stand-ins, and understudies, replacements, enablers, employees, confidantes, friends, and rivals, sometimes hapless victims and not infrequently long-suffering heroines.

Those caretakers rarely have an opportunity to openly offer their perspective on this pivotal relationship, and how it affects them emotionally, socially, and economically. My research for this book makes abundantly clear that the majority of live-in or -out, full- or part-time nannies have no official training or special education in early childhood development. More often than not their training is the sum of their experience, and their qualifications amount to little more than highly subjective references from previous employers. As a result, the status of "professional" will forever elude them, but the irony goes deeper than that: For the minority of nannies in the United States who actually do have professional training as well as legal working status, life is often a constant and frustrating battle to prove they are not "just babysitters."

After all, why would any young woman in her right mind actually choose to waste a decent education by going one-on-one with another woman's children, in a home that's not her own, and in a situation where no matter how good she is at her job she'll always be relegated to playing second fiddle? Professionally trained nannies may be in great demand among parents who can afford to hire them, but those who actually see this job as a career and stick with it for more than a few years before starting their own families, or branching out into more lucrative jobs in other areas of the child-care business, are still far and few between. As a result it is simply an accepted part of life in our supposedly color-blind and egalitarian society that most nannies do their work without benefits in exchange for cash and while under the radar from both the INS (now known as the U.S. Citizenship and Immigration Services Bureau) and the IRS.

Because there is no nanny union, they are, at best, considered domestic workers engaged in unskilled labor. As such the prevailing attitude continues to be that anyone can be a nanny really, simply by virtue of being female. Rarely are they recognized as the essential and extremely hardworking nurturers of society's working capital and most valuable future asset. In this new millennium women might be more liberated than ever, but mothers who work as well as the caretakers of their children continue to be deprived of anything resembling true equality, both financially, socially, and in terms of their professional status—the argument so powerfully made by Ann Crittenden in *The Price of Motherhood*.

One would have to be a true curmudgeon to disagree with the old chestnut that "the children are our future," but that is also where the national consensus ends. Babies? Always adorable. Motherhood? Wholesome as apple pie. Nannies? A necessary evil, but please—let's not talk about them. In fact, for purposes of immigration, labor practices, human rights, and our view of ourselves as "good mothers," it's better for all concerned to simply pretend that nannies don't exist. But they exist, thank God, and we should all thank our lucky stars that they do. How else could mothers blaze trails up the traditionally male corporate ladder? Not to mention toil away in midlevel white-collar positions or menial blue-collar jobs, contributing the crucial funds their families need to get by.

We certainly don't have a coherent national child-care policy to thank for that. What few feminists other than Barbara Ehrenreich have dared to point out is that nannies and child-care workers of every stripe are the unwitting victims, underpaid enablers, and questionable beneficiaries of the inexorable drive of the American female to achieve equality in the workplace.

The old chestnut *is* true, of course, and children do represent our collective future, not only because they will reap what we sow, but also because every society's wealth is directly related to the level of education and skills attained by its future citizens. Yet the vast majority of those who change our children's diapers, read to them, take them to the park, wipe their dirty noses, kiss, hug, and lug them about appear in no country's GDP. In the lexicon of economists and politicians the world over, "nonworking" mothers are not considered productive in the traditional sense, and therefore might as well not exist. It goes without saying that the same applies to the legions of illegal or undocumented child-care workers in this country.

And yet there is an awful lot riding on those nanny backs, particularly considering that working mothers are very much a part of the economic equation. With close to 70 percent of American women with children under ten engaged in the workforce, motherhood has long been a far more complicated affair than happy and impeccably coiffed housewives in 1950s commercials once suggested. Someone has got to look after our children while their mothers are away contributing to the economy—nothing new about that. Nor is there anything new about the debate surrounding the myriad ways in which modern, emancipated, or simply hard-pressed mothers should struggle with finding the right balance between career and family. Sadly, it seems the debate among women is becoming more polarized rather than less, as dedicated full-time stroller pushers and briefcase-wielding amazons face each other down with the mutual battle cry of "*I'm* doing what's best, so get out of my way."

Similar to countless how-to manuals on shattering the glass ceiling, since the 1970s a steady stream of books has been published on all the tricks of surviving working motherhood—juggling, multitasking, delegating, part-timing, rearranging priorities, and so on. What is comparatively new, however, is a strange and growing disconnect between the economic and political realities of our generally accepted social contract, and the messages women are getting. The contract states— explicitly in all manner of legislation and implicitly in our expectations and hopes for our daughters—that of course women should work. Not only that, it's obvious they need to and want to, which is actually so old hat it doesn't even bear talking about anymore. The other message women are getting, however, is possibly even more powerful, and has an equally legitimate claim to our hopes and dreams.

This message—Raise Your Own Children—comes not just via the expertly packaged legion of child-care experts, but also increasingly from other women and mothers, spread via an entirely new genre of books and authored by mothers who have found their true calling. Occasionally with humor but just as often with missionary zeal, these mothers write about how all other successes, ambitions, and challenges in their lives paled into insignificance once they were faced with the trials and sweet rewards of raising their children. While there is nothing wrong with reveling in full-time motherhood, the economic realities of our increasingly work-obsessed culture means that fewer and fewer women can actually afford to focus solely on raising their own children, even if they wanted to. Inevitably, while they are at work, child rearing becomes someone else's job.

Women are continually extolled to go forth and be anyone's equal in any area of life; to ever seriously suggest otherwise would be a most grievous violation of our current social and political code of conduct. Yet there are equally righteous voices, echoing all around us in the media and of course in our own hearts, that we mustn't forget to bond with our children, not to mention *have* them while we're still fertile.

And once they're here, let's be clear: Children need their parents. And while children don't screw things up, parents, on the other hand, do.

Well, mostly mothers do, actually. The language in the most recent editions of parenting manuals by Dr. Spock, Penelope Leach, T. Berry Brazelton, et al., may have been sanitized to reflect a politically correct view of parenthood, but a close reading of these texts reveals that very little has actually changed. Mothers are still considered to be primary caretakers, and even if Daddy now changes more diapers than he used to, let's face it—nannies have rarely been hired to be father substitutes.

It is no wonder then that the relationships between mothers and the women they hire as nannies should be such a pressure cooker of love, ambition, need, and misunderstanding. Add money, thwarted expectations, the potential for exploitation, and often profound differences in culture, class, education, and language to the mix and the only thing that is surprising is that mothers and the "other mothers" of their children have until now largely conducted their relationships without any real emotional guidance or insight.

The drama, not infrequently pathos and occasionally tragedy, of the stories told to me by so many women on both sides of the mothering fence is extraordinarily compelling. Not only do they provide an often entirely unvarnished look at what goes on beneath the thin, public skin of so many families, they also draw out the myriad ways, often harsh quid pro quos, unspoken conspiracies, subtle deceptions, quiet desperation, and millions of small and large compromises that mothers everywhere make in order to have someone else take care of their children while they take care of business.

The issues raised through the stories told in each chapter rarely have a single, "good" answer. The only thing they will demonstrate for certain is that one mother's Mary Poppins may well be another's childcare poison, and vice versa. However, my intention is to focus on certain universal issues and examine the whole spectrum of nanny/mother relationships, so mothers will feel less alone in their struggle for a formula that works for them. As in any relationship, it can be powerfully revealing to get a sneak peek at what the other person sees when they look in the mirror, and painfully surprising to hear how some of the things we all do and say with perfect conviction and righteousness become entirely warped in translation.

The stories in this book are all real, and the voices of the women who tell them genuine. I've taken great care to change all names and other obvious identifying features, such as the nannies' nationalities and family status; the mothers' professions; the names, ages, and genders of their children; and their location or nationality. I spoke to many more women than I have room to recount in these pages, and while each voice was unique in the same way that each child is unique, there were many strong and similar underlying currents of passion, struggle, and uncertainty that emerged over time. I met the women—mothers, caretakers, and often both—through friends and acquaintances; by word of mouth; occasionally through classified ads; in Internet chat rooms; and of course on countless playground or park benches and wherever children and their grown-ups congregate. Once I introduced myself and explained my project, the women I approached very rarely refused to talk to me, and once begun, I can honestly say that not a single conversation was ever brief or dull. In some way everyone had a new and interesting perspective to contribute, and above all each had her own inimitable voice, which I've done my best to capture.

The situations in which the mothers and their substitutes—for lack of a better word—found themselves were all as individual as the personalities of the women involved. The deeper I delved, the more I found that there was rarely a categorical right or wrong. With a few glaring exceptions each woman would look to what she perceived to be best for the children for guidance in where to draw the all-important lines in the complicated relationship with their mother or caregiver, just as I myself have done: My own family has endured virtually every variation of child care imaginable, not to mention the other obligatory, groaning-bookshelf reading list of the "modern mother."

It was only after reading Dr. Spock's famous opening, "Trust your-self, you know more than you think you do," that my confidence be-gan to waiver. Since then it's turned into a full-scale topple. Turns out I was pretty clueless, and what I know now, of course, is that the whole "having it all" shtick was a dirty, rotten lie. What's more, it has become clear to me that to have little Dick and Jane in safe and lov-ing hands while I or any other mom is at the office, occasionally has consequences that are not only unforeseen but also heart wrenching and deeply controversial in both a moral and ethical sense. Most im-portant, my view of how the catalyst of a child (or four, in my case) affects the relationships between women (never mind between hus-band and wife) has changed dramatically. Straightforward? Never. Honest? Rarely. Respectful? Sometimes. Intense? Oh, let me count the ways . . .

Above all, what I hope readers will take away from this book is this: Given the child-care options currently available to American women, having a nanny (legal or not) does not make any mother a pariah or a saint. I hope, too, that hearing the voices and stories of others who have made the same or different choices will make each reader more sympathetic to "the other side," or even to her own, and therefore bet-ter able to manage those issues that will inevitably arise. If reading this book leaves a mother—or a nanny—feeling more confident and com-passionate, and less guilty or resentful, and encourages her to step a little further out of the closet where this all-important relationship is concerned, then *And Nanny Makes Three* will have achieved its ob-jective. Not surprisingly, achieving it has much to do with my own ex-perience and a need I have perceived, not only in myself but in so many others, to synthesize what I have learned. Probably the most im-portant realization has been that the amount of emotional energy, fi-nancial resources, and sheer thinking time that I have expended on my relationship with the women who look after my children while I am gone is equal to none. Rather predictably, my husband has often complained that he comes a distant third, or perhaps I should say sixth: first the children—one, two, three, and four—then the nanny, and dead last: Papa.

the agony and irony of choice

PICTURE THIS: a supermarket cart filled to the brim, rush hour, a racing clock, a madly beating heart, a screaming, wild-eyed toddler writhing in his seat. People stare; tiny fists flail; a Baby Gap Velcro sneaker is ripped off and flung at the head of the cashier. You struggle to smile, but really what threatens to burst out, in an earth-shattering howl of "Enough!" is the rage, humiliation, and desperation churning just below the surface. This is a moment when your instinct is to drop everything and run, but still you carry on, grab the child, fumble with the bags, and where are the car keys? This is a moment when you would give anything—anything—for someone else to be pushing that shopping cart. "Oh God," you think, "where is the nanny, someone, anyone to take this child off my hands before I go absolutely stark raving mad?"

It's every mother's guilty secret that occasionally she wishes she could be anywhere on the planet rather than with her child. The smiling faces of lovely, well-behaved toddlers on the cover of *Parents* magazine, so provocatively displayed around the checkout counter, tell a different story, though. Shouldn't we all *want* to be our child's principal, full-time caretaker? Nurturing, teaching by example, staying calm when all hell breaks loose, exuding an air of saintly tolerance and Mary Poppin'esque control over the uncontrollable? It's only in our darkest moments that we admit to feeling positively murderous and full of a terrible rage toward our children. Anything, anywhere but this. Oh God, please, send me someone who can be the best of me at home while I'm away at work. Someone who is like the good mother I usually am, not the evil stiletto-heeled career woman who resorts to thoughts of infanticide in moments of stress and humiliation . . . Only bad, bad mothers could possibly have these thoughts.

Or could they? In fact, Adrienne Rich was the first to describe this perfectly human and entirely ordinary set of circumstances in her groundbreaking work *Of Woman Born,* written more than a quarter of a century ago. Unfortunately, Rich's insight that exclusive mothering by mothers is neither straightforward nor natural, nor even necessarily beneficial to either child or mother, has yet to make it onto the cover of *Parents* magazine. Nor, I suspect, will it ever.

Instead, in this twenty-first century no one is more conflicted about all the choices we theoretically have than the women who supposedly have them. This is particularly true given that these choices can often exist only at another woman's expense: those nannies, sitters, au pairs, and day-care workers whom we so desperately need but simply can't help exploiting (read: Pay as little as possible; expect more than is reasonable) if we are to have affordable child care. Without the nanny or the babysitter how could we ever be expected to fulfill our own destinies and those that society prescribes for us, as well as those of our increasingly achievement-programmed children?

But it's not so clear-cut. Yes, child-care arrangements are critically important to the smooth running of the hugely complicated machine that is any working family, but a closer look at the issue brings forth many difficult and often unanswerable questions. Such as: What is the value of one child's life over another? Or: Does a brilliant education automatically entitle a woman to an equally brilliant career? Or: Is every child actually entitled to his or her mother's exclusive love and attention?

Obviously the mother/nanny relationship is far from new. Nannies and mothers have grappled and dealt with one another for centuries, but with lines clearly drawn between the upstairs and the downstairs, and only the children moving freely across the divide. Mary Poppins is, of course, the archetype of the perfect nanny. Practically perfect in every way, particularly in the freedom her iron rule of the nursery affords her employer, Mrs. Banks, to indulge in her cause du jour of marching alongside the suffragettes in a pretty yellow dress and fetching sash. In every other way, however, Mary Poppins is really rather awful and unsympathetic—efficient perhaps, but also stern, unforgiving, humorless, and entirely lacking in the affectionate cuddle-and-giggle department. If it weren't for the fact that she could slide up bannisters and take Jane and Michael to magical places with racing carousel horses (accompanied by the irresistible Dick Van Dyke), I'm not too sure many mothers would hire her today.

In this century the once crystal clear line between mother and nanny is little more than a halfhearted smudge, no longer straightforward and heavily loaded with issues that have acquired the unpleasant patina of being politically incorrect or simply indefensible. Of course women have the right to work (not to mention, increasingly, the financial imperative). Naturally everyone's right to fair and equal treatment is inalienable regardless of race, gender, nationality, or religion. Without question education should be available to all, as should opportunity and the rewards of success. Would anyone really be so foolish as to question these things? In these ways all women are held up to be sisters, each with the same inherent potential as the next. The sad truth is that if we ever admitted to ourselves that inequality persists, racism continues, and money matters more than education (and that's just between women!) we'd truly be up the proverbial creek, and no working mother could ever go back to her job with a clear conscience again.

The truth is for the most part that most working mothers do the best they can, given the hand they are dealt. They want to be able to pursue the careers they were trained for and love, earn the money their families need, and somehow make sure their children are safe and taken care of in the best possible way while they are pursuing those goals. There is nothing wrong with that—but there are most definitely better and worse ways of doing it.

As Barbara Ehrenreich and Arlie Hochschild have pointed out in *Global Woman: Nannies, Maids, and Sex Workers in the New Economy*, feminism—and, by implication, modern motherhood—has in many ways reached a critical point. There is undoubtedly an unintended and bitter irony in the notion that those who live out the reality of the movement started by Betty Friedan and Gloria Steinem can do so only because of the availability of child care—which is not infrequently provided by nannies from poorer nations who have children of their own.

The notion that women with careers callously trample their less fortunate sisters in order to catch up with the men who still rule the world is a neat argument, but it is also a spurious one, for what else are we to do? True equality in the workplace may be inching closer, but it is no longer something I expect to see in my lifetime. I'm simply too tired and too busy with running our family's life to get particularly worked up about it anymore. What it boils down to is a new and impossible arithmetic, where the once joyous and triumphant notion of "having it all" seems to have quietly morphed into the vaguely threatening and barely sustainable state of "doing it all, or else." To be sure, the or elses are nothing to sniff at. Wherever we turn there are voices telling us: Spend quality time with your children, or watch them grow into social misfits. Make sure they are intellectually stimulated, mentally challenged, and educated every moment of the day, or forget about sending them to a decent college. Don't pressure them too much, though, or you'll watch them buckle under the weight of bloated expectations. Know where they are every minute of every day, or they'll end up addicted to drugs, smoking cigarettes, engaging in unprotected sex, or, God forbid, falling prey to weirdo Internet predator freaks. Set an example, be playful, don't forget plenty of affection, but also be honest, serious, and morally upstanding. Oh, and don't forget to pre-pare nutritious and balanced meals, make sure they exercise and brush their teeth twice daily to optimize their chances at long and healthy lives, and please check their heads for nits with a fine-tooth comb at least once a week. Phew! The question, it seems, is no longer, What's a parent (sorry, mother) to do? but rather, Is there anything we can af-ford *not* to do?

Sociologist Sharon Hays sums up this phenomenon rather bril-liantly in her book *The Cultural Contradictions of Motherhood*, as does Judith Warner in *Perfect Madness*. Both point out with increasing desperation that rather than earning working mothers a break, more success at work leads to ever greater expectations on the home and family front, particularly in the hands-on way we mother our children. Whatever one chooses to call it, the numbers don't add up. Having studied countless women's and parenting magazines and books, it seems to me that in each twenty-four-hour day every mother, working or not, is expected to find at least six hours of "quality time" for her children (refer to paragraph above for breakdown). Then, of course, she's got to put in ten hours of "dedicated focus" at work, devote two hours to "being sexy for her mate," put in at least two hours of "domes-tic drudgery," find one hour of "me time" for an aromatherapy bath, spend two hours commuting, and fit in one hour to power nap and an-other to exercise, as well as engaging in some useful philanthropic ac-tivity to "give back to the community." Doesn't add up? Yes, it does. If we stop and do the math, more often than we care to admit, what it adds up to is hiring a nanny or cobbling together some other form of child care, and feeling guilty and overwhelmed by the whole impos-sible mess.

Coparenting is as much a myth now as it ever was, and probably ever will be—with wonderful, heartwarming exceptions to the rule, of course. Every statistic confirms what we (well-educated, once fervent feminists) already know and resigned ourselves to once we had children: Mothers still change most of the diapers, get up at night, consult the pediatrician, and hire, fire, pay for, and deal with the nanny. For some this is a sad litany and cause for much resentment. But for many others it's a way to maintain some control over things they feel no one else could ever do as well—like being mothers to their children. In my own marriage, after four children and a couple dozen or so nannies, au pairs, babysitters, teachers, and various other helpers, my husband and I have finally reached a weary equilibrium. We each carry our part of the load and know without saying it that neither could get through it all without the other. At least not while maintaining our sanity, self-respect, and humor, as well as our capacity to love one another and the children. Through all of it an indisputable part of my load—and that of virtually every other woman I know and have spoken to about this—is to find, deal with, develop, and sometimes end the relationship with the woman whose job it is to look after our children.

I'm certain it isn't only in my heart and mind that there exists a large and dimly lit room, right next to the one Virginia Woolf so famously wrote into the consciousness of every thinking woman, mother or not. It is a room where one treads carefully for fear of upsetting the furniture; where one might hate the decor and knick-knacks on the mantelpiece but dare not touch them; where one feels like an intruder, sometimes welcomed as a friend and reviled as Boss, all at the same time. It's a room that is as much part of my house as the kitchen or the den where the children play, yet only I know exactly how to get there, how big it is, and how often it needs dusting, fresh flowers, or a good airing and occasional total slash-and-burn makeover. This is the room where the nanny lives, and this is the room where this book was written.

the other
extramarital affair

THERE HAS NEVER BEEN a shortage of advice on how to deal with the boss (male or female), the boyfriend, the lover and husband, and, of course, the female friend, whether sister, mother, or daughter. All of the relationships, in short, that form us, challenge us, sustain us, and occasionally drive us to the self-help shelf or the advice column. All these relationships, in all their diversity, are essentially between equals or involve situations where the lines are fairly clearly drawn, either in terms of gender, generation, or authority. They are also legitimate relationships that most everyone, at some point in their lives, has to grapple with in order to grow up or to move on.

The strange and often tortured tie that binds a mother to her nanny, however, is none of those things—or perhaps more accurately, it is all of them. Yes, there is a boss and an employee, but no mother I know can bring herself to describe the woman who takes care of her children merely in those terms. Yes, it is a relationship between equals in the sense that usually both are women and often both are mothers, but clearly that is where the equality ends.

Not only am I the mother of four daughters who range in age from five to fourteen, but I am also one of five daughters myself. For my sisters and me the birth of our one and only brother was an exception-proves-the-rule kind of event, and the world in which we all grew up seemed in every way to be made up principally of and for women. There was never the slightest doubt in my mind that I could and would be permitted and encouraged to do whatever I wanted, as long as I had a bit of talent and was willing to work hard. Reading the obligatory feminist tracts of my generation at university simply put into words all the things I felt and already knew in my bones. Once I graduated, married, and began my career as an editor in a New York publishing house, the fact that I might not be able to Do It All while simultaneously having lots of wonderful children and climbing steadily up the career ladder simply never occurred to me. What is more, relationships between me and the women in my life—colleagues, employees, sisters, all—would continue to be straightforward, honest, respectful, and equitable, always. How could they not?

The children are, of course, ours, not just mine. My husband is a very involved and loving father, as are a good majority of the other men of our generation of tail-end baby boomers. Together we read about the sordid custody fight between Mia Farrow and Woody Allen (fellow New Yorkers, after all), and took particular note when one of the reasons Woody didn't get the kids turned out to be that he couldn't tell the judge the names of his children's friends, the phone number of the pediatrician, nor the schedule and details of their afterschool activities. Since then my husband has always passed the Woody Allen test with flying colors, even though this is largely courtesy of the exhaustive lists of phone numbers, schedules, and names I've provided for him. Above all he knows the children intimately, loves them profoundly, and is often much better at helping them work through their problems than I am. Were it not such a ridiculous and outdated stereotype I would put this down to his ability to be more analytical in situations where an overabundance of emotion tends to make me irrational. . . .

Yet, when it comes to arranging child care for our daughters I have found that I am far from alone in mysteriously reverting to the gender stereotypes that our mothers sought to banish. I . . . obsess. After all, this is another woman doing things I probably ought to be doing! My husband . . . manages. After all, he is a management consultant, and the nanny is someone who works for us in return for a fair salary. He even wrote a contract with clearly phrased clauses, rules, and expectations, along with a convenient blank to insert a name and date. The only women who don't roll their eyes at the mention of this contract are my lawyer friends. Of course, as legal professionals they can be excused for trying to codify a relationship whose success depends on so much more than respecting the rules. One thing I know for sure is that if they felt they had to, ultimately they'd either break or ignore them just as much as everyone else. This, as we all know, is a contract like no other, and if violating some part of it means that our children are better off most of us wouldn't miss a beat in order to break a rule.

Clearly we are not alone. As Naomi Wolf admits in *Misconceptions: Truth and Lies On the Way to Motherhood* that after the birth of her first child she felt marooned and lonely in her new suburban home, trying to be a proper mother to her baby while her husband went off to the office. When she finally succumbs to the fact that she needs child-care help in order to resume her writing career, it is she alone who interviews potential nannies, and she alone who shares the care of her baby with the woman whom she eventually hires—at least during the day, while her husband is at work. Finally, it is her own relationship to this nanny that leads her to expound, briefly, on the hypocrisy inherent in this country's immigration policies and labor regulations in the child-care industry.

There is, of course, even for the most passionate, learned, and principled of feminists, a first time for everything—you hear about it from your mother, your sisters, and your friends; you vaguely know the statistics, the stories, the harsh facts, and the clichés. But still, when it happens to you it's a revelation, and as unique, new, miraculous, and painful as anything anyone has ever experienced. On top of the list there's love and sex, of course, but right after that there's childbirth and motherhood. Some people are incapable of change, no matter how earth-shattering the experience. For others these experiences carry with them the unexpected power of transformation, and I wouldn't be the first—nor certainly the last—to consider doing things for the sake of my children and family that never would have crossed my emotional or moral radar screen in an earlier, childless life.

I know I'm not alone in rarely stopping to consider the actual cost of having children on my husband's career versus my own. As Gloria Steinem so famously said, Whoever heard of a man having trouble with combining children and career? If child care was needed, in my mental calculation it would always—and still does—come out of the financial and emotional resources that are part of my contribution to our marriage. In reality, of course, the money we both make goes into the family pot, where it all gets stirred together and is ultimately dispensed without any regard to its origin. But that isn't the point. There is a mental spreadsheet tattooed onto my brain (and that of many women) that balances just what I earn against the cost of our child care, and neither logic nor fairness has much to do with the way the outcomes are calculated.

Where does this self-inflicted inequity come from? To be sure, at first my husband and I shared the nighttime feedings and 3:00 A.M. diaper changes, but very soon that simply ceased. Not, I hasten to add, because he wasn't willing (though he was grateful when I let him off the hook). No, it was simply because there was a part of me I hadn't known before suddenly rearing its head from the primeval bog of my XX-chromosome gene pool. It had me convinced that only I (mother, daughter, feminist!) could do these things properly, and in the way that my own baby daughter needed it. If someone else should be brought in to do it in my stead, I would have to be the one to pay for it, both literally and figuratively.

Blame it on biology, but not much later and ever since, I and countless other women have applied the same principle to choosing the nannies and sitters for our precious, most wonderful, and infinitely loved children. If there has to be an alternative to me (though of course no one could ever provide the unconditional love that I provide), well, she'd better be nothing short of "supercallifragillisticexpiallidotious"!

So where do fathers fit into all of this? Good question. Most likely they spend little or no time worrying about the nanny, what kind of mood she's in today, or the trouble she might be having with her boyfriend. Nor are they making unspoken deals on those mental spreadsheets, like, "If I quit bugging her about coming in ten minutes late every morning, then maybe she won't complain when I ask her to empty the dishwasher. . . ." The truth is, if the relationship with the children's caretaker were principally between a nanny and the male parent, at least three How to Manage manuals would have been published by now. They would be complete with sample contracts, sliding-scale salary calculations, performance indicators, and creative ways to provide incentives and maintain employee morale.

The sentence that keeps ringing in my ears time and time again when I try to talk to my husband about child-care issues is, "Well, let's just get somebody else!" Or, equally as absurd and laughable: "Just tell her to come in on time from now on. What's the big deal?" The deal, of course, is very, very big indeed, because the quid pro quo mothers expect from their nannies has to do with so much more than being punctual and orderly. Fathers, husbands, boyfriends, and partners do, occasionally, appear in *And Nanny Makes Three*. Neither as a writer nor as a mother would I ever underestimate their importance in a child's life. Nor do I pretend that the business of parenting is an exclusively female domain, with the father occasionally present merely as disciplinarian and role model. However, the whole point about the relationship this book sets out to explore is that it seems to exclude the male sex almost by definition.

What we long for in a nanny today—part-time, full-time, anytime— is very different from the qualities that made Mary Poppins such a prize catch for the Banks family on Cherry Tree Lane. What I really want is for someone who can, at least some of the time, be my partner in the messy and complicated arena of loving and caring for my children. Not an entirely equal partner, though—I am the Mother, after all!—but someone who is a sort of distorted mirror image of myself, better than I am at some things, and definitely worse at others. Someone dependable, discreet, affectionate, smart, kind, and, last but not least, affordable. In short, what I really want is the perfect mistress.

Over the years, as my children have grown older and we have attempted almost every imaginable type of child care, it has often struck me that the relationships I have had with my various nannies and babysitters have resembled nothing so much as a string of semi-illicit, extramarital affairs. While never a secret, each was somehow a furtive bond involving need, love, intimacy, secrecy, power, and money, as well as the unmentionable issues of class and race. That these relationships—for me and so many other mothers—are primarily between women makes the topic all the more interesting.

from nanny virgin to
serial monogamist
child-care relationship junkie

BECAUSE I'VE STRUGGLED with what kind of mother I want to be every bit as much as millions of women all over the world, it will come as no surprise that the writing of this book and the gathering and interpretation of the stories in it has been a deeply personal experience. In addition to growing up with many sisters and other opinionated women, I have also had the great fortune to have lived all over the world, both with and without children (three of my four daughters were born on different continents). In my life as a mother, and certainly as a writer, this has been both a blessing and a curse, allowing me to be an outsider and observer constantly on the edges of almost—but not truly—belonging.

To me the story isn't complicated at all, but to anyone who has lived all their life in one country it can seem quite exotic. My family is from and remains in Germany, where I spent a large part of my child-hood. My parents divorced when I was ten, and my mother, brother, one sister, and I moved to England, where she married an American writer and editor of a small literary magazine. German is my first language, as is my passport, but I certainly don't feel German. Neither have I ever felt free to feel English, despite the fact that when I think of those critical formative years between ages ten and twenty, they resemble nothing so much as a map of the London Underground.

As a student I managed to spend a year in Paris learning French, while babysitting and tutoring English to get the francs for my daily baguette. I met my American husband in our final year at university back in England, and after graduating together we moved to New York City for our first "real" jobs. Since that time we've spent a good part of our lives together in the Netherlands and Hong Kong, and even an ill-fated five-year attempt at being all grown up with four kids, two dogs, and a house on the outer fringes of Mega-City USA commuter country. Currently we are all still recovering from our latest move back to Asia, Singapore this time, where my daughters attend an American school with children of fifty-two other nationalities, and are growing up as "third-culture kids." In short, the only thing that seems safe and truthful to say is that regardless of where we are, we're not from there. If pressed, I would have to say that home is where my husband and children are—the sort of trite answer that means everything and noth-ing. In truth, culturally and socially there is no such thing as home for me. I'm like a well-built tree with shallow roots: Plant me anywhere, and chances are that before long I'll somehow blend in with the scenery and pick up the local accent.

Twenty years ago, as a freshly minted graduate with the world at my feet, I never dreamed it would come to this. Today I am forty-something, married with children, and currently "corporate commu-nications director (not active)," as the performing arts organization on whose board I serve so diplomatically states in my bio. What this also signals to those in the know is that I am currently unemployed, at least in the sense that I do not officially work "outside the home." People assume that once upon a lifetime I might have had a corporate career, but for the foreseeable future my career is my children. It was not supposed to be this way.

When I resigned from my first "proper" job at the age of twenty-seven, happily married and ecstatically pregnant, we decided to move to Europe for an opportunity that had come up with my husband's firm. For me, having grown up and gone to school all over the European map, this seemed like an entirely natural transition, nothing more than a temporary lull in my career. I'd have the baby, maybe start working on a book, learn a new language, do a few translations, that sort of thing. I saw it as not so much a break as a temporary sabbatical.

So in 1992 baby number one was born in the Prinsengracht Ziekenhuis, Dutch style: wracked by contractions I walked to the hospital along the canals, had the baby a few hours later, and walked home again the next morning with her strapped to my bosom in a baby carrier. My husband had been there, of course, huffing and puffing à la Lamaze, holding my hand and doing his valiant best to cut the cord with what seemed like a pair of blunt nail scissors. Neither of us thought for a moment what an unusual way this was to have a baby, particularly as the Dutch government sent a lovely midwife to our flat every day for two weeks postpartum. Her job was to teach us everything one needs to know to properly take care of a newborn—or to do laundry and get groceries, if that's what was needed. When she stopped coming we felt exhausted, exhilarated, and slightly terrified, but prepared.

This, as all fairy tales must, is where the fable of sailing through pregnancy and into motherhood comes to an end. It didn't take me long to realize that being alone all day with the baby was driving me nuts. With the inevitable naïveté of an eager and righteous first-time mother, I thought that a few hours of help here and there would be all

I'd ever need. I was beginning to feel rather smug about giving birth without any kind of pain medication (never again!), and loved to tell the tale of walking to the hospital and back home again the next morning with the baby. Nothing to it! Superwoman! The only thing I'd needed was for someone to carry my baggage to the hospital and back.

So in the way that momentous things often begin with one small and seemingly insignificant step, there followed my first encounter with a babysitter. I remember her well: She was an illegal eighteen-year-old immigrant from the Philippines named Catherine, who responded to an advertisement we had placed in the paper. She took my baby to the park for a couple of hours three times a week while I shopped, cleaned the house, caught up—and missed my daughter desperately.

Catherine did her job quietly and competently, in the practiced manner of an older sibling. One day, as many new mothers no doubt secretly long to do, I thought about following her to see where she went and what she did with my infant daughter. Did she talk to her the way I would have? Did she make sure the baby was always warm and dry? Was she really doing everything that I had so specifically instructed? Was there any bonding going on? And what did that mean, anyway?

Ultimately I decided against playing detective, feeling guilty and sheepishly paranoid. But with one thing leading to another I continued to wonder: Were we paying her enough? Where did she really go when she left for home at night? Who exactly was the mysterious uncle she was living with? Was it any of my business? Should it be? And then, that nagging question—would it be acceptable to ask her to do a teeny-weeny bit of the housework during the day, despite the fact that I'd explicitly hired her as a babysitter? After all, the going rate for cleaning women was quite a bit more than the hourly rate Catherine was getting.

It seemed the better part of valor not to probe too deeply. Instead I focused on the fact that the arrangement we had, as informal and short-lived as it was, served both our needs. After all, it was merely a cash transaction, where a payment was made in exchange for a service expertly performed, was it not? I always gave her a little extra, and paid for a taxi after dark. What could possibly be wrong with such an arrangement?

Our conversations in broken English focused on the one, and clearly the only, thing we had in common: the baby. What sweet things she had done that day, how many diapers she had filled, and how her lopsided smile seemed to come out whenever she saw a particular toy. All that, for seven guilders per hour. Just like the MasterCard commercial says: The rest? Priceless. Unbeknown to me, this short-lived encounter with Catherine clearly marked the beginning of my transformation from child-care virgin into serial monogamist child-care relationship junkie.

One day Catherine simply failed to show up in the morning. Not knowing where to find her, I found other sitters: The first was Johanna, a Bible-thumping milkmaid with blond braids who was reliable but about as cuddly as a Gouda cheese. After her came Tsivia, a chronically late teenager who had recently immigrated from Israel with her family. She immediately got the baby purring like a kitten, but had the disconcerting habit of taking her for walks and disappearing for hours on end. She ultimately stopped working for me to start training as a security guard for El Al at Schiphol airport. "Good money, and lots of travel!" she told me cheerfully, as she quit with one day's notice—as if this made up for the fact that I now had to scramble for someone else to help with the baby while I planned, packed, and organized for our return to the United States in three weeks.

Not long after this I found myself sitting on a mattress on the floor, surrounded by our life's possessions, waiting to be unpacked into the minute closets of a cramped brownstone walk-up. With my daughter crawling around eating dust balls, for the first but definitely not the last time I wondered: How the hell am I supposed to manage all this: plan and supervise her toddler life, look for and actually do some decent work, and not kill my husband in the process? The answer was, and has been ever since: If I could possibly help it, or afford it even if it ate up almost everything I earned, Not By Myself.

love

*t*HE BEATLES KNEW a thing or two about love, but they were dead wrong to think it can't be bought. For today's mothers, their children, and their nannies, sitters, au pairs, or anyone else who is paid to look after them, love is a currency just as much as dollars, health insurance, and overtime. Parents are certainly not the only ones to endure or do things for the love of their children that no sane person would otherwise put up with, and nannies have been doing the same thing ever since their job was invented.

Among the nannies I interviewed for this book I heard endless variations on the refrain of "I couldn't stand the mother, but the children made me stay." In other words, "The pay stinks, the hours are horrible, I get no respect from my boss, but I love the kids and they love me, and it would break my heart to leave them." Actually, all things considered love is pretty cheap, given the current average market value of a week's worth of cuddling, schlepping, bathing, playing, wiping, and all the other verbs that are routinely part of a nanny's job description: as little as $150 per week for an au pair, to anywhere between $250 and $1,000 per week for a nanny, depending on the specific combination of location, hours worked, housekeeping or not, number and ages of children, overtime, off the books or on, live in or live out, health insurance, gas subsidies, Christmas bonuses, paid sick leave, overnight stays, and so on. While New York City is certainly at the high end in terms of compensation, it is still a good barometer for other urban moms and their nannies in terms of pay. Word on the playgrounds is that right now you'd have to fork over a minimum of $500 (*not* including taxes) to get someone decent, and at least $100 to $150 more for someone with good experience and references.

Money aside, not infrequently the web of love, need, dependency, devotion, and deception spun within the triangle of a mother, her children, and the "other mother" is as complicated and relentless as a Greek tragedy. According to Imelda, an experienced nanny who has been trying to have children of her own for years,

> It's definitely a love-hate thing. There are definitely days when it looks like they've got everything and all the things I'd want for my own kids if I could have any, and I've got nothing. But I guess that's not really true. I've got those kids, and I love them to death, and I know they love me back. I mean, you just know that they do, don't you? And then you realize how messed up it all is, the two of them working like crazy all hours of the day, and I'm the one who gets to hang out with their kids, doing all the things they pay so much money for, classes and stuff. It's no picnic, but it's always easier if you're not the mother. The kids definitely bottle up all the crap for when the mother comes home, dads, too, sometimes, but never as much.

There certainly seems to be something profoundly wrong about a situation where the majority of a child's waking hours are spent in the company of someone whom the child's mother pays in order for her to be able to hold down a job that pays enough for her to pay the nanny. Why do we do this?

For love, of course. The love that almost every mother naturally has in abundance for her children, and in considerably less abundance for herself. It is, after all, the one thing that for time immemorial has ensured the survival of the species. As general rules to live by, the ten commandments work very well, but once a woman becomes a mother society adds an umbrella clause that really changes everything: "Thou shalt give thy offspring the best of yourself and of everything you are capable of giving, for henceforth your life shall be worthless without them."

Unfortunately, at the turn of this millennium the definition of "the best of oneself" has all too often come to mean all of oneself, including every drop of energy, every dollar earned, every waking minute of the day, and every remaining shred of sanity. As Judith Warner has written so convincingly, contemporary American motherhood resembles nothing so much as *Perfect Madness,* the title of her book. No wonder then that our relationships with those women who actually get to spend time with our beloved children are so often fraught with so much resentment and complicated double standards.

Regina's full-time job was to look after six-month-old baby Violet and four-year-old Janie while their mother and father worked.

> Janie is such a sweetheart, a really affectionate child. She just loves sitting on my lap and giving and getting hugs and kisses. But if her mom caught her doing that with me she would just get so mad, she'd take it out on me in some way. So now I just have to go to another room or something, and keep having to sort of push Janie away because she doesn't know what the heck is going on, she just wants to love everybody. And then she's got to go and give her mother the business and run away from her like she's punishing her or something. It's ridiculous, I end up having to tell her that she should go give her mom a hug, and then that just makes it worse.

It's hard not to sympathize with the uncomfortable double bind Regina found herself in at times, but jealousy's other name isn't "the green-eyed-monster" for nothing. Meena, a mother of two children who were both in school all day by the time we talked, practically exploded with resentment and emotion when I asked whether there ever was any rivalry between her and the nanny.

It was totally excruciating. The worst time for me was when Anjeli was two. I'd finally stopped nursing a couple of months earlier. That at least gives you a way to stay connected to your child, I mean literally—pumping breast milk at work, usually in the toilet, that was one way for me to express my grief at having to leave her with someone else. Sitting there crying, with the milk rushing to my boobs. It was really hard to give it up, and then when I did, Anjeli just seemed to totally fall in love with our nanny. She would light up like a Christmas tree whenever she arrived, and at nighttime I'd have to literally chain the front door because she would scream hysterically when Dara left and try to follow her. I never talked to Dara about it, but I must admit that I felt really strongly that she enjoyed Anjeli's feelings for her way too much. I could never put my finger on it exactly, but sometimes it was almost as if she was sort of smirking at me. I mean, how could you not feel horrified and humiliated as a mother when your child basically screams and runs off the minute you walk in the door?

Luckily our whole dynamic changed when Sanjay was born, because he was such a mama's boy, and of course for a while Anjeli was beside herself with resentment over this new baby that was taking everyone's attention away from her. Dara was so good with them both, she really was, but I swear there were times when I could have ripped my baby out of her arms and killed her. I never could stand for her to be around once I was home, I still can't. I'm not sure if she was ever really conscious of the impact she had on me, how for a while I felt as though she was really trying to undermine me. Now that they're older, when I think about it, I realize that it was all probably just in my mind, but all the same, it was truly awful.

What should be a moment of sweet reunion, a highlight of the day for every working mother, instead so often turns into a frenzy of disappointment, built-up resentment, and need. Oh, the handover. That place where, more than any other, worlds collide and the lovers' triangle of mother, child, and nanny gets crushed into an excrutiating nugget of stress and good intentions gone awry. Judging by what each side has said to me in numerous conversations on the topic, it's a situation uniquely designed to bring out the worst in each of the three players involved.

This account by the mother of three children age seven, three, and one sounds a lot like a train wreck waiting to happen. You will recognize the plot and know that there's about to be an epic crash. You realize full well that the touching scenes among passengers of the doomed train will be their last before the inevitable meltdown. Followed, in turn, by heroic displays of bravery and emotional reunions among the survivors of the wreckage. We've all seen the movie, or another one just like it, in our own home.

Meet Alexa and nanny Claudette. Although the two women don't actually work together, their situations, background, and families are similar enough to show how their days might develop along parallel lines.

Alexa prides herself on her professionalism, on being a good manager, an effective leader, and a really good problem solver, as well as a devoted mother. Until she went part-time so as not to miss out on her children's formative years, she used to work in a demanding, fast-paced, and often disproportionately high-testosterone type of job. She constantly struggled—and frequently failed—to squeeze her work into an 8:00 A.M. to 6:00 P.M. schedule so that her nanny could leave on time to be home for dinner with her own family. Alexa is happily (or at least uneventfully) married to the children's father, and in theory they continue to be equal partners in all aspects of parenting and life, including making the money that's needed to pay for it all. In practice, however, now more than ever, Alexa makes virtually all the child-care arrangements and decisions, hires and fires nannies and additional sitters when needed, and somehow ends up bearing the responsibility of making it all work.

Claudette is in her forties and from "the islands," with two grown children of her own. She's been working as a nanny for eight years, and is finally approaching the end of the long, arduous, complicated, and expensive process of getting her green card. The family she works for resembles Alexa's in many ways, not just in the number of children and the general setup, but also in the sense that as the nanny her relationship is with the children first and their mother second. Their father is occasionally around, though Claudette is fairly certain he isn't aware of all the details that go into making the logistics of their day. Most often she'll see him in the evenings, taking over from her in case the mom couldn't make it home on time.

Just as the nanny-to-parent handover often resembles a train wreck, so does Alexa's thinking bear comparison to a complicated network of trains, each running on a carefully calibrated timetable and heading to different destinations. Each of her children is one little locomotive chugging through the cycle of his or her day with fairly constant and predictable needs: fuel, rest stops, maintenance. Her home is another, and so is her husband, her work, and her nanny. They all run alongside one another, and Alexa has each schedule internalized. Yet although she's the official district manager of the network, the job doesn't come with the perk of a company train for her personal use. She's used to getting around by hitching rides on all the others. If you asked her to describe the trains in her husband's head, she would tell you that there are probably just two: home and work. Oh, and maybe there's one for sex and the husband-and-wife thing.

It's clear that on balance Alexa loves her job, though she has resigned herself to the fact that her new situation is a sadly diminished version of the work she was trained to do. She doesn't bother to mention the other sad and boring litany of modern working motherhood: half time really means three quarters; a lot less money; being sidelined into boring assignments; little no or prospect of ever getting the big promotion that once seemed so imminently within her grasp. It's the price you pay.

Still, she's doing something worthwhile and using her brain and her talents to contribute to something other than just the insular little universe of her own family, not to mention earning some money and justifying her existence in a material way. Now more than ever that family, and in particular her children, are the most valued and unconditionally loved center of her world. They are the place from which it all radiates and the anchor that gives it meaning and value. Anchors, however, have a disconcerting habit of being both a source of strength and stability and an impediment to making a quick getaway—especially in the morning when you are late for work.

> In many ways the children are the thing that keeps me going: Either I'm missing them desperately and can't wait to get back home, or I'm dying to get away from them and to hand all their gazillion little needs over to someone else. In between there are the times when we just enjoy each other. For one reason or another though, these almost always end too soon.
>
> Generally, in the morning, by the time the nanny shows up, I've been up for hours and I'm just fit to be tied. Waiting for that moment when I hear her key in the door is always intense. For some reason there's never, ever enough time to do all that needs

to be done, but I guess that's just the nature of mornings. Of course the children can sense that all I really want is to leave, and that, in fact, my mind is already somewhere else, so they cling and protest all the harder. At first I thought having me around more would make it easier for them to let me go, but actually it's just the opposite. Much as I love them, they're just like little parasites, it's as though the more they have of me, the more they're hungry for more.

If the nanny is on time, and it looks like she's in a good mood, it makes a huge difference to the start of my day. There are times when I'm so absurdly grateful, I feel like kissing and hugging her like a long-lost relative. But God forbid she should be late, or looking grumpy. There's almost nothing guaranteed to make me angrier or more frustrated, though, of course, I've got to bite my tongue in front of the children. It just seems so incredibly selfish and thoughtless, because I know she knows how much pressure I'm under at work, and that I'm completely dependent on her to show up in order for me to be able to leave. I really wonder sometimes whether she fully realizes that my getting to work on time, especially now I've got to cram so much more into fewer hours, has everything to do with the both of us getting paid!

This is not, Claudette admits, something she thinks about a great deal. Trying not to get overwhelmed by her own morning rush, however, is. "It's hard to get going in the morning. Just look at everybody's faces on the subway; you know they're all still half asleep. I hate that, when nobody wants to look nobody else in the eye 'cause they're just putting one foot in front of the other. I just get there quick as I can, but even a good day takes at least an hour, maybe an hour and fifteen."

For Alexa, "After the stress of the whole getting-up-with-the-children routine there's almost always a sense of relief at getting to work and cranking up the energy and excitement I get from doing what I do. But then that old mother clock kicks in because, inevitably, at some point, I start to miss them. I might be looking at a document or sitting in the middle of a presentation, and suddenly I'll start wondering where they are, hoping that my oldest daughter liked the special little treat I packed for her snack at one in the morning the night before, and wishing I could see her face or just close my eyes and smell the baby's hair, things like that."

Claudette's transition into her workday is anything but gentle. "It's always a mess when I arrive. We're supposed to have these ten minutes when we talk about the day, you know, who's s'posed to go where, get picked up when. Nine times out of ten, she'll be holding the door for me and trying to catch the same elevator I came up on to go back down. It's like Grand Central Station, is what it is. Oh, and then the kitchen usually looks like a bomb's gone off. So, first thing I do is get everyone calmed down, get things organized. It's no good when the mom and I are there together. She's rushing, I'm rushing, everybody just gets all worked up."

Alexa may leave her children, but they never completely leave her.

> Naturally no day that I'm actually at the office goes past without at least three or four phone calls, sometimes more. Even though they can be kind of irritating when I'm in the middle of something, I do love how the sweet, banal minutiae of their lives contrasts with the Big Important Stuff I'm supposed to be working on. It never fails to put things in perspective. But, you know, that mommy clock keeps ticking. At some point in the afternoon the pressure inevitably starts to build toward this point in time that I know I absolutely cannot pass if I want to get home on time. And I want to, I really, really want to, because as much as I love my job, at the end of a long and busy day I'm completely certain that I love my children more, and that I want to get home to

them *now*. Don't you think every mother feels that way? Every day I'm a sucker for that moment when all's right with my world because I'm home, I've got my children back, and work is over.

And yet, the reality is that more often than not it turns into a nightmare. To the point where on some days I just wait in the hallway for ten minutes decompressing, imagining the scene I would like to be rewarded with rather than the one almost certainly awaiting me.

I would look like someone out of a commercial, and there'd be music playing in the background as I, the happy, beneficent mother unlocks the door of my home to be greeted by my beaming, excited children chattering about some sweet detail of their busy day. Have you noticed all those ads lately, with these models who look like they're fifteen, briefcase in one hand and naked baby in the other? It always makes me think, "For God's sake, put a diaper on that baby, and how come you don't have spit-up on the shoulder of your suit?" So here's the rest of my fantasy: standing discreetly on the sidelines would be the respectful, loving, big-bosomed nanny, smiling Buddhalike at the wholesome family reunion. The closing shot of the scene would be of Nanny stashing my briefcase in the hall closet before slipping quietly into her coat and out the door. In the background my brood and I head to the kitchen for milk and warm cookies. More music, movie over, time for real life. Sometimes when I open the door there really is a sweet reunion, but on most days, in one way or another, everyone just dissolves.

Claudette is usually ready for her day to end way before it actually does, anticipating and dreading the handover just as much as Mom. "It's a long day. I'm ready to be done. I mean, it's my job, it's hard work, you know?"

For Alexa it feels as though the pressure hardly lets up.

More often than not the nanny will be pissed at me because once again I'm twenty minutes late, which will make her miss her train. Then the two little ones come running out in their pj's all excited to see me, but clutching some stupid chocolate cookie I'd told her specifically *not* to give them, accompanied by the sound from the TV of a stupid cartoon that I'd asked her specifically *not* to let them watch. Lately my oldest has started to grab onto her and start whining, "Don't leave, don't leave." Talk about an awkward moment. I mean, of course I know it's a good thing that they're so close, but it's pretty hard all the same to just stand there and get shoved aside for the nanny. Or maybe she does it because it's the only way for her to get any attention while I'm being smothered by her siblings. I don't know. Either way it's hard.

Then the little ones will wipe their snotty chocolate faces all over my jacket, and I'm just about ready to either kill the nanny or physically push her out the door. Because I do think it's up to her to somehow control all this better and not just hand me back a great big mess when I come back after working all day. I know it's not easy taking care of three little kids, but that's her job after all. I have my work, and she has hers. I'd be home with them more if we could afford it, or if there were a way to somehow do what I do and not work these long hours on the days I'm at the office, and not have too much to do in too little time. But there isn't. It's not as though I actually have a choice about any of this.

Claudette claims that most of the time she likes her job and adores the children. Yet she still has plenty of resentment of her own built up, particularly in the lack of choices she has in the way it all turns out.

I just hate that she is always late. I hate that for some reason my time isn't supposed to be as valuable as hers. I hate that she expects me to clean up after her and her husband in the morning—they've got enough money to get somebody to clean! I hate that she gets to give the kids junk food and candy and lets them watch cartoons on the weekend, and I'm supposed to just give them carrots for snacks, and read books. I hate it that she tells everyone those kids are her most precious possession, and yet she argues with me about every dollar I make. I hate it that she always blames me when I come in late even though I've got an hour and a half commute by train or subway or bus, and she takes a ten-minute cab ride to work. I hate it that she just takes for granted that I can stay late and doesn't pay me overtime, as if it's some sort of wonderful privilege to look after her children. I hate it that she comes swooping in at the end of the day like some goddess and gives the kids everything I've been telling them they can't have, and then tells me she thinks they're getting spoiled. I hate it that she blames me for getting sick and not being able to come to work, when half the time it's something I picked up from the kids. I hate it that she just can't stand it when the kids say they miss me or want me to do something for them instead of her.

I hate it that I've got to be looking after somebody else's kids so my own kids can go to school and have a life—without me! It makes me so mad, not getting respect for what I do, when half the time the reason I'm here is that she can't stand being around her own kids day in and day out. I hate all that. But I love the kids. And I love that they love me, because if they didn't I'd rather be cleaning toilets.

When pressed neither Alexa nor Claudette actually felt there was much about their respective relationships that they would change. They didn't like it all that much, they weren't even sure how much they actually liked the other woman, but they both wearily accepted that this was probably the best compromise either could expect given all the other demands and needs they had to contend with.

By the same token, the mothers and nannies who liked one another all had one thing in common: Respect. R-E-S-P-E-C-T! Such an obvious and critical ingredient for any good working relationship, yet sometimes the hardest thing of all to give. Love? Easy as falling off a log. Especially when you're looking at the adorable face of *your* baby or the toothless smile of *your* toddler, and some overwhelming chemical reaction turns your insides into mush and makes your heart ache. Respect? Oh brother, let us not count the ways in which mothers disrespect their nannies, and vice versa.

This is what Sarah, a recently divorced and single mother in her early forties, had to say when I asked her how it could be that she was onto her third au pair in ten months:

> Well, you know, I've found that they just don't have a clue, do they? If I could afford something different I would. I really wonder what the education is like in these Eastern European countries. I mean, not a single one of these girls was anywhere near my son's league intellectually. He's just eight! If you ask me, it's pretty obvious that all they wanted was to get into this country and then stay illegally. I mean, what a chance we're giving them! Coming to America is obviously the best thing that ever happened to them. Well, I'm sorry, but if they can't even keep up with my son's homework then they just can't stay in my family. I think I'm done with this au pair thing. Maybe I'll try to get a Mormon girl; at least they've got good values and speak proper English.

I managed to catch up with Maryna, the last of her au pairs, before she relocated to the West Coast to stay out the rest of her year with another family.

She was impossible. She treat me like I am little baby and can't do anything right. Always she was interfering and telling her son what I say is wrong and not to listen to me. He was nice kid, I guess, but really badly mannered. Is not surprising, with the mother always putting the pressure on him and criticizing. Before I come I think it will be easy to have just one kid, and older, that's why I choose this family. Big mistake! My new family have three little children, two, five, and seven. Will be more work, but I don't care. If they don't treat me like baby, and let me work and take me serious, I can manage.

Last I heard Maryna was doing well with her new family and thinking of staying another year.

Most mothers who rely on nannies or au pairs do agree that the second, third, and fourth year the nanny stays with the family is a good thing for all concerned. It provides wonderful stability for the children; everyone knows the system so no more explanations are necessary; and generally the children become just as tightly woven into the life of their caretaker as she is into theirs, and their mother's. Familiarity may breed contempt among adults, but with children it's more often the opposite, as the caretaker watches them change and grow—perhaps even from infancy—into that first "look what I can do!" stage of toddlerhood, and then into the beginning of speech and real conversations, and little personalities that develop into big and bigger ones, and finally real people. That, in truth, is how love really grows—over time, every day, in constant baby steps, to the point where the nanny might as well be a child's mother because she's been with him and cheered him on and cared for him at virtually every single big moment of his little life.

Eileen is thirty-four but looks about forty. She came to the United States from Jamaica when she was just twenty-two, leaving her five-year-old son in the care of her much older sister. Coming first on a tourist visa, she has since been married and divorced, and now has a green card, a three-year-old daughter, and a boyfriend with whom she lives in a one-bedroom apartment in Brooklyn. In the high-stakes world of Manhattan nannies Eileen is a true prize, the kind that some mothers would kill for. She's legal, she's articulate and street-smart. She's worked with only four families in her twelve-year career and has great references. She tells me that she uses the word "career" on purpose when she talks about what she does, because she gets a kick out of seeing how it startles people, but also because she wants to be taken seriously. She works at least fifty-five hours a week and makes seven hundred dollars, cash in hand; she gets two weeks' paid vacation and buys her own health insurance. Her daughter spends her days in a jerry-rigged day-care facility in the basement of a Brooklyn brownstone, where for two hundred dollars a week one caretaker and sometimes her sister look after Aneesha and seven other children. Aneesha's father shows up from time to time to buy "his little girl" presents, but doesn't make any regular support payments. Eileen doesn't waste any time trying to get more out of him—he's a loser, and she's the one who got the kid, so screw him.

Back home Eileen's son is in trouble. Lately he's been skipping school, keeps getting into fights, and his aunt just can't handle him anymore. Eileen is worried sick about him, and about her sister, who seems to have just given up on the boy. Eileen wants to bring him to the United States to live with her, but her boyfriend isn't particularly thrilled with the idea. She feels helpless and guilty, and spends a great deal of her hard-earned money sending him stuff, haranguing him endlessly on the phone, and paying to get him out of yet another "bad situation."

While she makes sure he has all the cool gadgets and hip clothes he could ever possibly want, she has actually seen him just once, at most twice, a year since he was five years old. Eileen admits to becoming defensive and furious in equal measure when he asks her, as he frequently does in his arrogant, seventeen-year-old rage-at-the-world manner, where the hell she comes off telling him about right and wrong, since all she ever did was hand him off to other people to raise. The one thing that gives Eileen hope is that on the two occasions he's met his little sister he took her everywhere with him, and was more patient and playful than Eileen thought he could ever be with anyone. "He was tender," she said, "just tender as could be."

I talked to Eileen in New York City's Central Park, on a bench in one of the playgrounds on the West Side. She was there with a three-year-old boy named Jackson, and I approached her for no other reason than that she looked friendly. I'd been lurking around the park benches for a while, trying to pick out someone who might actually speak to me and answer some questions, and the two bulging, distinctive orange and white Zabar's shopping bags hanging off the stroller handle-bars gave me what I thought was a perfectly innocuous opener. Once she'd dispatched the little boy toward the sandbox I put on my best "isn't he cute" smile and launched forth. That must have been an awful hassle, I wondered aloud, navigating the narrow aisles of Zabar's with a shopping cart and a stroller. Her response was a suspicious look and a question: "You looking for a nanny?" I stammered yes, then no, then yes again, and so we began to talk.

Eileen's employers at the time were a married couple with two children. The family lived in a "classic 6" on the Upper West Side, with a view of the Hudson and the George Washington Bridge, and Jackson's four-year-old sister Molly was enrolled in a private pre-school three mornings a week. This was the second marriage for Jackson's father, a lawyer in his fifties (Eileen didn't know his exact age), and the first for the little boy's thirty-five-year-old mother, Nancy. Jackson had two older half siblings, a boy and a girl of nineteen and sixteen. Their mother had been a stay-at-home mom, and now lived with her daughter in the old family home in Princeton, New Jersey, while the oldest son was in his junior year at Syracuse University. It only occurred to me after Eileen had finished her story and I was writing up my notes that I knew everyone's first name (given only on the promise that they would be changed for this book), except that of Nancy's husband. On the few occasions she referred to him at all, he was simply "the dad," while his wife was mostly "Nancy" or, occasionally, "my boss."

Nancy and Eileen appeared to have a good routine going, at least on those days when everything went according to plan. Eileen had to drop Aneesha off at her day-care center by 6:30 A.M. in order to get to Nancy's apartment by 7:45, though she admitted with a shrug that it was often 8:00 or even 8:15 by the time she could get to the Upper West Side by bus and subway. Nancy's job as a human resource manager for a large PR firm in midtown allowed her to stick to a fairly predictable nine-to-five schedule, and the nanny's official workday was supposed to be over by 6:00 P.M.—in theory. In practice, Eileen told me, "she's almost never back on time. If I come in late by fifteen minutes, she adds like twice that much onto the end of my day. I'm not sure how that's supposed to be fair, but there's not much I can do about it." On Mondays and Thursdays Eileen was able to leave on time because the housekeeper came from 2:00 to 7:00. Known to Eileen only as Neema, she was from Sri Lanka, fiftyish, and a widow, living with her grown daughter and two grandsons in the Bronx. She'd been working for Nancy "for forever," and Eileen said that she tried to stay out of the house while Neema was there because she'd stuff the kids' faces with candy and coo over them like puppies. All of Jackson's hand-me-downs went straight home to Neema's grandsons, but Eileen didn't want any of that for Aneesha. "I like getting her new stuff. She doesn't deserve it any less than these kids do."

Watching over little Jackson, playing happily with a pal just ten feet from us, we talked about the curious convergence of the lives of these four families, right here in a New York City park sandbox. Little would Jackson and his sister, Molly, know, now or probably ever, how many heartstrings they once held in their grubby little hands. Give them a tug, and eventually it would be felt all the way across the world, from Manhattan and New Jersey to the Caribbean and a dirt-poor tsunami-ravaged country on the edge of the Indian Ocean.

Eileen's eyes rarely strayed from Jackson's busy little figure, pushing his dump truck, dragging his shovel, and making sand piles. The two of them obviously had an easy and well-practiced intimacy, literally touching base with each other every few minutes or so for a nose wipe, a hug, a sip of apple juice, or some help with rolling up the too-long sleeves of Jackson's hoodie. "He's a pretty easy kid, sleeps well, good eater too. His sister's another story, hell on wheels she is. But brother, that girl could charm the pants off you. I get mad at her sometimes when she acts like a little princess, but I know it isn't her fault. In my house these two'd have proper manners, I can tell you that." This isn't the only time during Eileen's narrative that I wince inwardly and have to ask myself—whose side are you on, anyway?

Nancy certainly doesn't sound like a bad person, nor a bad mother or even a bad employer, though the irony of her profession does not escape me. There can be few areas of human resource management where theory and practice are potentially further apart, or where the term seems more like an oxymoron, than in the relationship between mother and nanny. The longer Eileen and I talk, the more I realize that these two women are engaged in a relationship far more intimate, profound, and complicated than any contract between an employer and an employee that Nancy is likely to come across in the manual for her "real" job.

So here's the picture: Nancy loves her children. Eileen loves Nancy's children too, but she also loves her own—let us not venture to guess whom she loves better. Nancy loves the fact that Eileen so clearly loves Molly and Jackson, because that allows her to pursue the other thing she loves and needs—her work. When it comes to Eileen's children, however, Nancy would probably have to admit that she'd rather they didn't exist, at least not in a way that would require Eileen to be a constant, hands-on, loving presence in their lives—at the expense of Molly and Jackson. Clearly neither woman can afford to be a full-time mother, and so they somehow make their love for their children fit into each other's lives like one glove inside another—and another, and another.

At least Eileen has reached a point in her life where she has a somewhat reliable support network of her own, a little shaky and improvised but mostly ready to kick in at those times when the demands of Nancy's job stray into that bottleneck witching hour between six and eight in the evening. That's the time when Eileen herself is supposed to be getting home to pick up her child, do the grocery shopping, and fix dinner. Eileen freely admits that there are days when she is so mad at Nancy for every minute Eileen must wait that she could practically kill Nancy. Eileen's boyfriend, Wayne, is a security guard in a factory warehouse with pretty steady hours, and on most days he can get off work to pick Aneesha up at six. Usually, when Eileen gets home, though, the little girl is watching TV and hasn't had dinner or been bathed, so Eileen's got to scramble for something for the three of them to eat. It's a long day for everybody.

It is still better than it was. As annoying, disorganized, inconsiderate, bitchy, and late as Nancy can sometimes be, at least she does occasionally pay Eileen overtime, has so far always remembered Aneesha's birthday (it's exactly three months before Jackson's), and occasionally even asks about Marley, Eileen's son, with genuine interest. "She gets mad at me sometimes," said Eileen, "but at least I feel she respects me. Anyway, she'd be up a creek if I left, but actually right now I'm kind of happy how things are working out. We get along. It's okay."

Not that long ago, seven months pregnant with Aneesha, Eileen was up a creek herself. It was her fourth year working as a full-time sole-charge nanny to three children in a family on the Upper East Side of Manhattan. "The dad was something on Wall Street, never saw him really, and the mom was one of those real-estate brokers, selling people apartments." Eileen had looked after two of the children since they were born, and would regularly work sixty-hour weeks.

> The money was good, but the hours were real bad. She always had some deal going down, you never saw anybody so stressed. Half the time she'd have me working weekends too. With her always rushing around, my coming there regular was the only thing those kids could rely on. There's just something about having a baby to look after right from the time it's born. I mean, you don't have a choice about loving your own, but when it's somebody else's and they get to be so dependent on you, man, that gets under your skin.

The mother went back to her job full-time just two months after each baby was born, and would regularly tell Eileen that she was truly a part of their family and that she didn't know how they'd ever get along without her. In the end Eileen figured she had just gotten suckered and started to believe the fairy tale.

"I never saw it coming, you know, figured I'd earned a break and some more regular hours, maybe even that I could bring my own baby to work for the first couple of months to make it easier on everybody." When she told her boss that she was five months' pregnant, that she'd like to have two months off—unpaid—to have the baby, and then return to work but for slightly fewer and more predictable hours, she wasn't prepared for the reaction.

> You should've seen her. I mean, she knew I was married and all, wasn't like this should be such a surprise. She was ice, man. Ice. Part of the family, my ass. She said she'd have to discuss it with her husband, but that she was quite sure he wouldn't want anyone working for them who couldn't make his children their first

priority, made it like he was the bad guy. "His children." Jesus, what a bitch. I stayed another month, 'til she found somebody else, gave me a check for what she'd have paid me for two months, and I was outta there. Don't even ask me about the kids. They got over it faster than I did, that much I'll tell you— they were so little, still had their mom, and then there was just someone else to pick up after them and drag them around all day long, doesn't make much of a difference, does it?

I went back home to Kingston for a while but had to come back here to have Aneesha, so she could get her American passport. You don't want to hear the rest. I'm doing all right now, and Jackson and Molly and me, and even Nancy, we get along okay. I guess I respect what she's trying to do; she just wants the best for her kids. Nothing wrong with that.

On my way home that afternoon (riding the commuter train in sweet anticipation of reuniting with my own daughters after a long day in the city) I tried to fill in the blanks in the picture that Eileen had drawn of her previous employer. It would have been so simple and satisfying to dismiss her as the villain of the piece, but playing devil's advocate was also alarmingly easy. To the extent that she was a "bad mother," she was probably no worse than millions of other incredibly busy, overextended working women with children under ten, trying to make sure their families didn't get shortchanged between her rushing from one appointment to the next. As a wife she did what was probably expected of her and what clearly she had come to expect from herself as a mother and a professional: keep child-care issues out of her husband's hair and allow him to pursue his career (probably more lucrative than her own) free of babysitter hassles. As a professional she was obviously dedicated to her clients and their interests, including making herself available at all sorts of odd hours.

As an employer, however, it is very tempting to say she was a louse. But she paid Eileen well, gave her a severance package comparable to what most blue-collar workers in America can currently expect, provided her with an excellent reference letter, and gave her a clear reason why she felt she could no longer employ her. What actually screwed it up in the end was none other than the whole love thing. The sort of I'd-throw-myself-under-a-truck-to-save-them kind of love that she probably had for her own children, that you have for yours, that I have for mine, and that she naturally assumed Eileen would come to have for the baby she was expecting.

This hypothetical truck is a doozy indeed. It's big and it's deadly, and Eileen's former employer is surely not the only mother to have made an imaginary close encounter between it, her children, and the nanny a condition of that nanny's continued employment. I did not get to meet Eileen again, much as I would have liked to, and I only hope she does not regret having talked to me. As for Nancy, in the event that she recognizes herself, all I can say is—your nanny would surely pass the truck test with flying colors.

As Jane, mother of two and an English professor at an Ivy League university told me, "It's part of the contract—actually, it *is* the contract. As much as Rina gets on my nerves sometimes, as much as I constantly struggle with her over all the junk she gives the kids and the stuff she lets them get away with, I know she would die for them. In the end that's all that matters—all the other crap I can deal with."

Jane and Rina's situation is a good example of a relationship that works almost in spite of itself. The fact that both women are totally devoted to the children is probably the only thing they have in common, but it is a powerful bond and the grease that keeps their engine running. Jane knows Rina well enough to recognize her strengths, to compromise on the things that she will never be able to change, and to realize that she needs to give up on some things that just don't work. Jane hasn't yet figured out how to conquer the handover beast either, but tells herself that the children obviously have a need to melt down before they can put themselves back together again to be with her in something resembling a normal state. "I just try to let it all wash over me, and eventually we all calm down. Rina definitely likes to huff and puff and glower when she's unhappy with me about something, and it's hard not to take it personally. But as long as we both have our time and space with the kids, it usually just simmers down and goes away."

After almost eight years in the family Rina is pretty set in her ways and doesn't make many compromises, but the routine they have works. Jane knows full well that an occasional break from Rina is essential if the two are to not drive each other crazy, and she encourages Rina to travel to Arkansas to visit her own, grown children several times a year. Inevitably, while she is gone, other, temporary babysitters are hired. At first they appear refreshingly novel, young and fun, but ultimately, when she returns, Rina is always greeted with open arms, great relief, and renewed appreciation.

To the children, Franny and Jacob, Rina is certainly part of the family, not in that they see her as a substitute mother, nor a sort of kindly aunt, but rather a dependable, warm, and friendly fixture in their lives and another person besides their parents who loves them unconditionally. What could possibly be better than unlimited, unconditional love? Ask Franny whether she loves Rina, and the answer will be an emphatic "Well, duh! Of course I do!"

According to Jane there is not much of a downside to her children having a close, loving, and independent relationship with someone other than their parents—but Jane is an uncommonly generous, self-confident, and thoughtful mother who knows her own limitations and who does not have a problem giving Rina complete control over some—just some—aspects of her children's lives. Having grown up with a working mother and nanny herself, jealousy has never been a significant part of her lexicon when it comes to recounting the story of Rina, Franny, and Jacob: "There might have been moments when I was still nursing and the children were very, very small, when the act of handing them over to someone else's loving arms was a real gut wrench. But I never blamed Rina for it, and for better or worse I've always been able to rationalize that for them to be with someone who loves them, and with whom they feel as safe and loved as they feel with me, has got to be a good thing. Difficult, but good. And just as often a relief, actually."

Anna, a former schoolteacher from Bolivia now in her seventies and recently retired from full-time nanny work, hasn't always been so lucky.

> I had many families where they think, just because they're rich and I'm from developing country, they're better than me. Nothing I can do as good as the mother, never mind I am educated person, too.
>
> So they want me to love their precious children, and I spend time with them all the day, and we play and do the homework, and I give them dinner when the mother stay late, and she act like she is shocked and nasty to me when she come home and the children scream, "I don't want you, I want Anna!" What am I supposed to do? Why they have children in the first place? Is not good when they have no respect, not just for me like another educated person, but for the children's feelings, too.
>
> The children learn from the example, so if they see that mother not look me in the eye when she speak to me, they learn that is okay, that is way to treat another person. But I always look them in the eye, and I speak to them like they are real people. And all the children I look after, when we're together

and mother is not around, we get to love each other, it's beautiful. Is only when the mother comes and acts like her love is better than mine, it becomes a problem. I tell you for a fact, some mothers, with everything they go to do instead of coming home to be with the children, like go to gym and shopping and have nails done, their love's no better than mine, not one bit. But then I'm just the nanny, right?

"Just the nanny." How often that phrase has echoed through my conversations I truly cannot say. It might pop out apologetically, accompanied by a shoulder shrug if the nanny is mistaken for the children's mother. Sometimes it has been flung at me defiantly and with more than a touch of exasperation, as in the case of Anna; or, finally, declared with pride and an almost territorial sense of sovereignty from the mouths of mothers. "After all, she's just the nanny," is so often only part of what they are saying, with the unspoken words ringing just as loud and clear: I, on the other hand, am the real deal, the one who actually makes decisions, the one who really has control and who loves them in a way that no one else could possibly ever comprehend."

Unlike Jane, many mothers I spoke to admitted that sometimes the knowledge that their children, especially when they were very little, seemed to love another woman as well as themselves was close to unbearable. Gaynor, a dentist in her early forties and mother of two little boys, told me she knew full well that her feelings of rage and hurt at her youngest son's refusal to come to her when she got home at night was probably irrational, and certainly unfair. Yet she simply couldn't help physically wresting the little boy away from the nanny and asking her to leave the two of them alone in what she admitted was "the nastiest, lady-of-the-manor tone I could muster."

I'm just like a woman scorned, the long-suffering wife who comes home to find her husband shagging the parlor maid or something. I know it's disgraceful, the way I speak to her sometimes, but I just can't help it. Charlie's only just turned two, and he's at that delicious age when every little piece of him is totally adorable, and the thought that someone else has touched him and kissed him and smelled that gorgeous spot in the crook of his neck, it simply drives me wild. I kind of have to take possession of him again every night when I come home, and bloody hell, does he make me work for it. I know Sue is scared of me, and I've apologized to her God knows how many times. But if I'm really honest, I also sort of like that about myself, that I can turn into this mother beast and roar like a lion, and God help anyone who stands in my way, including the nanny, bless her heart. Poor Sue, it's really not her fault at all. She's really so sweet with them both, but Charlie does insist on following her around like a besotted little puppy . . . Oh God, there I go again.

The last word in the "for love or for money?" debate must go to Joanna, who is both a mother and a nanny, and who has loved more children than I can shake a stick at—though none, of course, as deeply as Molly, her two-year-old daughter.

I'd have to say it is a job, but at the same time it's so much more than that. It's easy to get in over your head as a nanny, especially when you don't have kids of your own and you're handed this gorgeous, gorgeous little baby to look after. There was one time when I got too close to this one little girl. I'd had her since she was born, and I didn't realize just how attached I was to her until the mother let me go. She never really said why, but I knew the reason, and to tell you the truth, I was devastated.

I've had lots of kids since then, all ages, all types, and I can honestly say that in one way or another I've loved them all. But I've never found a child who's chosen me over their mother, never. It's this thing that most kids just instinctively know, that because you're their mother you've got to love them no matter what. Now when Molly gives me the business if I've been out all day and she's having a lovely time with the babysitter, there's two things that go through my mind—the first is, "Oh God, hand me that knife," and the second one is, "Hang on, it's all right, she's just acting like this because she loves me."

need

*a*S MUCH AS love is the currency of the mother/nanny relationship—or any relationship, for that matter—need is its fuel. Just like there are many kinds of love, the kind of need that compels us to eat, breathe, and sleep is a totally different animal from the one that tells us that little Johnny needs his diaper changed, or Mommy really needs to nail this deal if she's ever going to get that promotion. Not to mention the kind that borders on panic because you absolutely, positively have to have the babysitter show up on time if you're not to be late for that critical meeting.

In the mother-nanny-child triangle the only one whose need is never actually questioned, nor considered selfish, unreasonable, or even excessive, is that of the child. As anyone who has spent any time looking after toddlers and babies can tell you, it takes at least three years before a child's life stops resembling anything other than a never-ending stream of needs, with any luck anticipated and met with a modicum of love and affection before it turns into a full-fledged scream-until-you're-blue-in-the-face existential crisis. By the same token, and speaking from four babies' worth of personal experience, there can be little in life more satisfying to a mother than being the only one able to come up with the solution when your baby is distraught with hunger, or tired, or fussy. Think of those times when your infant would scream bloody murder at everyone who held her except you, but would stop magically the moment you picked her up and tucked her little ear right next to your heartbeat. She might as well be pointing right at you yelling, "Mommy, it's *you* I need!"

No wonder it's so hard to turn those little bundles of hunger, fatigue, and nerves over to someone else so we can go back to work, or simply out to dinner for that matter. It has always been a simultaneously excruciating blow to my ego as well as a tremendous relief when, rather than clinging to me with desperation as I headed out to the office in the morning, one of my daughters would rush to the nanny and give me the cold shoulder. "She needs this," I would tell myself. "She needs to pretend she doesn't need me or want me, so she can let me go without falling apart." What's more, little children can be far more cunning and manipulative (or let us be more kind and call it "practical") than we tend to give them credit for. Here's Mama, who's leaving. There's Nanny, who's staying. Who'll be playing with me and getting my snack, and with any luck letting me watch a bit of SpongeBob before nap? Hey, I know on which side *my* bread is buttered. Plenty of time to give Mama the business later! That morning departure, or departure in general, is a cause of much eye-rolling among nannies, and comes a close second to the end-of-the-day handover as the part of their working day that they want to get over with as fast as possible. Particularly for those with quite a bit of experience, to be alone with the children *sans Maman* is, after all, what they're there for. Who wouldn't feel like a spare when the mother continues to hang around?

Rhiannon is a soft, plump, and reassuringly redheaded Irish nanny of indeterminate age who "just loves kids, but not all the responsibility that goes along with having little ones of your own. Well, maybe one day . . ." Sipping tea from an old-fashioned thermos at a playground ("My office!") she chats away unself-consciously. I'm just as charmed by her lovely lilting accent and the unexpected emphasis in her speech as by her laid-back, slightly loopy attitude. "Like I've always said, there's got to be at least a bit of a scene, hasn't there? I sometimes think the mums feel cheated if there isn't one. You know, wailing, 'Mummy, Mummy, please don't leave me or I'll die,' and then they're happy as little clams practically as soon as she's out the door. Truth be told, I usually can't wait for the mum to be gone. I won't take a job anymore if I haven't got sole charge. I mean, if the mum's there the whole time, what does she need me for?"

Oh, Rhiannon, we need you for so many reasons and in so many different ways. For most mothers the answer to this question is like the proverbial tip of the iceberg—that fraction of the frozen peak floating above the surface and hinting at the much greater hidden mass below: The children need to be okay. They need to be happy, with any luck loved, but above all safe.

As Jeannie, mother of eighteen-month-old Lucy so succinctly put it, "Oh my god, if I ever felt that I'd left my daughter in a situation where she wasn't safe, or with someone who didn't care about that as much as me—actually, it just doesn't bear thinking about. When you don't have children you just don't realize that that's what being a parent is really all about, you know? Keep them safe, keep the bad stuff away, and then with any luck at some point they'll be able to fend for themselves. But until she can, that's my number-one priority. Fend for her, I guess. Surround her with people and things that are good. If you can't do that, or at least try to, I'd say you're a pretty crappy parent. Plenty of those around too, though, right?"

Jeannie is in her late twenties and has a midlevel administrative job in a government agency. She is not married but lives with Lucy's father, who works in construction. For her and the little family she helps to support, staying home after the baby was born was never an option, and neither was working part-time. Her child care consists of a combination of Lucy's grandmother and a day-care center, and there isn't a lot of room for error. Her mother is still fairly fit, but she has diabetes, and the car they depend on to get everyone to and from where they've got to be is a temperamental ten-year-old Honda that they can't afford to replace. So much could go wrong. For now it works, and Jeannie is never in doubt that Lucy's in good hands, and that she's doing the best she can for her daughter.

Speaking about her child care Jeannie admits that "it helps that she's my mother, you know? I mean, it does get me mad sometimes, the way she does things with the baby so old-fashioned and different from how I'd do it. But she's my mom and I've got to respect that, and anyway, I know for a fact she's been acting this way since I was a baby, and I figure I turned out okay. And this is her granddaughter we're talking about! So I know she'd never hurt her, and there's just the two of them. I do wonder sometimes about the day-care people, though. They're really nice ladies, but with so many kids there it's really more about keeping things under control than giving any one of them individual attention."

When I press Jeannie about her relationship with her mother when it comes to Lucy, she does her best to be diplomatic, surely because I know, and she knows, that to be critical of this linchpin of her child-care arrangements would be akin to looking a gift horse in the mouth.

> Look, it is what it is. I really don't have a choice. I'd love to have a relationship with my mom that's got nothing to do with babysitting Lucy, and I am really grateful she's around to help me out. I need her, is all there is to it. You know how people always say that every woman's afraid of turning into her mother? Well, the weird thing is, three days a week, my mother kind of turns into me, if you know what I mean.
>
> It drives my boyfriend crazy, but with him in and out of work

like he is, I need to have someone there I can depend on. He does his share, but it's not as if he's jumping at the chance to babysit nine to five, Monday to Friday!

Few would dare to quibble with the legitimacy of Jeannie's needs, much less with how they all fit so nicely into our social puzzle. A steady job, a bit of family, kids taken care of, everyone fed and housed pretty much under their own steam and without the assistance of tax-payers or the government. The modest upward mobility and self-reliance of people like Jeannie are what makes life work for the rest of us: Together she, her boyfriend, and her mother do what they can to keep our institutions ticking along, build our houses, and take care of their families without bothering anyone else.

Ultimately, Jeannie's current job may not have fabulous prospects, but it does have one advantage that many other mothers with nannies, children, and pressing work commitments would kill for: basic health insurance and regular hours, no matter what. Try getting the post office or the DMV to stay open past 4:30, and all you're likely to get is a stony-faced stare. "Yep, that's me," Jeannie said. "I used to get mad at people shutting the door in my face, but now I'd do the same thing. Ten minutes to get my act together, another ten to get to the car, if I'm lucky forty-five minutes' drive over to the day-care center to pick up Lucy, and I'll just manage to sneak in under the wire before they start charging us extra." It's a good thing that so far, knock on wood, Lucy hasn't been sick a whole lot or had any special needs. It's also a good thing that Jeannie can't afford to worry too much about the rate of turnover among the employees at Kids' World (80 percent per annum is the current, countrywide average for day-care centers), or about the fact that the vast majority of women who work there are engaged in one of the worst-compensated professions in this country. "It's not great, but it keeps her out of trouble. And you've got to figure that if they didn't love kids, they wouldn't be there."

Choices. It may seem that it's terrible when you have none, but sometimes it's just as bad when there are too many, none of them perfect. Instead of thanking your lucky stars that you can afford a babysitter or nanny, you end up feeling that no matter what or whom you end up with, both you and the kids are getting shortchanged somehow, and that there's got to be a better solution, somewhere. Carla is a pediatrician, but her actual profession matters little—she could be any one of millions of women who have a job they love, a career they are proud of, children to raise and cherish, and many imperfect choices for managing their collective care.

> What it really boils down to, I guess, is to somehow create a situation where you never have to make a choice, between children and career, I mean. And that just doesn't happen, right? I'm not talking about emergencies here, I mean, those are obviously no-brainers. I mean the day-to-day, Are they happy? Are they safe? kind of stuff. Because in order for work to work, I need to know that the kids are okay, and in order for them to be happy, I need a happy nanny, right? But a happy nanny is usually one who gets to go home at five, and who gets paid more than I can afford, and who doesn't have to do anything she thinks is beneath her, like doing the ironing and taking out the garbage, God forbid. So everything is one huge compromise. Except I feel the person doing all the compromising is me.

It seems that unless a mother is extraordinarily lucky or extremely wealthy the best she can hope for when it comes to finding and keeping the nanny she needs, not to mention wants, is four out of five. Here's the wish list, give or take a few attributes, diluted down to its highly unscientific essence from the dozens of conversation I have had; everything else could probably fit loosely into one of the following categories, listed in descending order of importance:

1. First and foremost there is safety, or the ability to make certain that at the very least in our absence the children come to
   no harm.
2. Love, or at a minimum some affection and a knack for actually creating and maintaining an emotional bond with the
   child.
3. Reliability, which is less about being punctual—though that
   does matter—than about being there consistently, where
   and when a nanny is needed. (Of course, having found
   someone who meets criteria one, two, and three, four is
   likely to be a problem.)
4. Affordability. Someone that wonderful deserves to be paid
   very well, particularly if she is also going to stand up to
   scrutiny when it comes to the last attribute on the wish list.
5. Flexibility, of course! Under which heading I would include,
   by the way, not just flexible hours but a willingness to look
   after the children as well as clean the house, do the laundry,
   and cook meals. All with a smile, thank you very much.

As Carla said:

> I'd have loved to put my kids in day care, and it really doesn't
> have anything to do with the money. I just think it's so much
> healthier for them to be exposed to lots of other children and
> adults in a structured environment, getting socialized, and with
> any luck actually learning something. But the way day care
> works in this country means that it simply isn't an option for
> someone like me. There's simply no way I could ever commit to
> being there by six every single day, no matter what. It'd be nice
> to say I could, but it's just not realistic, at least not if I want to
> be able to do my job the way it's supposed to be done.
>
> For a while I actually had an afternoon nanny who would

pick the girls up from day care every day and bring them home, and sort of bridge the gap until we got back, but that didn't really work. First of all it was really expensive, second she didn't have much of a relationship with the kids, because she mostly ended up being a sort of taxi service, and then she always hung around for a few hours with me home as well, because otherwise the whole thing wouldn't be worth it for her. And I hate that. So I ended up hiring her full-time.

The stupid thing is it still costs as much as ever, because I want the kids to do lots of activities, and then of course I still end up getting other sitters for weekends and things.

Sounds like Carla is managing her menagerie with a pretty mediocre score of three, maybe three and a half, out of a possible five.

And then, of course, there are the variables—those things that are negotiable to some but absolutely essential to others. One mother admitted to me, "Of course I need someone I can rely on to use their best judgment when tricky things come up and I'm not there, but you know what else I need? It sounds stupid, but I've always craved my nannies' approval. I hate it when I think they don't like me much or look down their noses at me for the way I've handled some situation with the children." Respect! Don't we all need a bit more of that? Other talents with which mothers wished to endow their personal Mary Poppinses ranged from the sublime and the ridiculous, to good table manners and an impeccable accent.

Accents can be important: "She used to say 'ax' and 'barf' instead of ask and bath, Oh God, it drove me crazy! Now I won't even interview someone if they don't speak in proper sentences on the phone. So shoot me, I'm a snob. But that kind of thing really matters to me."

Looks can matter too: "Well, you know, I'm sorry, but there's just no way I'm going to have a pretty young thing in the house with a better arse than mine. It's bad enough having your boobs ruined with all that breast-feeding, I'm not going to pay some Bo Derek type to jiggle my baby on her hip and make me feel fat and ugly every day. I guess that's why we've never had an au pair. I just couldn't handle a luscious babe from Sweden over breakfast while I'm propping up the bags under my eyes. Bottom line is, she's got to have a weight to height ratio worse than mine."

Star signs? Go figure: "Once I actually put in the ad 'Virgos preferred,' can you believe that? I should have said, 'Virgos and Capricorns.' My nanny now is a Capricorn, and I like her a lot. But the only others I've really loved were Virgos."

Kids or no kids? "No kids, I can handle the love and affection and responsibility stuff without any help; what I need is a nanny who's got the energy to schlep the stroller up and down the stairs, who'll get messy with them in the sandbox and have snowball fights. A big sister type. I think if you're a mom yourself you're always going to try and preserve your energy for your own kids. Look at me! Actually, if that weren't so weird I think I'd get a guy nanny."

She has to drive. She has to sing better than me. She has to like cats. She has to be a vegetarian. She has to be Jewish, no, Buddhist—no, Christian! She must never, ever smoke. She can't have a boyfriend. Actually, she should be married. She's got to have children of her own. She needs to be legal. It just wouldn't work if she were fat and out of shape, and body piercings or tattoos may be okay on my yoga instructor but definitely not when it comes to setting a good example to my kids.

The list goes on. Whatever the individual bottom line, it has been chosen by mothers as a way to minimize the feeling that ultimately this is a shot in the dark. This, after all, is no ordinary job—it is *the* job. It's the one that could make or break your family, the one upon which your career depends, the one that hovers at the borderline between your sanity and general mayhem, and the one that allows you to have a life outside of, oh God, motherhood.

For Rhiannon, the Irish nanny with the thermos of Lipton's, it was all very different when she was growing up: Catholic, working class, kids of every age in a big and close-knit family, and the whole nine yards of factories, poverty, pubs, and church. "There was my mum and my aunties and my grandma, everybody all together. So whoever was around and out of a job or whatever would just sort of pick up and look after the little ones, that was just life, you know? When I was thirteen and chomping at the bit to get out, if someone had told me I could get paid fifteen dollars an hour for wiping snotty noses I'd have had a good laugh! Don't think I can remember a time in my life when I wasn't minding *some*one younger than me."

When I asked Rhiannon why she works as a nanny, her answer was simple: "It's easy, I like it, and I need the money." Her employers at the time were a well-to-do couple of (her emphasis) "*artistic* types" who did a fair bit of traveling, lots of entertaining, and lived in a funky loft full of "weird stuff on the walls." They had two small children of two and four, let's call them Jack and Emma, who were happily making pigs of themselves and their obviously expensive designer clothing in a muddy sand pit as Rhiannon and I chatted and watched them.

So: Rhiannon needs work, her employers need a nanny, Jack and Emma need looking after. Problem solved? Well, no. It never is that simple. Rhiannon thinks it's all pretty funny and sort of silly, really, but she likes to play along because, well, because she needs the job.

> These people are really well off, I mean, you can just tell, can't you? No way does she *need* to work, and to tell you the truth, I still haven't quite sorted out what it is that she's actually supposed to be *doing*. But she's always talking about how there's this meeting for *work*, and how so-and-so is an important *contact*, and that she's so happy the children are in such good hands while she's *working*, and things like that. Actually, I think she doesn't really *do* anything; she just can't be bothered to be with her children and

do a *proper* job on them! But she leaves the house when I get there and comes home at five, good as gold. Honestly, though, I'm not complaining, but why someone like that would need a full-time nanny I really just can't fathom, can you?

I chuckle and nod, but rarely has my chummy consent sounded, or felt, so hollow. I make a quick getaway and follow up with copious writerly notes on our conversation to avoid admitting the obvious: Rhiannon has hit a nerve. Whatever it is that Jack and Emma's mother does—"something *artistic*"—surely what I do as a writer (or, as I sometimes describe myself, "a mother who writes") is not so very different. And yet, to imagine my life either without regular and reliable child care or without the satisfaction of chiseling away at a chapter, an article, or some other project until it's just right and ready to launch is pretty much akin to torture. Where, on a scale of one to five, does that kind of need fit in? There is some compensation, to be sure, and my pride would never allow me to pursue this calling without some kind of payback and recognition. Yet it is impossible to argue that I have ever labored under the same kind of financial imperative as mothers like Jeannie or Carla. What it really boils down to is that what to me is a fundamental, existential need to be and think of myself as something other than a mother is nothing short of a luxury to women like Rhiannon.

While she never said so directly, I got the distinct impression both from her and many of her colleagues "at the office" that as far as they were concerned, and for middle-class mothers with small children, the concept that work could have another (higher?) purpose than simply making a living was really kind of redundant. With the exception of a couple of nannies who were also students, not a single one of her own volition expressed any kind of female solidarity with the mothers they worked for, in the sense that they felt it was important for women to have careers and achieve success. They all worked at being nannies first and foremost because they needed to pay the bills, make the rent, and just get by. The fact that by and large they really did love "their" children did not mean that, if they had their druthers, looking after someone else's kids would come a distant fourth after better money, decent benefits, and regular hours. Not to mention something with better prospects: The best an experienced nanny can hope for after many years of devoted service is more money and, paradoxically, the closest she'll ever come to a promotion is getting the children to a point where they no longer need her.

Legal status and working papers are probably another thing to add to many a nanny's wish list, but given current immigration requirements it is also the one factor most likely to elude the legions of illegal child-care workers in this country. An uneducated woman from a country south of Mexico, Esmeralda's idiomatic take on her situation certainly put my existential musings into context:

> I need this job, what else you think ugly old Latina like me can do? Speak no good English, no have the papers, but hey, you look me! I got strong back and nice smile and big arms for give hugs! All the white kids I take care, they all need hugs! If I no hug them and wipe their smelly bottom, my family in Ecuador no eat, no pay medicines, no go to school. Is so simple.

This much is clear: Having listened to Esmeralda's story, in order for me to carry on researching this book and not guiltily rush home to wipe my own children's bottoms, I must (and do) accept one thing unequivocally—all needs are relative. My need to do what I do and have child care while I'm at it may not be as pressing as Esmeralda's grandkids' need to eat, but it's still valid and real. What I and anyone remotely similar to me should obviously strive to do is not exploit anyone less fortunate than ourselves, or pay them less than what is fair. After all, none of us would hesitate to unceremoniously dump Esmeralda if we ever thought that, with her nice smile and big hugs, she didn't hold up her end of the child-care bargain. That sob story is neither here nor there if it turns out that she's chronically late, neglects to buckle your toddler into the car seat, or lets him watch R-rated movies while she's talking on the phone.

Yet when it comes to pinning down what it is that nannies need from their employers, I invariably find my vocabulary subjected to some serious readjustment. The concept of need, as Rhiannon would say, is generally considered redundant, since only someone truly clueless would bother to ask such a thing. I might as well have been one of her three-year-old charges when Helena from Haiti told me, "Honey, what you talking about? I need myself a job. Wanna hear what I want? Got enough pages in that notebook of yours?" This, to put it mildly, was turning into an awkward situation. Accompanied by much hilarity and many guffaws and patronizing looks from the other nannies around us who were clearly enjoying her performance, I quietly took notes and tried not to leap up and interfere as Helena's charge, a bundled-up little boy of maybe two, toddled ever closer to the metal swings being energetically pumped back and forth by some big kids. When the inevitable happened and swing and boy collided, Helena made a great show of admonishing him for his careless toddler ways. Last on her wish list, after "a nice SUV, a couple trips home every year, paid vacation, a big apartment, and no trouble with the landlord," I should probably have added "obedient easy-care toddlers who look after themselves."

As in most other professions, among nannies there is most definitely a hierarchy of who feels entitled to ask for what. Not surprisingly, class, experience, nationality, and the great big unmentionable of race play a large part in determining where on the spectrum of what-I'd-like to what-I'll-actually-get a nanny is likely to find herself.

Charlotte, also from Ireland, is at the very top of the heap, considerably higher up than illegal Rhiannon. Not only is she married to an American, and therefore a resident with a green card, but she also has a bona fide, twenty-year-old diploma from Britain's venerable Norland College for Nannies. I found Charlotte through an agency, whose representative told me, "Someone of her caliber could pretty much write her own ticket. We've got families on our books who would kill for a nanny like Charlotte." When I asked the agency rep what exactly it was that made her such a catch, his answer made me smile. "Well, she is highly experienced, and qualified of course, and she has the most wonderful references from the Earl of Something-or-Other as well as Lord and Lady So-and-So." They might have had nothing more than threadbare tweeds and a freezing old castle with the roof falling in, but it seems that when it comes to getting someone else to raise their children, Britain's aristocracy still knows best.

Charlotte herself, however, was truly lovely, and by the end of our conversation I myself would have happily ransomed my children to have her come work for me. That might not have been enough, however. Her package, informally noted by the agency as a suggested list of perquisites, included a base salary of between nine hundred dollars and one thousand dollars per week; a car and a cell phone for her use, to be furnished by the employer; three weeks' paid vacation; a "voluntary" contribution to her health insurance, and a Christmas bonus (two weeks' salary was average). All on the books, of course. Should Charlotte be required to live in, she would expect no less than a private suite with her own bathroom, use of a car, cable TV and a phone line, access to laundry facilities, and free meals. Finally, Charlotte would not be expected to be on duty for more than fifty hours in any given week, at which point she would be paid overtime, and she should not be expected to do any housework, with the exception of tidying the children's rooms and preparing their meals.

As it happened, Charlotte was living out so that she could be home with her husband on evenings and weekends, and had found a "lovely family" of two working parents in Washington, D.C., who obviously felt this nanny was well worth her package, and then some.

> Even though I say so myself, I've been with so many families that by now it's as much about me interviewing them as them interviewing me. I always insist on meeting the children and spending a bit of time alone with them. I won't stand for bad manners, no matter how good the money, I'll tell you that! And yes, at this point I wouldn't take a job if I didn't have my independence. I get a lot of the perks, that's true. And I have been very lucky. I've had to turn down lots of offers and families begging me to come back. I've kept in touch with all my families; it's lovely, it's like having children all over the world! Once I was with a family in Saudi Arabia, and I had a car and driver and a cook, my goodness it was lavish. But I didn't like it there in the end, so far away from home. I do like to work with the young ones, that's when you can really have an influence on their lives. I do love it. It's such a privilege to be part of someone else's family. I really appreciate that they want someone like me to look after them. I mean, if you don't mind my saying, some of these women coming here from foreign countries, they don't speak proper English, they're illegal, calling themselves nannies. That does bother me, to be honest. So I suppose I do think I'm worth it. What's too much for someone who loves your children?

Not only are there plenty of mothers who could tell me exactly how much is too much, but there are just as many nannies who'd scarcely allow themselves to dream of the sweet deal Charlotte is getting, never mind actually feel entitled to it. Much of this has to do with the fact that unlike for Charlotte, for so many women becoming a nanny is a profession of last resort, very much on a par with menial, hands-on housekeeping or cleaning work that also doesn't formally require any special skills or qualifications. For equally as many it is merely a stopgap job, something to do for a couple of years to pay for school while they're waiting for their papers to come through, or for something better to come along. The truly remarkable thing about Charlotte is not so much the fact that families are falling over themselves to pay her upward of seventy thousand dollars a year, including all the extras, but that for her being a nanny is nothing less than her chosen lifelong profession and career. Go to any playground or Gymboree class in America and ask the women there—"Did you *always* want to be a nanny?"—and the likely response will be a combination of eye rolling, laughter, and disbelief.

Nevertheless, while looking after another woman's children would not be many a nanny's first choice of job, there are situations that are more bearable than others. While some nannies' perspectives on their employers was just as idiosyncratic as that of the mothers' on them, what many of them spelled out for me was surprisingly consistent. Lissa, a forty-two-year-old former elementary school teacher from Dubai, would have made an eloquent and articulate nanny union representative, stating her own and that of so many of her colleagues' position politely but firmly:

> So, first, tell me what to expect. I cannot guess what the mother want and read her mind, everybody different. Some people like lot of discipline and want to know every little thing, some people give me all the freedom. I don't mind, I can do it the way she wants. I do not want to be the best friend. If someone hire me, is because I'm grown-up woman with experience, who have children before. I don't want to hear the problems with her husband or her boss; is not my business. I got problems in my own family, I got friends. My business is with the children, and if you hire me you got to trust me, be honest with me. Be straight.

If you want housekeeper, hire housekeeper. If you want nanny, you want someone to teach your children, be patient with them, look after them, I do the job. Don't mix the two. Show me some respect. Don't tell me I do something wrong in front of the children, make me look like I am servant. I got to work like a team with the mother, we have same goal, to love the children and to teach them to be good.

If she does not believe I am good person, why she let me stay with her kids? She need to trust me, we must be on same team together. You need teacher, driver, cleaner, cook—okay, I will do that, but how much you will pay? I am human, too. If a kid hurts himself with mother is no big deal. With nanny is very, very big deal. Sometimes I think, "Lissa, go away from this kind of job, is so, so big responsibility." But is good responsibility too. Children are good. Is grown-ups that make the problems.

This, then, might be Lissa's wish list: a decent salary, no changing the rules midgame, respect, honesty, and trust. Perhaps, above all, an understanding on the mother's part that even though to be a nanny is real *work*, this doesn't also mean that the caretaker's attachments to the children isn't genuine or deep. In fact, it would seem that the whole business of nannies meeting the needs of mothers and vice versa could be pretty straightforward. If only it didn't involve our children.

Other than through a mother's instincts, the only way to figure this out is to go to the books. Even then it helps to have an idea of what answer you want to come up with before you even start looking, because this sort of research is primarily focused on justifying the choices that we make in our lives. So what do the experts say? If we were to take Dr. T. Berry Brazelton at his word, America's "favorite pediatrician" would in one fell swoop eliminate probably a good third of all nannies currently working for working mothers. In his *Touchpoints: The Essential Reference to Your Child's Emotional and Behavioral Development,* he says, "A nanny or mother's helper must be reliable and be able to make the baby her top priority. She mustn't have young children or a sick husband at home who needs her."

Dr. Brazelton's other ideas concerning what small children need from their caregivers, as well as the general lack of adequate child care in this country, are much more sympathetic and make a great deal of sense: He stresses a need for safety, attention to good nutrition, and a child-centered rhythm to the way the day is organized. He also feels children need a bright and pleasant atmosphere and as much individual attention as possible, in order to respect and encourage each child's emotional development. Despite this eminently sensible advice, for hard-pressed working mothers in need of guidance and reassurance this may not be the best place to look. In the very last paragraph of the *Touchpoints* chapter, "Allies in Development," Dr. Brazelton wonders about how difficult it must be to be forced to leave a child in substandard care by asking, "What does that do to the grief a mother feels anyway in entrusting a child to another person?" In this way, and even with the best of intentions, the tone of this expert's writing still makes it abundantly clear that while *some* nannies can certainly do a good job, no one can do it better than Mother.

While the more recent, post-Brazelton crop of parenting books is much more consistent in addressing and advising parents, one general, underlying message hasn't changed a great deal. What is more, the parents who read these books, myself included, don't seem to mind particularly. As one mother put it:

> Oh yeah, I'm all for forcing people to be politically correct in their language. And frankly, it would really rub me up the wrong way if some book or article about whatever, sleep problems or homework strategies, just said, "Mothers do this, mothers try that." But I still know it's me they're talking about, at least most of the time. I mean, doesn't it make you laugh when you go to a

PTA meeting and they thank the "parent volunteers," and every single person in the room is a mother? And if there *are* a couple of dads, let's face it, everyone's just going to think they're unemployed. And no one takes offense when they read a magazine called *Working Mother,* do they? I mean, how ridiculous would it be to name a magazine *Working Father?* Actually, if for the sake of magazine demographics and gender equality one had to come up with a P.C. companion title to *Working Mother* magazine, it should probably be *Stay-At-Home Dad.* Those guys probably need more help than anybody.

While I won't venture to speak for stay-at-home dads, there is another category of need among nannies that bears mentioning, and that probably should not be a surprise: quite simply, the need to be needed. As a mother I must admit that often I wish my children didn't need me quite as much as they obviously do, or that their demands for my help, attention, or a bedtime story didn't always, mysteriously, come either all at the same time or at the very moment that I'm settling in to read a book, go out for dinner, or have a quiet conversation with another adult. While children definitely have a sixth sense about just when it is that they can bug you the most, their caretakers don't seem to find this nearly as irritating as mothers, sorry, "parents," do—quite the contrary.

Carol is quiet, well spoken, and childlike. She has moved around quite a bit in her twenty-six years, trailing after a couple of boyfriends and looking for a good place to settle. She obviously loves babies and talks with tremendous affection about the little ones she has looked after.

> There's nothing more helpless than a little baby, is there? It's just wonderful the way you can teach them things, like when they look at you and kind of try to mimic the expressions on your face.

You do get terribly attached to them, it's impossible not to really, when they get to know you and rely on you, like, for everything. Food and sleep and a cuddle. I just love babies, they're so gorgeous. Some of the mothers I've worked for, they didn't know how lucky they were! I hate to say it, but some of those babies, they got more of what they needed from me than their own mothers. The little boy I look after now, we just have the best time together. He's always happy to see me, it's so cute.

Liana, a feisty, jovial, and loud nanny from Mexico, relishes the relationship she has with the older daughters in "her" family, and while she obviously doesn't think much about their mother and her choices, the girls make it all worthwhile. "I tell you, those kids, they need me; their mother doesn't care. They come to me for advice on *eeee*verything. Boys, clothes, stuff at school, I mean, they tell things to me they could *never* tell their mom. She just treat me like I'm the maid or something, but the girls, sometime they come to me and they say, 'Liana, we're really embarrassed Mommy is so mean to you, please don't take her serious.' I think I go to them for reference when I get another job."

Whether it is something that happens quietly and in private or openly and with the parents' approval, the sense of intimacy and pure affection between a nanny and her children was possibly the only aspect of the relationship between nannies and mothers that all caregivers agreed on: It is good, and it is essential. You've got to like the children, and they need to like you. The money might be terrible, the mother might be a witch and a hard-ass or neurotic and impossible, but if the kids love you, you could just about hang in there and bear it.

While the criteria for what makes either a good employer or a good nanny are broad and often quixotic in the details, the core values (to use a business term my husband likes to bandy about) are surprisingly consistent. We might be looking for that perfect nanny who is both a Virgo and has a big butt, but if she isn't also loving, trustworthy, and reliable we won't even let her in the door. Prioritize and compromise: When it comes to getting what you need, that's what it's all about.

Good feminist that I am, I'd guilt trip myself out of a job pretty quickly if I allowed my actions to be dictated by the fact that my freedom to pursue interests other than my children rides entirely on the backs of women less fortunate than I am. In truth, that peculiar territory of need connecting mothers to their nannies and vice versa is regulated by something much more prosaic than my bleeding-heart-liberal conscience on the one hand, and ferocious mother-hen instincts on the other. Much like oil and water, child care is a commodity for which there is a market. In order for it to function, there have to be buyers and suppliers, and in order for the whole thing to not get completely out of whack, everyone needs to follow certain rules. I should say: Break them, and you will do so at your peril, but the one aspect in which this market is different and more complicated than all others, and therefore immune to economic theory and logic, is that if we break them it isn't just us but also our children who will bear the brunt.

Here is my personal checklist for minimizing the risk that my children don't get the short end of the stick as I head out into the world without them, while maximizing the likelihood of finding and keeping a nanny type of person whom we love and who loves us. First and foremost, no price gouging. If you pay for one thing, don't turn it into something else, expecting to have a freebie thrown in. Not only is there no such thing as a free lunch, where my children are concerned I'm under no illusion that there is such a thing as free babysitting either (other than that provided by their father, which of course isn't actually babysitting at all), and that's just fine. The next thing I would urge every mother to do is to find her inner hippie, take her by the hand, and chant, all together now: Love is good! More love is better! Love is a gift! Having another person in your children's lives who truly cares for them, even though money is exchanged in the process, is nothing to feel guilty about.

The other person to get in touch with is your inner Napoleon, the most charismatic of leaders and brilliant of strategists (that is, until his grandiose ambitions to conquer the unconquerable got the better of him). Getting most of what you need and want from your nanny most of the time is the most any mother can expect. Don't get greedy, or it might literally drive you insane, in which case both your children and their father would be far worse off as well. I always think that my child-care situations and those of so many of my friends and the women I have talked to are a lot like those impossible and ubiquitous FDA-recommended food pyramids plastered on the walls of every school cafeteria in America. They really serve no other purpose than to remind us that most children manage to thrive and grow despite the fact that the proportion of fats to carbs to proteins that they ingest is probably all wrong. Just like the undisputed expert in nannydom said: A spoonful of sugar does make the medicine go down, even if it is just a pile of empty calories. We might as well admit that we need our nannies, that our nannies need us, and our children, God bless their innocent hearts, need us both.

guilt

*a*RE YOU A good mother? The best mother you can possibly be? The kind of mother that those amazingly wonderful, adorable, and unique children of yours deserve, all the time? Me neither. I know precisely one person who would happily answer that question in the affirmative, and she's almost as insufferable as her children. Another friend, who at first answered my question with a confident "Yes!" followed what was a very accurate assessment of herself with a long pause, and then started to backtrack for half an hour, overjustifying every decision she'd ever made and ending apologetically with a description of herself as "a disgusting control freak." There are many others, in fact almost all in my circle of friends and acquaintances, whom I think of as wonderful mothers. Unfortunately, the images they have of themselves, and those that others have of them, rarely line up. Part of this has to do with the tendency many women have of immediately downplaying or deflecting any compliment they might be paid, instead of saying "Thank you, yes, I really am very good at that, and I'm so glad you noticed." Even more unfortunate, where their perceptions of themselves as mothers are concerned, for some reason doubt seems to weigh even more heavily than in areas of professional accomplishments or other talents. In fact, a healthy measure of self-deprecation regarding our mothering skills appears to have become almost de rigueur, as much part of our conversations as bemoaning the fact that everyone is working too hard, traffic is getting worse, and the weather is increasingly weird. What kind of world is this for our kids to grow up in?

Philippa, a good friend of mine and a constant inspiration to me in almost all aspects of combining motherhood with a serious career, summed it up for all of us: "A good mother? Oh Lord. I don't really know how to answer that. I do all right, I suppose, but I could do better." Given a "very helpful husband," her almost superhuman attention to every detail of her children's lives, and the tremendous competence with which she solves her clients' problems on top of managing her family, it's hard to imagine how Philippa could do better. And yet . . . it doesn't take much to also imagine a little voice in her head whispering that a good mother would surely be available to help with homework every night; that a good mother would most certainly not schedule a business trip that coincides with daughter number two's opening night performance in the school play; and that only a really *horrible* mother would send her son to school on a breakfast of oatmeal and Tylenol instead of staying home with him to nurse his runny nose and sore throat.

One doesn't have to look far to realize that there are few mythical creatures in American culture as revered and as fantastically endowed as the "Good Mother" (GM for short). She is beautiful, kind, patient, and wise. She never yells, she is always fair, and even though she does the world's most important job, she wants little for herself. She is play date, secretary of transportation, general, cook, cleaner, teacher, and dispenser of hugs and sugar-free sweets. And lest you think she can't possibly be all that and not also a lumpy old frump, beware: With one swipe of the Maybelline wand and a cleverly draped silk scarf she'll turn right back into the sex kitten she was before the kids (she learned that trick from her subscriptions to *Good House-keeping* and *Parents* magazines). It is generally preferred that she not work outside the home, but should she be forced to nonetheless, we all know that nothing compares to the satisfaction she derives from her children and the charity work she does in her free time while her children are conveniently away at school. She does not, by the way, have a nanny, and she manages to get all the exercise she needs to stay fit by doing lunges as she vacuums her immaculate home and jogging while pushing a stroller. Yeah, right.

With the possible exception of losing weight, very few issues have generated as many tomes of advice, guidance, and analysis as that of how women can be better mothers (sorry, parents). As a first-time mother eager to do the right thing, it can make your head spin. As a second-, third-, or fourth-time mother who is trying to finish a chapter in her book (or at the very least the advice column in *Working Mother*) before she dozes off at midnight, it is sure to make you feel hopelessly inadequate, confused, or simply exhausted, yet again. The only thing I know for sure after two decades of observing, reading about, and interpreting people's attitudes toward motherhood is this: *It's not fair.* It wasn't fair when my mother made me go to bed earlier than my older sisters, and it still isn't fair now that I'm writing yet another book about mothers, parenting, and children while my own children are enjoying McDonald's for dinner with the au pair instead of a home-cooked meal with me. It's sad, but given a choice between broccoli (Good Mother!) and French fries (Baaad Mother!) they'd go for the fries every time. Not fair!

Damned if you do, damned if you don't. Either way there's never a shortage of things to feel guilty about. At the risk of sounding Oliver Stoneish, it does appear as if there is a universal conspiracy afoot to make sure mothers never feel completely good about what they are doing, because just when you think you've got it figured out, "they" move the goalposts yet again. It's not that the advice is bad. It's hard to go to Dr. Spock, Penelope Leach, T. Berry Brazelton, or any of the other child-care gurus and point to any one thing and say, "Are you insane? How could you actually expect me to *do* that? It's simply impossible!" It never is, in theory or in isolation. Quite the contrary: Bonding is lovely; proper nutrition is essential; consistency, warmth, discipline, spontaneity, and stimulation are all undoubtedly needed if our children are to have an optimum chance of thriving in the environment that we as mothers (sorry, parents) create for them. It's the cumulative effect of all of this advice that is so insidious. We're supposed to do *all* of it, all the time, with the result that forty years after the "problem with no name" first reared its ugly head, it hasn't acquired just one but more like thirty-seven names. Guilt, however, is definitely the glue that sticks it all together: Be warm, but don't smother. Be spontaneous, yet consistent. Show discipline without losing your temper. Be fun, but not frivolous. Give them their freedom without losing control. Keep your promises. Never tell a lie, yet don't tell them more of the truth than they can handle. Make mistakes and there will be consequences! Give them everything they need, and some of what they want, but whatever you do, don't spoil them. Remember, you're the mother (sorry, parent). Whatever happens is on your head, and yours alone!

With this kind of baggage tucked away in their briefcases, pocketbooks, and diaper bags it's no wonder that many working mothers tend to be ever so slightly neurotic when it comes to handing over their children to a nanny, particularly for the first time. Sandra, a newly retired accountant in her late forties, remembers it like this:

> Oh God, those first few months I was just a mess. I cried every day. I called twice an hour. I used to have this little newborn baby picture of my son on my desk, and every time I looked at it my milk would come gushing out, and then I'd start to cry again because I thought I wouldn't have any left for him by the time I

made it back home, sopping wet shirt and all. My nanny at that time, well—a baby nurse, really—was just wonderful, though. She was so kind. I think she was at least a grandmother, with grown children, and it showed. Knowing she had that kind of experience really helped. It made me feel like I wasn't quite the worst mother in the world to leave my baby behind. Steven (Dad) was just completely bamboozled by the whole thing. I suppose it was a bit of postpartum, but it was also more than that. He kept saying, "If you hate it so much, why don't you just stay home? I'd love it if you stayed home; we'll manage some-how." I suppose it might have helped, for a while. But what I re-ally remember was this overwhelming feeling of inadequacy. Almost panic. Like I had given birth to this child, this perfect little person, and suddenly all these things were expected of me that I wasn't sure I could handle. I still feel that way sometimes. Like I am the biggest fraud. I mean, what do I really know about being mother to an eleven-year-old boy?

It seems obvious to me that Sandra knows an awful lot about mothering preadolescent boys, but neither her friends nor her hus-band's reassurances seem to count for much.

Steven says I shouldn't obsess so much, that he'll be fine, that he's always *been* fine, that he's survived four nannies and three moves and that we'll always be his parents. But I do wonder. I don't regret any one thing per se, I think, but I'm still sure there are things I could have done differently, different people or places we could have chosen that would have been better for him and the girls. That's why I've decided to stay home now, while the girls are still little. And I do feel better about myself as a mother now that I don't have a nanny. But I'm also older, and we're more financially secure, and I know I have a place to go back to at work if I want to. At least for now, and it's only been a couple of months. I know perfectly well that the really hard decision for me will come in maybe two years, because if I don't go back to work then, in some way, shape, or form, I'll truly be past my sell-by date.

For every professional woman who finally makes the decision to give up work in order to be a "proper" mother there is a honeymoon period. Finally, you're on the other side, where the grass has been so much greener in all these seasons of doubting and rushing and compromising. Now that you're here there's no end to all the things you're going to do, not just for the kids, but also for yourself: volunteer at school; get in shape; cook dinner every night; read more; catch up on all the movies you haven't had time to see in the last ten years. . . . If you can still afford a housekeeper once or twice a week that would be nice, but really you're looking forward to doing it all, and without a nanny. Until you try. You find out pretty quickly that "proper motherhood" is far from idyllic or easy, and that there still isn't enough time to read the books piling up by the side of your bed. Without the child care you used to take for granted, being in charge of your family is just a different kind of job, and one you don't get paid for. Sandra, too, is coming to the end of her I-stopped-working honeymoon, and although she doesn't regret her decision, she is beginning to realize that the thing she longed for all these years doesn't actually exist.

I so desperately wanted a break from the grind. It hasn't been such an easy adjustment for the children, either. On the one hand they love it, and on the other I know they really miss Eva sometimes. I miss her, too. It was just awful having to let her go. And I do miss work. Not just because I know I let down my partners and all the younger women in the firm; they all used to hold me up as some kind of an example—"look at Sandra, it *can*

be done!" That's bad enough. But it's also that sense of achievement and belonging, not to mention financial independence, in
a productive, adult environment. It's something you really don't
get when you're "just" a homemaker.

I mean, I do admit I used to get pretty fed up with the other
mothers, who didn't work, partly of course, because they would
always schedule the damn parent coffee at nine in the morning,
and I could never go. But now I've been home for a while and am
getting increasingly sucked into the whole volunteer and PTA
thing. It's hard not to. I'm beginning to understand those mothers
who turn their children into another career. Perhaps it's just a
matter of time before I end up doing the same. But so far, so good.
It's just the nature of the beast, I guess. You're always just kind of
groping along, pretending you know it all when you don't.

The thought that we might be letting our children down somehow
is rarely far from the surface, despite plenty of evidence to the contrary. If, as one interviewee put it, a mother should feel that "there
isn't really anything to feel guilty about, but I just can't help it," she
wouldn't have to look much farther than her TV or a copy of *People*
magazine for a bona fide reason. As any consumer of various mass
media channels knows, a slow news day is the perfect time to run yet
another story about yet another study that shows how children in day
care or who are farmed out to regular babysitters are somehow not as
well off as those who have "proper" mothers at home with them all
day. These reports seem to appear with crushing regularity once or
twice a year, as do hideous tales of children left unsupervised and
falling prey to Internet stalkers, toddlers falling out of windows carelessly left open while their mothers are out shopping, and teenage
girls turning tricks for pocket money after school because there's no
one waiting for them at home. You might not feel guilty for what you
are doing (or not doing, as the case may be), but you're not in this

alone. Go talk to the nanny and figure out what *she* could be doing better. There must be something!

A closer look shows this illusive something is not only in our heads, but not at all supported by the facts. It's always easy to blame the mom. From Bruno Bettelheim and his infamous "refrigerator mothers," whom he held responsible for their children's autism as early as the 1950s, to the equally infamous 1997 nanny trial of Louise Woodward, during which it turned out that selfish, careerist moms rather than careless babysitters were to blame for their children's suffering, public opinion has pretty much held firm: When it comes to shortchanging and therefore damaging our children in the love and nurture department, working mothers are by definition guilty until proven innocent. Before Woodward's controversial murder conviction (her sentence was eventually reduced by the judge to involuntary manslaughter, and yet again to time served after she had spent 279 days in jail), there was a veritable feeding frenzy in the media focusing on all the ways in which the dead baby's mother had failed her son. Talk-show callers and their popular conservative hosts alike vilified the mother for being a callous yuppie who was clearly working not in order to make ends meet, but just because she wanted to "improve her lifestyle." What kind of a mother would leave her baby and his brother with a low-paid teenager who had "come to the United States to seek adventure," when she obviously didn't even need the money she made at her part-time job as an ophthalmologist? Certainly not popular talk-radio star Dr. Laura Schlessinger, who led the attacks on Mrs. Eappen with her signature slogan.

Yet, the proof for a mother that doing a job does not equal doing damage to her children is also abundant and remarkably consistent: Despite considerable effort and decades of painstaking research on the effects of women's employment on their children, study after study after study has concluded that to merely have a mother who works outside the home has virtually nothing to do with how happy, successful, and well adjusted a child is likely to be, both in the short and the long terms.

Other factors however, make a great deal of difference, although each of these is also fraught with the possibility of mother guilt. Material constraints are right at the top of the list (are they getting enough of all the stuff they need and want?). Others issues include stability (well, this marriage sucks but let's keep it together for the kids), quality time and attention (oh God, please don't ask me to help with homework tonight), and the extent to which we're able to make our children a priority and truly focus on them (the meeting ran late but I *promise* I'll make it to your game next time). In short, once we get to the point where we can agree that Bettelheim was wrong, where work is something that we do for *everybody's* benefit, and where fathers actually begin to do as much of the nitty-gritty parenting work as they say they want to, guilt still has a way of making us doubt ourselves.

Indeed, many of the mothers who talked to me, particularly those with infants and toddlers, seemed to feel that the guilt they carried with them to the office every day was nothing less than the price of admission—accepted, expected, an annoying thing to have to deal with but really par for the course. How could one, as a mother, possibly feel good about leaving one's children in the hands of another, no matter on how many levels and in how many ways this choice or state of affairs can be justified? And if you do feel good about it, well—you ought to feel guilty about *that!*

According to Jane, a radiologist and mother of two boys,

> It just comes with the territory, doesn't it? My mother always worked. I remember that, even though I never questioned the fact that she had to be out there having a job, if I wanted to I could always turn the screws and make her feel horrible. You know, the sort of thoughtless, manipulative thing teenagers do and say, like, "But Kathy's mom is *making* her Halloween costume. I don't want

one from the store." My mother should have just told me to cut it out, and that I was damn lucky, and that Kathy was a bubble-headed moron. But she never did. And I don't now, either, when my son pulls that stuff. I know I should, but it gets right down to that insecurity I have that somehow I don't actually deserve to be his mother, and that maybe, God forbid, he's right! Maternal guilt can be very lucrative for children, you know!

Oh God, and the nanny. Don't even ask about some of the stupid things I've let my nanny get away with because I was feeling guilty—for coming home late, changing plans on her at the last minute, that kind of thing. It's really a sort of cause-and-effect thing, what's it called? A self-fulfilling prophecy. Yeah, my husband feels guilty, too, but it's about different things, and then he tends to be much more practical about dealing with it. You know, "I'm sorry I can't give you this now, but how about next week at seven sharp I'll give you that instead, deal? Deal. Done." With me, my son knows to spin things out ad nauseam. I don't even think he does it deliberately. I do it to myself, as if to be a good mother I have to worry. So, he gives me something to worry about. And if he doesn't, I give it to myself!

Given how much the media and all the voices all around us constantly exhort us to love our children (and despite the fact that we all occasionally want to kill them), the notion of "good enough" simply doesn't cut it anymore. My older friends tell me about a brief and shining moment in the 1970s when for a few years the female characters in movies and television sitcoms were flawed and real, and far more loved for their imperfections, anger, and resourcefulness in dealing with whiny kids, philandering husbands, or patronizing bosses than they were for sacrificing themselves at the altar of perfect motherhood.

One of these was Ann Romano, played by Bonnie Franklin on *One*

Day at a Time; another was Alice in the movie *Alice Doesn't Live Here Anymore,* and later in the TV show *Alice,* both major hits. Erica, a scientific researcher now in her early fifties with a grown-up daughter, remembers both characters well.

> Ann was never supposed to be perfect, but she was funny, really funny. And she tried so hard to do the right thing to bring up her kids with a little help from a lot of people. I used to watch it all the time. It was a really good, old-fashioned sitcom, with genuine characters. Sure, they were caricatures to a certain extent, all the stupid macho men she had to deal with, but they were irreverent and funny. Also, she was divorced just like me, and had these daughters she was struggling to raise, so I really identified with that. Babysitters or day care never featured in the show; that would have been too much for TV at the time, even if it was the seventies. But you know, there was a sense that it was okay for her to make mistakes, as long as you knew she was trying her best; that she was a good feminist; actually, that it was good to *be* a feminist, even. There is no one on TV nowadays I can really identify with. I don't mean that because I'm not young and sexy anymore. I mean, there's a lot of great women characters, but they're either childless and brilliant and powerful, like CJ in *The West Wing,* or kind of weird and wise and beautifully single, like Carrie on *Sex and the City* or Grace on *Will & Grace.* Or they have kids and are completely overwhelmed by them, like that one character on *Desperate Housewives.* It's hard to imagine them dealing with child-care issues in anything other than a trivializing way, isn't it?

Even I am old enough to remember that *Roseanne* was funny, and so were reruns of the *Cosby Show,* but the working parents in both of those sitcoms never seemed to need so much as a hint of child care.

In this way the most implausible character of them all was probably Claire Huxtable: a well-educated and well-to-do African American lawyer with her physician husband and four children, in the most successful family sitcom of all time *ever,* and yet she does it all without any babysitter other than her own older children. Another media vehicle in which babysitters, nannies, or any other form of child care is consistently and conspicuously absent is the celebrity profile. There is Joan Lunden, giving *Redbook* a tour of her nursery and talking ecstatically about the joys of having twins after fifty; Elle Macpherson, "the Body," producing two beautiful sons with nary a stretch mark or increase in the size of her minuscule, butt-hugging, belly-baring jeans; Madonna taking up writing children's books to entertain her two little ones with wholesome morality tales in between recording albums and impersonating Christ on the cross during a concert tour.

These stories do, of course, make for good copy. I'm as much a sucker as the next person for looking through pictures of one celebrity offspring after another, artfully arranged in gorgeous photographs and accompanied by their beautiful, devoted, besotted mothers. No nanny in sight! She must do it all herself! No wonder I feel fat today, and more than usually guilty for letting the kids watch *SpongeBob* so I can catch a break and have a glass of wine. Leafing through *InStyle* magazine (November 2005 issue) in search of wardrobe inspiration doesn't help either. There she is again—superstar supermom. This time it's Julia Roberts leaving others dumbstruck in the wake of her "new mommy glow" while "illumination radiates from her maternal core" all nicely packaged in a fantastic Dolce & Gabbana gown. So who *is* looking after the children while she's hosting that awards show? It's obviously not a topic anyone in our celebrity-obsessed culture likes to dwell on.

One doesn't need to be a supersleuth reporter to realize that celebrities must have to rely on babysitters and nannies and various other forms of child care just like all other working mothers, and probably even more so—nor that they love their children any less because of it. How could anyone possibly look that gorgeous and go to so many glamorous parties without a whole coterie of nannies, sitters, cooks, and drivers? I don't begrudge the Madonnas of this world—if I had fame, beauty, talent, tons of money, and absolutely no privacy whatsoever I would do the same. I do resent, however, the fairy-tale notion that this is what motherhood can and should look like for some people: guilt-free, low-cal, and always just delightful.

In the mother-child-nanny triangle guilt takes many forms, and it has a way of sneaking into and distorting many perfectly good relationships. Clearly, Mama guilt vis-à-vis the children is the one we can all relate to, but just as many mothers manage to saddle themselves with a guilty conscience when it comes to their nannies as well, often with good reason and awkward consequences. In fact, in terms of employer/employee conversations there is probably none that is quite as awkward and steeped in paranoia, guilt, fear, and, not infrequently, lies as the one when you tell the nanny that she no longer has a job—or, for that matter, tell the parents and the children that they no longer have a nanny.

This mother and her caretaker had had an unusually long, close, and loving relationship, which is of course the reason why it was ultimately such a dreadful wrench to end it.

I'm telling you, I stayed in that job for at least six months longer than I really wanted or needed to. I knew I couldn't afford to quit without cutting back on our expenses, and of course the only way to really do that was to let Gina go. At that point she'd been with us since both my girls were born, more than ten years, can you imagine? She spent more time with them than she did with her own kids, for heaven's sakes! And she was always there, always, for everything. When they were sick, when they had concerts and birthday parties. Jeez, she probably taught them how to walk, even though she managed to pretend I was the one who did it. And they loved her, they really did. So now I want to change careers and try freelancing from home, and all of a sudden I'm supposed to just fire this woman who's been through just about everything with me and my children? I just couldn't do it. I'd lie awake at night, rehearsing things I would say. For months on end I just couldn't look her straight in the eye. Of course she figured it out before I did, in the end. She basically forced to me say it, that we'd have to let her go, that we didn't really need her anymore, that everyone was growing up. I was crying hysterically, really, it was one of the worst things I ever had to do in my life. Oh God, and the girls, they hated me for months afterward. They still talk to her on the phone a lot, and sometimes she comes to visit, always remembers birthdays, all the big events. She's with another family now. I know them. I know she can't be making as much money as she did with us, which also stinks, you know? She builds up ten years of experience with one family and then she's got to start from scratch with the next one, not to mention that she's ten years older and kind of running out of steam, and really getting to the age where she'd like to sit down most times and not chase after some toddler on the playground. She really deserved to grow old with us, you know? I wish *so* much that we had enough money to be able to do that. God, it still makes me cry just thinking about it.

When I spoke to Gina she confirmed how hard it had been to leave "her" girls and how she'd seen it coming for months, dreading the inevitable and feeling guilty about secretly looking for another job when she hadn't even been let go yet.

But I had to, really, didn't have much choice, did I? I felt so bad. Going out behind their backs and talking to people. Oh, that was bad. I'm not their mother, I guess, but I was just as close to them as a mother would've been. *Anytime* you got to leave your kids you feel bad. It wasn't anybody's fault, you know. It wasn't mine! You just can't help but look for somebody or something to blame. Stupid that I should've felt that way, but I felt so guilty, like I was deserting them or something. It turned out all right in the end, we're still pretty close and talk sometimes, but in the beginning they were so mad at me for leaving! It kinda teaches you not to get too close, you know, but they do, they become family. And nothing can mess you up like family, can it?

My friend Marianne also had a nanny, Celia, who was dearly beloved by everyone in the family and especially her two small daughters. She had looked after both of them since birth. The oldest was maybe five when quite by accident Marianne found out from the nanny's sister that Celia was illiterate.

I was just devastated! I started to leave little notes around the house to figure out if it was true, but there was just one excuse after another—"I didn't see it, I forgot"—so clearly it was true. I didn't know *what* to do. I mean, I just knew we couldn't keep her, but I couldn't tell her why, I simply didn't have the heart. She was such a proud woman, and so wonderful in every other way. In the end I made something up. Oh, I cried and cried, it was one of the worst things I've ever had to do."

Marianne might have succeeded in allowing Celia to maintain her dignity, but the cost of propping up what had become the facade of their relationship was considerable for both of them.

I suspect that in no area of employer-employee relationships are white lies, particularly about sick or dying relatives, quite as rampant as between child-care givers and takers. "My father died." "My mother is in the hospital." "My sister's decided to move in with us, so she's going to look after the kids." I lost my passport and missed my plane." "The doctor says I've developed an allergy to dogs." "I just want to take a break from work for a while and stay home." "My husband thinks it'll do him good to be with lots of other kids in day care." I've heard them all, and even used a few myself, and I know too that more often than not these lies are told for two reasons: to alleviate our guilt for not being honest about our true motives, and to avoid retribution. The fear that somehow the nanny will take out her resentment of us on the children is a powerful motivator for fudging the truth. Most nannies I've spoken to insist that if anything the opposite is true, but of course there are always those few genuinely bad eggs who will poison the atmosphere for everyone and strike fear into every mother's heart.

Victoria is a marketing executive with a big demanding job, a husband with a big demanding job, and two big and—according to their mother—far too demanding children. Given her deadline-prone and often unpredictable schedule, replete with trips and late nights, her experience with nannies is long and checkered. Like most mothers, the times she remembers most vividly are those when things went horribly wrong.

> I think George was four, and every day he'd come home from his little preschool program on the bus. So obviously I was expecting his nanny to be at the bus stop waiting for him, and to walk home together. There weren't a lot of streets to cross, but at least a few. And once they were home, I had told her, I didn't want them to watch TV but really to play—some craft project, go to the park, kick a ball around, whatever. So one day we're in the car together, just the two of us, and he said something about the nanny that just made me stop in my tracks. I don't even know what it was anymore—I just knew I had to get to the bottom of it, whatever it was. So I stop the car and get in the back with him, and we just

sit there, and I kind of try and get him to talk, tell him how much I love him, that he can say anything to me, that I really need to know everything that goes on when I'm not there, that I'll never ever get mad, all those things. So he climbs into my lap and starts talking in this tiny, scared little voice, and basically the story that comes out is that he's been terrified of telling me because he thought I would get mad at the nanny, and then she would get mad at him, and he's afraid of her.

Some days she didn't come to pick him up at the bus at all, and he'd walk home by himself—by himself, four years old!—and then, when he did get home she would lock him in his room so she could watch TV, "Because your mommy thinks TV's bad for you." Oh my God. I can't even describe to you how I felt. I honestly think that was one of the worst moments of my life, ever.

The stupid thing was that *I* felt like such an ass for trusting this woman; that, you know, for some reason *I should have known*. I fired her right away, and I didn't even tell her why! I didn't say to her, "I am firing you because you put my child in danger, and because you locked him in his room, and because he was scared of you," I just said, "Goodbye, we won't be needing you anymore. Please don't come back." Of course my husband was horrified, too, but once she was gone he just said, "Okay, chalk that one up to experience; next time get better references, and we'll both make a point of dropping in unannounced a *lot* in the first couple of months," and he was over it. Me? I've been paranoid ever since. I ask everyone to spy on them—literally! The neighbors, the storekeepers, the bus driver, anybody who might see them out and about. I used to laugh at people with nannycams, but not anymore.

Almost nothing, ever, will get under a mother's skin quite as much as the feeling that somewhere along the line she screwed up her kids, regardless of the fact that whatever it was that she did might have looked like the only viable option at the time. Maxine is a Caribbean nanny who has worked for three families since coming to the United States when she was twenty-six, leaving behind her seven-year-old son. By the time we met, her son Wayne was twenty-five and a young father himself, living with Maxine, his girlfriend and six-month-old baby, and with his ten-year-old sister, in a small house on the outer edges of a sprawling American city. Maxine has finally given up nannying, although the money would probably be better, in favor of hospital work in a pediatric ward. Speaking of the children she used to look after, an unmistakable note of sadness and resignation creeps into her voice, and she explains that "it just got to be too hard to part with them. I mean, you tolerate the parents because you love the kids, and whatever else you want to do doesn't even matter—you love them, and they grow up in your hands, and then someone else decides that you got to separate. It's so arbitrary. I just used to feel cheated; it was always such a letdown. I mean, you watch them grow up and change, and then, 'boom,' you're supposed to be out of their lives just like that."

When I ask Maxine how it felt to leave Wayne behind, it takes her a long time to answer.

> I really can't even describe it. I was carrying so much guilt, all the time. All little boys used to look like him, any little boy riding his bike in the street. I was so angry, just full of resentment, blamed everybody but myself. I know it messed him up. He knows it too, all those things he couldn't have when he was a kid. Oh, I spent so much money on phone cards and sending them stuff, food, clothes, everything. And then when he started to come on visits it was almost worse, because I had to make him go back. He was always in trouble. Then I had to start using the visits with me as incentives. Like, "If you don't have a good

report card, then you can't come see me." No child should have to grow up like that, like, "You can only see your mother if you get a good report card." I didn't know what else to do. I left him with my mother because I thought she'd do a better job. But she didn't use the strong hand with Wayne that she used with me and my sister. We have a good relationship now, but when she had Wayne it was bad between us. It was like everybody resented everybody for something—like me having to leave Wayne with her was proof that she'd been a failure with me. And now, with his sister, he'll still bring it up sometimes, things like, "She has stuff I never had." I don't know if he says that to make me feel guilty or whatever. But it's true.

Maxine still struggles with the bills every month, and she relies on Wayne and his girlfriend to help pay the mortgage. Her granddaughter, Keisha, has a nanny of her own who comes to the house to look after the baby while her mother is at work. Maxine is trying not to get too deeply involved, but she admits that she can see the young couple breaking up. She doesn't like being a grandmother much. Much as she loves Keisha, more than likely she's just another baby that's going to disappear from her life and cause heartache. Maxine insists, however, that she never did feel any resentment toward her employers and their children. "Just wishes. Like wishing I could have my own children with me. That I could give them all they wanted. The families I was with, they were always generous with me, that wasn't it. There're days when you'd get mad, but every job has that. It's missing your own kids. Really missing them so much it hurts. Wishing they were with you."

Clearly nothing in my repertoire of guilt, nor the feeling that I might be missing some small part of my children's lives and that they might be missing me, can quite compare to the heartbreaking dilemma of the absentee mother. The basic narrative is usually the same: start with grinding poverty, lack of opportunity, and no money for the schools, the education, and the bribes to corrupt officials that might lead to a better life. From there it's easy to see that some parents feel they ultimately have no choice but to seek their fortune among the hardworking, sometimes illegal, and often exploited armies of domestic workers who clean the houses, cook the meals, and look after the children of richer people in richer countries. They come to the United States from everywhere, but particularly the Caribbean, South America, and Southeast Asia, and to a lesser degree southern and Central Europe. Striking out for unfamiliar shores in search of a better life is, of course, a great and cherished American tradition, a well-worn stepping-stone on the way to achieving the mythical American dream. At this point and in this century it would be pretty much inconceivable for the average (if there is such a thing) American mother to do what hundreds of thousands of other, less fortunate mothers still feel forced to do in order to support their children: essentially, abandon them to someone else's care, pray for the best, and find work in a faraway country that pays enough to send money home every month to give them all a better future.

Irma is a bright and pretty Filipina in her midthirties. By the time I met her, she had been living on the West Coast for eight years, long since separated from the American family of midlevel diplomats with whom she first legally entered this country from Saudi Arabia. She has three children, age fifteen, thirteen, and twelve, all going to private schools and living with her husband in the Philippines, leading what she calls a "better class lifestyle in a big house, nice neighborhood." The last time she saw any of them was nine years earlier, and her visa—and with it any chance of going home to visit her family—had expired twelve months after she arrived here.

> You see, this is how it works. When you're from the Philippines, nobody wants you in their country. Except to do the dirty work,

you know? So this is how lot of people come to America, with some family from overseas, like me—they bring me with them from Saudi because it's so cheap there to have domestic worker, and they can get me tourist visa to get through immigration when they move back to home posting. It was a good family, twin boys, lovely lady, I like them. But then we are in America, and after a few month I ask them to pay me like they would pay American worker, and they say no! It's not enough we bring you over here, pay you more money than before? A few months longer I say nothing, but then I see other people get paid more, they get vacation, no work on weekends, all that, and I say this is not fair! And other ladies in the park, they come to me all the time and they ask, "You're so good with the children, so nice, you want to be nanny for me?" So I get in a fight with my family, and the father, he says he can't pay so much, that he won't sponsor me to renew the visa, and I have to leave them. It was one day to the next! Just one day to say good-bye to the boys, after four years! I don't know why he is so cruel, he says to me he thinks it's better for the children to make a clean break, but of course no one thinks about my feelings. I cry and cry and cry, I feel like I have nobody!

All my children gone, no family, nothing. So I stay with a friend, another Filipina I meet in church, and she helped me find another job. I went to family with two children and one more born three months later. So there I have this little baby, all day long, he sleep with me, I get up for him at night, I take care of his brother and sister all day long, I really love them. They love me! Their mother loves me! I just try not to think of my own children, it hurts too much. In beginning, I close my eyes and kiss the babies and pretend they are mine, try to remember how they smell, how they feel. It's so hard. I talk to them every week,

they say, "Mammi" to me on the phone, and they write me letters, send pictures. But, you know, now mostly it's, "Mammi, we
need computer, Mammi, we need camera." And whatever it is, I
send. What else can I do? It's how I can show them I love them.
How else can I show them? Two more years. Then I save enough
money for all the school, we buy a house, we can buy a little
store, my husband wants to start a taxi business. And it's true, is
all with the money I make to be nanny for other children. It's not
right, but this is how the world is. I feel I do the best I can for
my children, but it means they grow up without me. I am lucky,
my husband is good man, I have my sisters and my mother look
out for me, so they tell me what is going on. It's hard for him,
too. Nine years he is father alone, no wife, it's not natural. It's
not natural for a mother not to see her children grow up. I hope
I do the right thing. I hope I have grandchildren, and one day we
all have enough money to keep family all together.

   Irma's current employer tells me she would have been willing to
sponsor her for a working visa, but that the immigration lawyers she
consulted told her that with no qualifications, no property in the Philippines, and no family in the United States, Irma's chances of being
approved are precisely zero—as is the likelihood of being allowed
back into this country even as a tourist once she does return home.
And yet, with the social security number and the driver's license Irma
was able to get during the time she still worked for the family who
brought her over here, she is very much part of the establishment—
just in a permanent state of "application pending" limbo.
   Her employer said:

   You should see her with children, she's just a natural. I really
   think she has a gift. They gravitate toward her in a way I've almost

never seen with anyone else. The thought that she will leave us one day just makes me desperate, but then sometimes—only rarely, but sometimes—when I go into her room and I see that every single surface is covered with pictures of her own children whom she hasn't seen or touched in all these years, oh God, I do wonder what I've done, to keep her here with us, away from her own family. In the end it's her own choice, I do know that, and there is just so *much* she is able to do for them with the money we pay her. Literally, all these things we take for granted: food, an education, clothing, medication, just basics. She really does love my children like they are her own, and I can see that that, and the money, in a funny way, puts her in a terrible bind, every year when it's time to renew her contract. Her family has come to depend on her so much by now that if she went back to the Philippines she'd be cutting off their lifeline, literally. What emotional bond she's got with them is all about material things, and I think she's almost scared about going back and facing them after all these years. My children just love her for who she is, no strings attached. That's kind of the drug that makes her stay. It's what she craves, you know, like an addict. It's a good thing I'm not one of those mothers who get jealous, but the truth is I probably love her almost as much as they do.

Though Irma is clearly constantly tormented by feelings of guilt and longing for her children, it could be argued that both she and all the various children in her life are actually the lucky ones: As their mother she may have made the ultimate sacrifice in leaving them, but at least they are receiving genuinely good care from other family members. As a nanny, the quality of care Irma provides for the children she looks after is also probably superior to that received by the majority of American working-class children in day care. In fact,

Irma's employer insists that her children are far better off with the nanny looking after them day-in, day-out than they would be with her: "I know that for me, having a nanny is by far the best solution, and I know how absolutely blessed we all are to have Irma. She's so much better at it than I would be. In the end, I'm probably a better mother because of her."

In general, however, "probably" is not a concept we can tolerate easily when it comes to deciding what's best for our children. And yet, they are "probably" safe, they "probably" get enough attention, and—as many low-income mothers hope when they leave their kids in day care in order to get to their jobs—they "probably sort of, kind of like it there" is the most many of us can realistically expect. This is not to say that day care by definition leaves children worse off than having either their mothers or someone like Irma all to themselves—far from it. Study after study confirms that good day care allows children to thrive physically, emotionally, and intellectually just as much as, and occasionally even more than, home care or relative care. The operative word is "good." While some of the dozens of studies that have been conducted on this subject over the last three decades might differ in the details, they all agree that the quality of care a child is likely to receive in a day-care situation is determined by a combination of factors: the adult-to-child ratio; the staff turnover rate; training; the level of experience and staff compensation; an emphasis on proper nutrition and hygiene; the availability of age-appropriate toys and activities; and space. All things that, not surprisingly, cost money—to the point where a spot in a well-regarded, licensed day-care program can cost almost as much as in-home care. Not to mention the fact that snagging a place in one of the better programs in low- or middle-income neighborhoods is often the equivalent of winning the local lottery, doesn't cover those days when a child is sick, nor the evenings when the parents need to work late or would maybe like to catch a movie, or any domestic chores whatsoever.

It isn't hard to imagine that horrible, sinking feeling of despair, guilt, and resignation that millions of parents go through every time they're forced to leave their babies in a substandard care situation because they simply have no choice—either because it's all that's available to them, or because it's the most they can afford and still have enough left to pay for food and the rent. Marilia and her husband are recent immigrants from Bolivia, where they led a relatively comfortable middle-class existence, both with steady jobs. However, once her husband, a professor of economics, fell foul of the local authorities as a result of some critical articles he'd published, they felt they had no alternative but to leave, and they managed to come to the United States on student visas with their four-year-old son and one-year-old daughter. With the help of some friends and relatives they are now eking out an existence, with the father working as a short-order cook and the mother as a housekeeper and babysitter, in-between scrambling for the expensive college credits they need to maintain their student visas and avoid deportation. They've no family to fall back on, and while their son is now in school and doing well (at age six he's often called on to translate for his parents), Marilia must work, often six or more days every week, and long hours every day. The day care for their now three-year-old daughter is subsidized, but the help she gets from the government is neither enough nor, in Marilia's eyes, is the care itself good enough.

> Everybody say, "You lucky," but I don't think so. The place Nisia goes is old, is not clean, all the time there are different ladies take the children, sometimes I don't even know the name! I wish I don't have to leave her there; every day she cry and I cry, and I worry, what they do with her? How they look after all those children? She's so little, she need her mother, but I'm not there. What they do when the children cry, when they need something? Nobody tell me nothing, feels like nobody cares about my daughter, just like an animal with all the other little children in

that zoo place. I don't want to leave her there. But is not possible
to complain, nothing else to do. I need to work, my husband
need to work, we try to study English; to be legal, all costs
money. And I can't find job where I can take Nisia with me; nobody want that. All the time I worry about her, all the time. I
don't want to be mother like this.

Clearly, even the knowledge that she has no or little choice in her
child-care arrangements allays even an ounce of Marilia's feelings of
guilt and despair in the matter. In truth, nobody wants to be the kind
of mother for whom choices about where and with whom to leave her
young children, and where or even whether to work, are unattainable
luxuries. But then again, many women are just too tired with the business of mothering and working and holding it all together to think
about it too much—for them, even the effort of worrying about whether
or not they're doing the right thing is more than they can bear. Why go
down that road if you haven't got any options in the first place?

Dolores is a child-care worker in the very day-care center where
Marilia drops Nisia off every morning, and while she's sympathetic to
"our clients' concerns," she too is a single mother, with a teenage son,
who is "barely making ends meet."

You know, I love children, I really do, but all these kids—it's too
much sometimes. The people who run this place, they're always
scrimping and saving on everything. We do our best, honestly
we do. It's really hard work, and you just can't make everyone
happy! The parents, I mean I appreciate that they want the best
for their kids and all, but sometimes they just don't realize that
one person simply can't get to every dirty diaper and every little
boo-boo right away! And it isn't as if we're getting paid the big
bucks exactly. I've been here more than a year now, but most of

the girls, they're come and gone again in six months, maybe a year. No surprise, really; something better comes up and they're out of here like a shot. They think they love kids when they start, and then reality hits—there's too many kids to really spend time with any one of them, and it's a good day if you manage to play some games, get them all fed, stop them from hurting each other or themselves.

But the bad days are bad, man. There's nothing like a room full of screaming and crying toddlers with runny noses and dirty diapers to make you want to curl up and die, is there? I try to let it all roll over me when that happens. Keep smiling; remember they're only babies. And then the parents come to pick up, and you're supposed to tell them what bowel movements little Johnny had that day, or why his shirt's on inside out. I mean, give me a break! Yeah, I've thought about getting a nanny job—the money'd probably be better. But the hours here are good, and at least I get some health insurance for me and my kid. Thank God he's old enough to look after himself when he's out from school. That Nisia? Yeah, she's a real cutie. Bit of a mama's girl, though. And so quiet. Needs to learn to stand up for herself.

The relationship between Marilia, Dolores, and little Nisia is not necessarily typical—there are plenty of wonderful stories of mothers and day-care workers who work closely together, respect one another, and recognize that the mutual blame game of "she should do more" and "she can't expect me to do everything" ultimately solves nothing and only hurts the kids. But it is an extreme example of a system that either fails or manages to just barely meet the needs of everyone in its orbit. In this case the women who are mothers and the women who look after their children might as well hail from different planets, so far do they fall short of each other's expectations and hopes.

Becca is a sweet, extremely bright, and devoted "Quality Child-Care Provider—I am not a nanny," she said, "not a housekeeper, *not* a babysitter who cleans, let's just make that clear." She has worked for many years with children of all ages, teaching preschool and privately, living with families and commuting to work, and she wants one day to open her own school.

When I was teaching, there were always other teachers who would look at the parents as problems, like somehow we were all adversaries and it would be all about getting the better of someone else. It's easy to fall into that trap, to be honest; there are always parents who seem to be completely unreasonable or just not getting it, or wanting you to pay way more attention to their child than everyone else's. So, yeah, everyone needs attention: When I teach I need the children to pay attention to me, the parents need me to hear them, everyone has these overwhelming needs.

You can never get away from that, whether you're teaching a whole class or working in someone's home with just a couple of kids. But at least now I try to start out new situations and relationships with a different point of view, and I always make it really, really clear in the interview—and it's that we, and I mean the adults in this situation, need to be *partners*. Forget equality here, I'm not talking about being equal partners, but in my work I need the parents to be my partners so we can work together, not doing the same things, but together. And parents need that too, I think, when it comes down to it; they need to have a partner in raising their kids, and that's what the best child-care providers are. So now, in interviews, I have this whole spiel where I kind of look at the mother and see if I like her, and then I say, "If you're looking for a nanny to work for you, I'm not sure I'm the right person" (and then I give them the bit about me not being a housekeeper), and then I tell her, "If you can look at me like a partner with your children, if you need someone to bounce ideas off of, if you need someone with a lot of experience, then I think we can work together."

Becca, I think I need you!

money

W HAT IS THE PRICE of love? Is there a "going rate" for indulging in ambition and building a satisfying career? Of course we could go the Hallmark route by clutching our hearts and declaring that a mother's love is priceless, but unfortunately that doesn't help a whole lot when it comes to calculating exactly how much to allocate for child care in the family budget. Speaking of Hallmark, have you ever tried buying a card for your son's or daughter's nanny or childcare provider, that VIP in both your lives without whom you'd most likely be up the proverbial creek? No category for them—secretaries have one, as do teachers, aunties, grandmas, friends, daughters, stepchildren and stepparents, husbands and wives, widows and widowers. For nannies, look in "miscellaneous" and/or blank, and you'll probably end up with one of those one-size-fits-all floral ones.

Nor are statistics much help: Whether compiled by the Department of Labor or various industry service organizations, all acknowledge that since by definition the private child-care sector operates in large part off-the-books; any accounting of exactly how many women do approximately what for whom, where, and for how much is never going to be more than an educated guess, and will vary significantly depending on your location. What is more, it has become clear to me in the course of my researching that nothing in the business of looking after children raises hackles and gives rise to resentment quite as much as the issue of money. This could be nothing more than the old chestnut of "trying to get as much as you can for as little as possible," but calculating the value of child care is hardly the same as buying groceries. The real reason for the bitterness of the money conversation is most likely that no one wants to actually have to put a price on their children's heads. Yet that is what parents and those they hire to take care of their kids do every day. More often than not it's an unpleasant and highly emotional business, and consensus of what constitutes a fair dollar value for the work performed is rare.

As a parent on a limited budget with a stressful job I would like to pay at most a couple of hundred dollars per week for nine quiet, one-on-one-attention, worry free hours a day, with a sleepy, bathed, and contented toddler or two at the end of it. Throw in one weekend night of babysitting so my husband and I can have our regular date-night, and while we're at it some laundry, cleaning, and grocery shopping, a bit of leeway on the hours, all delivered with a smile and without the considerable hassles of filing taxes and social security, or of providing health insurance. After all, that (the hassles, I mean, and minus the cash) is what I would get if I gave up my job and stayed home with the children: no social security benefits during the time I take off to raise the kids, and health insurance and other perks like paid vacation time and child-care tax credits only if I'm lucky enough to be covered under someone else's policy as a dependent. Staying home full-time with two toddlers is one of the hardest things I've ever done, and there are days when I wouldn't wish the tedium and isolation on my worst enemy. But really—isn't this a job that anyone could do?

As a nanny with a possibly dodgy visa, a child or two or my own, and most likely a few years' of experience doing other people's "menial" jobs (including babysitting), I would like this: Depending on where you live, either between twelve and fifteen dollars per hour, or no less than four to five hundred dollars per week net in my pocket, for no more than fifty hours of child care (that means no mopping the kitchen floor while the baby's asleep, thank you very much). Preferably all cash, because what's the system ever done for me, anyway? Pay me overtime at the rate normal people get overtime, including nights, weekends, and holidays. Ten paid vacation days every year, or more, depending on how long I've worked with you; and paid sick leave when I need it, especially if it's because of that flu bug I caught from your kids. A Christmas bonus would be nice, and I don't mean a twenty-five-dollar gift certificate to Wal-Mart. I'll also take a contribution to my health insurance or medical costs, at least a month's severance pay if you no longer need me, plus a decent reference.

Clearly what seems perfectly fair to some (usually the employers) often appears nothing short of miserly to others (guess who). It's quite remarkable how often the phrase "most precious," "most valuable," or "priceless possessions" can be found in all manner of parenting books, articles, and other sources of how-to advice for those trying to figure out what to do about arranging affordable, adequate, and age-appropriate child care. Then again, as far as the sector of "child-care workers" that appears in government statistics is concerned (i.e., the minority of those who are in the system, and therefore legally employed), one thing is also clear: When it comes to valuing their contribution to the nation's economy, they rank somewhere between janitors and restaurant workers, not much below preschool teachers and their assistants, and barely a smidgen above the girl flipping burgers at McDonald's. (The current minimum wage ranges from $5.15 federally to $7.35 in Washington State. The national average is $6.15.)

The most recently available estimates, the annual "Occupational Employment and Wages for Child Care Workers" report published by the Department of Labor's Bureau of Statistics in May 2004, puts the mean hourly wage for child day-care workers at $7.65, and their average annual wage at $15,910. In some parts of the country their hourly wages are estimated to be as low as $5.90, with annual wages of $12,270—in short, if you work in a day-care center looking after a large proportion of this country's population of preschool children so their parents can keep our economy going (nannies do not make up a statistically significant part of the government's estimates), there are only eighteen other occupations out of the total 770 identified by the BLS that earn less than you. Those who earn more include service station and parking-lot attendants (finally—proof that we as a nation value our cars more than our children?), taxi drivers, bellhops, and (yes, really) "animal trainers." If you think that this state of affairs leaves lots of room for improvement, you would be right—but also sadly mistaken in the case of twelve states (Alabama, Delaware, Georgia, Kentucky, Missouri, New Hampshire, New Jersey, Ohio, South Carolina, South Dakota, Texas, Utah, and Washington, D.C.), where wages for child-care workers have actually decreased since 2002. No matter how you look at the numbers, one thing is clear: This nation's child-care workers are predominantly women and often mothers themselves. As such, they suffer from a higher concentration of poverty-level jobs than almost any other occupation in the United States.

Unfortunately, the talents that make for a good nanny or day-care worker, or, for that matter, a good mother, are only fully appreciated as "transferable skills" by those whose voices will never be counted by the Bureau of Labor statisticians: The infant getting rocked to sleep by a lullaby, the toddler having *Good Night Moon* read to him for the millionth time, the preschooler getting help with his coloring, his sister being buckled into her car seat, and their friend looking for a reassuring hand to hold on the walk home from school. Sometimes, of course, these very moments are their own reward. Children really are an extraordinary gift, and the time we spend with them is precious and fleeting, and occasionally incomparably wonderful. Yet while there are always times to sweeten the drudgery, thank God, there is still no getting away from the fact that looking after children, especially the under fives, is, as one mother who I interviewed put it, "brutal." It's real work, sometimes hard, often monotonous, loud, dirty, and exhausting, usually repetitive, occasionally sweet and funny and rewarding, but always work. It isn't work that suits everyone just because they're female and capable of reproduction, and it isn't even work that anyone who is functionally a parent ought to be trusted with—and, just as much as any other profession that requires a very particular skill set in order to succeed, some people are naturally and effortlessly brilliant at it, while others are simply awful.

With all the talk about "our most precious possessions" one would have thought there'd be a direct correlation between a family's ability to pay their skilled nanny a decent wage and their willingness to actually do so. Not necessarily so: One of the most astonishing conclusions I have come to in the course of researching this book is that it often appears to be the most well-off parents who are the meanest about money, at least if their (frequently disgruntled) nannies are to be believed. Of course, it is also true that disgruntled nannies out to tell all on their former, or sometimes current, employers were invariably at the front of the line when I went out in search of women to interview. Another curious fact is that while most nannies were more than happy to volunteer exactly how little they were being paid by a miserly boss, the same was not true when it came to divulging how much they were getting from employers who were more generous: To put it plainly, if the number was low, I'd get the number, including decimal points, pennies, and possibly deductions. The higher the salary, however, the fewer the specifics, as if all of a sudden the mention of an actual dollar figure had become faintly obscene.

Either way, high or low, this goes to show that just as in many a bitter divorce, when it comes to parents and their children's caretakers money either becomes a substitute for a satisfying emotional relationship or the currency in a complicated game of emotional blackmail. Similarly, among mothers hanging out and talking about their nannies, sitters, and various other child-care arrangements, the down and dirty numbers are almost never mentioned, but rather couched in vague terms like "the going rate." Many mothers would undoubtedly perceive it as a greater invasion of their privacy to be asked exactly how much they pay their nanny than it would be to divulge how many times a week they have sex with their husbands—or with anyone else for that matter. While I had no trouble bringing up any number of difficult and intimate issues during my interviews, when it came to "how much?" the question would be lobbed back and forth between us like a hot potato. Not only did I rarely get a direct answer, but it was almost always accompanied by a wide variety of qualifiers, ranging from, "But she's only been with us a few months," and "I pay her a bit less than the going rate, but I make it up to her in other ways," to "Of course, she's grossly overpaid, but I don't care as long as I get to keep her."

So let's stick to facts: Not only are children work, they're are also darn expensive. To get any one of them unscathed, reasonably well-fed, clothed, housed, and decently educated from birth through adulthood requires a sizable investment in cold, hard cash. The actual numbers vary depending on whom you ask, where in the country you're doing your research, and how much disposable income a family has to start with. Nonetheless, there is a national average, as calculated by the United States Department of Agriculture in an annually published paper entitled "Expenditures on Children by Families." In 2004, a middle-income married couple with two children spent between $19,020 and $21,120 on expenses related to child rearing. Considering that the average pretax income of such a family is calculated at $55,500, that is a hefty chunk indeed. Not surprisingly, the various data available from the USDA, the Census Bureau, and the Bureau of Labor Statistics also show that the more a family earns, the more it spends per child, although the overall proportion of child care–related spending does not go up nearly as much. In other words: The more people make, the more they have to spend on their kids; *but* in families in the upper income brackets this is likely to be well below 10 percent, whereas at the other end of the spectrum (i.e., poor families headed by single working mothers) 40 percent spend at least *half* their cash income on child care, according to *Poor Familes in 2001,* by Richard Wertheimer, published in 2003 by Child Trends.

Buried in the mounds of data on exactly who spends how much on their families and where, the same USDA report also contains this astonishing little nugget of government-sanctioned cluelessness regarding the actual cost of child care in this country: "It is assumed that the number of unregulated family day-care providers far exceeds the number of regulated providers, though it is impossible to determine by how much. . . . No single data source provides comprehensive information on wages of child-care workers." Ah, well. I guess we're back to calculating the going rate by making a good old-fashioned educated guess, particularly since I trust neither my neighbor nor yours to tell us how much she's *actually* paying. The only ones who will happily discuss wages are employment agencies that specialize in providing various household personnel. Even they will tell you that the range is vast, and that everything depends on the nanny's experience; her exact responsibilities; the number of kids; live-in or live-out; weekends or not; with newborn experience or without; and so on. Right off the bat, in what is arguably the most expensive city in the United States, New York, forty-five hours of child care per week can easily run anywhere between approximately $250 for an au pair (including agency fees, but excluding his or her room and board), to upwards of $1,000 for a true blue-chip nanny-to-the-stars. Everybody who is anybody else, including those who opt for good full-time day-care programs, will fall somewhere in-between.

Let's not kid ourselves though. We, the mothers, might pussyfoot around with one another about exactly how much we do or don't pay, but the unspoken pact that guards our dignity and lets us maintain at least an illusion of privacy where our personal finances are concerned does not exist in the nanny world. Marisol doesn't waste any time beating around the money bush.

Sure I know. We all know how much each other makes. We talk about it all the time. There's some that are generous, and there's some that are just plain mean, but if you work around here [Central Park playground, Upper East Side of Manhattan] everybody kinda knows what's what. I got my network, if you know what I mean. See her over there, with the blue coat on? She's getting' $1,000 a week, but I hear the family's nasty. "We payin' you, so shut up and do it" kinda situation. Me, I'm making $650. I've been there, like, almost a year now. I'll be asking her to raise me to $700 next time it comes up, been working longer hours lately. Six hundred dollars is pretty much where you got to start out if you want someone good around here. Maybe $550 for someone with no experience.

They're like vultures, some of them. I seen one mother, she hang around the playground couple days just kinda watching, then she says to this one girl, "How much're you making now? I'll pay you a hundred bucks more if you come work for me." But that's kinda extreme. You got to wonder what a person who'd do a thing like that would be to work for. You've got to know what to ask for, that's key, and there are some things that are worth more, others you avoid like the plague. Like the best setup I know, moneywise, is this girl, she's got three families going, and they pay her by the hour—twenty bucks, cash! So yeah, you do the hourly thing you can earn a lot, but it's not always steady work. Living in is, like, the worst. 'Cause you're never done, can't have a life. And it doesn't pay that great, either; even if you got a room, most girls living in still have a place somewhere.

Mara is one of the few mothers who's not afraid to go into detail. Her two daughters are old enough to be in school all day except for vacations or sick days, so they no longer have a single caretaker who works for the family full-time. Instead, Mara ("I arrange everything— my husband gives me free rein with this stuff") cobbles together a fairly complicated system of overlapping, part-time babysitters and caretakers, each of whom is paid at a different rate, depending on how long she's been working and, to quote Mara,

what she is good at. One of them is kind of our anchor, because she's been with us for years, started out as Lola's camp counselor. She gets twenty an hour. That may seem like a lot, but when she comes I know she's got homework covered, the house is spotless, they listen to her, they're totally comfortable, and I literally don't have to worry about a thing. The other two are both students, one gets twelve dollars and the other fifteen dollars an hour. The younger one is fairly new, and she still doesn't totally know the ropes yet, so I don't use her on the really tough days. But she's sweet and fun, has tons of energy, so that's great. The older one is, well, older. She really knows our routine by now, she's been totally reliable, and it's a good steady gig for her as well.

I must admit, though, with all this juggling sometimes I think my head's going to explode. And even though I think what I pay them is justified, I definitely wouldn't want one of them to figure out that the other is getting more. Luckily they don't really know each other that well, but who knows what they all talk about behind our backs.

For Tricia, who has worked with "maybe a dozen families" every which way (live-in and -out, part-time, full-time, with housekeeping and without), the formula is also clear. She insists that any client who

won't stick to the formula will get the boot, and that she has any number of people asking her to work for them at any given time.

Look, I'm too old for this crap, if you'll excuse me. I've got like a
million years of experience, I'm a nice person, I've got references, I'm reliable, and I love kids, and I know what I'm worth!
If you think fifteen dollars an hour is too much, that's fine,
thank you very much, have a nice life. Go get some inexperienced little Mexican, but don't come crying back to me because
you're paying her two hundred bucks a week, and she speaks no
English, and it turns out she's been feeding your kids doughnuts
and using your phone to call her relatives for two hours every
night. I got no sympathy for that, really.

I don't mind doing a little bit of cleaning, that's okay, comes
with the territory. If I'm in the house anyway, I'm not the type to
sit around doing nothing. I'll drive your car if you want me to,
but I use my car, you pay for it—forty cents a mile. Standard. I
looked it up. This one woman, she just couldn't believe it. One
week I was driving her kids all over creation using my car, and I
gave her the bill, and she refused to pay! Said she thought that
"should be included." You seen the price of gas? No way, José,
no way. I make that really clear now, before I do diddly-squat for
anyone, or their kids.

And you know what? It pays off. People like to know where
they're at. They appreciate it. You pay me like a professional, I
work like a professional, that's the bottom line.

And that isn't all: Tricia's families know she has a four-hour minimum and likes to get at least eight hours per week. A twenty-four-
hour stint is $165, and an overnight stay $125—a whole menu of
choices. She tells me she only came up with these rules because she
was "sick and tired of getting nickel-and-dimed to death."

I've seen it all, man, you wouldn't believe some of the stuff people try and get away with not to pay you. Like when the mom comes home early, and suddenly I'm supposed to leave and only get paid for two hours? You've got to put your foot down, you know. And this one woman, she kept saying, "But I don't think I should be paying you fifteen dollars an hour once the children are asleep; you can just sit and watch TV." I told her, in that case I'd go home and watch TV at my house. She still didn't get it.

Fifteen bucks an hour and $125 for an overnight might make some people gasp. However, if you do the math, figuring in Tricia's expenses, the cost of housing in her area and the fact that she actually ends up with an average of twenty-five, at most thirty-five paid hours a week, and is constantly wondering where her next job is coming from, financially she's no better off than a salaried nanny (though quite a bit better than workers at a local day-care center, who earn approximately nine dollars an hour before taxes). Marisol's hours might be long—7:30 A.M. to 7:00 P.M., Monday to Friday, but on most days that includes several hours of downtime while her kids are at school, weekends off, and a steady paycheck. Basically it's a toss-up, particularly given the fact that hiring some "inexperienced Mexican" (read: an illegal alien who might in fact be highly educated and have a great deal of experience) is the only affordable option for many parents.

One cannot write about the cash-for-care economy that all illegal nannies participate in without at least a passing mention of Zoe Baird and Kimba Wood, both of whom were forced to withdraw their nomination by then president Clinton for attorney general in 1993, when it was revealed that they had hired illegal alien women as nannies for their children early in their respective careers. The hypocrisy of those cases has been well documented, but what is equally clear is that unless a mother (or her mate) is planning on running for office, is a lawyer, or for any other reason truly loath to engage in any illegal activity, very little has changed in the last decade. Most nannies still prefer to be paid mostly in cash, and most employers still prefer to pay them that way, because it's generally more lucrative and a lot less hassle for everyone involved. What's more, given the constantly rising cost of child care, the number of parent employers who bother to file the nanny tax form (also known as Schedule H) is actually decreasing: According to *The Wall Street Journal* in March 2005, almost 24 percent fewer employers paid the tax in 2003 than had done so in 1997. Legally, anyone who employs household help at $1,500 or more per annum is required to pitch in Medicare taxes of 7.65 percent on the nanny's gross salary, as well as social security. Then there is federal unemployment insurance of 0.8 percent, state unemployment insurance (between 2 percent and 4 percent), and a variety of other taxes depending on your state. The nanny's share of social security, Medicare, and local taxes would add up to at least another 7.65 percent, which means that if all the proper taxes are withheld and other contributions are made by both parties, the employer ends up paying approximately 10 to 12 percent more. In the event that some of those taxes are also deducted from the nanny's take-home pay, she might end up with as much as 20 percent fewer dollars in her pocket. Add to that the paperwork that's required (quarterly) to keep it all aboveboard, and giving Uncle Sam his due adds up not only to a significant chunk of change but also a whole bunch of time that most parents would rather spend, well, with their kids.

There's no doubt: "The system" is complicated, and once you're in there, it can be difficult to get out. Many think: much better to keep this "between us." What goes on between a nanny, a mother and father, and their children is by definition kind of a private transaction, anyway. Thus far, and with a few oversubscribed exceptions like the Head Start program, the government doesn't have a leg to stand on when it comes to helping parents out with arranging and paying for child care. Why let them have a piece of the action, or, God forbid, provide them with an excuse to sic immigration on the nanny? Given a choice, and unless they have little or no financial constraints, most people would rather put more cash in their caretaker's pocket now than help her put something away for the proverbial rainy day.

Take Tricia. American and proud of it, worked hard all her life, smart head on her shoulders, trying really hard to be a good, upstanding citizen.

> You know, I do my share, really I do. I pay my way, keep up with my Social, but with all these families I got, forget about anyone paying my taxes. What really gets me is the other stuff, and that's where being honest just hurts you. Like a couple of months ago, we lost the tuition subsidy for my daughter. So I ask, whaddaya mean, I got too much money, because I don't report that much income, you know. Turns out it's my "assets." Like, my car! It's got a hundred thousand miles on it, for God's sake, but it's still valued at whatever the hell it is, and that puts us over this limit they have. So what am I supposed to do? Get rid of the car, forget about getting to my jobs, and then my daughter can get a break on her school fees? It's just all ass-backwards, it really is.

Nonetheless, Tricia was one of a distinct minority of nannies interviewed for this book who'd gladly have one of her employers file taxes and pay social security on her behalf, if only one of them were willing.

This is not to say that employers who choose to go the under-the-table route are lawless delinquents out to exploit their staff and get away with the most child care at the absolute least expense to themselves—far, far from it. Take Andrew and Miriam, a couple of highly educated and grossly underpaid professionals, both of whom are totally committed to working long hours in their respective management positions in nonprofit agencies. It's obvious that their exemplary social conscience will always compel them to do the right thing wherever and whenever possible. On the other hand, they also struggle constantly with the knowledge that where getting adequate child care is concerned, doing the right thing would eat up a far larger portion of their disposable income than they can afford on their meager salaries.

Miriam told me:

> We both work such long hours, and we've got to be available for all sorts of emergency situations. Day care just makes no sense. Also, much as I hate to say it, the programs around here really aren't very good. Lots of overcrowding, staff turnover is huge, and the kids just seem to get sick all the time. But the sitter thing is just as complicated, especially because we've never felt comfortable with this white family, black servant thing that so many people seem to have going on. I'm sorry, but I just can't use the word nanny—it makes me so uncomfortable! I truly hate it that we've never been able to offer anyone health care, you know? I know what having no health insurance can do to a family, believe me. And because we've never been able to pay that much, no one who's worked for us has ever wanted us to pay taxes, though that's another thing that makes me really uncomfortable. The first sitter we had, when Sarah was two months old, she had a six-month-old of her own, and we let her bring her baby here, so I felt good about that for a while. I mean, we weren't paying anywhere near what some people got, but at least she didn't have to leave her baby. She just wasn't really that good a sitter, you know? I came home during the day a couple of times, and she'd be on the phone with Sarah in a sopping wet diaper and her son plonked in front of the TV—I just had to let her go.
>
> That was a real epiphany for me, to realize that I just wasn't prepared to leave my own child in a situation like that, and that my conscience wasn't the issue—but that *Sarah's* being looked

after by someone who really cares about her is the issue. I get paid jack shit, and I make a real difference in the world, I do, I really believe that. But Sarah deserves the best we can afford as well, she really does. I don't like breaking the law, believe me. But I'll do what it takes to make sure we can hire a good sitter, and unfortunately, for most the thing with the taxes is just a deal breaker.

When I ask Miriam what percentage of her family's combined after-tax income goes toward child care, the calculation she makes on the back of her napkin comes to a whopping 24 percent—and that's before she's even factored in any of Sarah's other expenses (tuition, medical, clothing) or any extra babysitting. She looks at the number and shrugs. "It's a huge chunk, but that's kind of what I expected. The really scary thing is, there's this whole other family that's got to live off of what I pay the sitter."

Miriam's concern for her sitters' welfare and the fairness of her arrangements is exemplary but not necessarily rare—many nannies told me that the mothers they work for are fair, and even generous. Occasionally, this can lead to another, wholly unexpected kind of dilemma. Josie is a high school teacher, her husband an electronics entrepreneur, and the couple is, in her words, "extremely well off. I'm so lucky in that for the last few years we've really never had to think or worry about money, knock on wood." Josie "always has and always will" work full-time, and she and her husband have employed the same nanny for their four children for the past seven years. However, not having to worry about her own financial situation has not stopped Josie from being concerned about that of Maureeah, the family's "much-loved, long-suffering, and simply wonderful" caregiver.

Maury's in her fifties now, fifty-three, I think. I know for a fact that she doesn't have a single solitary cent in savings. I mean, think about it—after working for us for seven years, she really ought to have a nice little twenty thousand dollars nest egg squirreled away—hundred dollars, two hundred dollars a month, that wouldn't have been hard on her salary. She doesn't have a lot of expenses, she lives with us, her kids are all grown up. I mean, this really ought to be a time in her life where she should be focused on saving as much as possible. We've always paid her taxes, so at least she'll get some Social Security, but it's very little.

Problem is, she's just this insanely generous person, and she's forever buying presents for her grandkids and her friends and going off on these ridiculous cruises that she really can't afford. It's like she simply can't bear to have money in her pockets; it just sits there burning a hole until she's spent it. I've tried to talk to her about it, but it's pretty clear that she just couldn't care less. I guess she thinks her kids are going to take care of her, though God knows they can barely afford to take care of themselves. We've offered to set up a retirement account for her, or a savings account where she earns a little interest, but week after week she just goes out and blows it all. I thought of forcing her to do it, you know, like withhold a part of her salary and pay that directly into a separate account, but she did *not* like that idea.

And then my husband said, I guess he's right, that that wasn't something he's prepared to do because it's patronizing—it's her money, she should be able to do whatever the hell she likes with it.

She's figured out by now that if she wants to get an advance or borrow money, she's got to go to Dave, because I "disapprove." The one small thing I *have* managed to do is switch the day she gets paid to Mondays—at least that way she's got to wait until the next weekend to spend it all. But she spends it, that's for sure. And while we're on spending, there is one other thing I wish she wouldn't do—she keeps buying my kids presents!

I mean, expensive presents! That's what I mean, it's lovely and so generous that she wants to get them gifts, but that is just so inappropriate.

I've tried to ask her not to, but what does that make me look like? It's like I'm the mean one, (a) because I don't want to get Max yet another stupid video game, and (b) because I don't want her to spend her money on my kids for things that, of course, I can perfectly well afford to buy but just don't want in my house. Dave says it's her life and her business, but how can I not feel responsible? It's really frustrating.

The experience that Josie had with the nanny prior to Maury is another example of how the for-love-or-money conundrum can be played out between parent and caregiver.

This was a completely different time in our lives, the kids were younger, Dave was just setting up the business, and everything just seemed like this one big risk. To the point where I would have done almost anything to have some stability, you know, "one sure thing" in our lives. So there was Maury's predecessor, her name was Lila and she was from the Midwest, somewhere in Ohio. Farm country, farm girl, everyone in her family still on the farm and farming. So her brother-in-law, lovely man, three kids, young wife, gets leukemia and dies. We'd all met him one time when they'd stayed with us a night on their way to the city, so it was kind of personal—it always is, I guess, when it's someone you know, doesn't matter how little. So, of course Lila was horribly upset, very close to her sister and everything, and I, like an idiot, make this big ostentatious donation to leukemia research in his name. Well, not like an idiot exactly, it is a horrible disease and just as worthy of donations and research as anything else, but what the hell was I trying to prove?

When she quit a few months later, you know what the first thing was that went through my mind? "How can you quit on me now, you disloyal, ungrateful woman, especially after I donated all that money to leukemia research?" Of course I didn't say that, but it was definitely what I thought. What a perfect cliché, you know, the one about "no good deed ever goes unpunished." I should have just given the money to her sister, but then *that* would have been patronizing, or inappropriate, or something. And now we've got good old Maury, who can't waste her money fast enough. We just redid our wills, and she's in there. I'm *not* going to tell her that.

The as yet only vaguely acknowledged situation that Josie and Maury are finding themselves in after having "worked together" for seven years is another inherent dilemma faced by longtime nannies whose charges are slowly but surely growing up: In the early years, when the work is the hardest, you get paid the least. Still, you stick it out, you build a relationship, you get your raise every year. But then, unlike almost any other profession, the better you are at your job the more your responsibilities—at least according to the original job description of "nanny"—will begin to diminish. You're still important to the family for all sorts of reasons, and making more money than ever, but it doesn't take very long before everyone starts to realize that your original value proposition simply makes no more sense. With the children all eventually at school, those empty mornings begin to loom large, and then, inevitably, the questions come: So, what about the housekeeping? How about a little shopping, some cooking, the laundry? Before long this is the choice that presents itself: Either you cut back your hours, which you can't afford, or you swallow your pride and start to do the housekeeping that is just crying out to be tackled in those empty hours when you were supposed to be enjoying a well-earned rest from toddler tantrums, smelly diapers, and schlepping the stroller. This murky intersection between exactly what constitutes a nanny and what a housekeeper is possibly the hardest obstacle to navigate on the long road of a nanny/employer relationship, and more often than not money becomes its lightning rod.

Kate, a first-time mother with a six-month-old daughter, is adamant:

> All my friends say I'm crazy, but I just want the nanny to be totally focused on Amber. I'd never ask her to do other things, I'm paranoid about that. My husband's always telling me—couldn't she do a bit of this, a bit of that, I mean, she's home all day. She probably would, if I asked her. But I just can't bring myself to. As it is I'm really uncomfortable with the idea of someone else raising my child, and we're not actually paying her the going rate, so whatever she does I want it to be for Amber.

It isn't hard to imagine the day when both Kate and her nanny are going to regret not just those words, but the expectations they created and will be forced to rearrange.

Valery has been through the nanny/housekeeper cycle a few times, and by now she knows to ignore the pie-in-the-sky "it's all about the baby" talk from overeager young mothers like Kate.

> Comes with the territory, don't it? Sooner or later they all ask, is only natural. I always say I'll do a bit of everything, the light stuff, but for the big things they need to get themselves a cleaner. The worst is when they sneak it up on you. Is always better you spell things out up front. This one lady I had, six months into the job with twins, she start asking me to stick stamps on these envelopes she was doing for some mailing when those kids were napping. So I ask her, what you gonna pay me for doing that, what you pay your secretary at the office? She just said, well, you're sittin' there doin' nothing,

thought you might like something to keep you busy, help me out. Is like I'm there to do anything she wants, just because she's the boss.

It depends, though. There's some people, they treat you right, I don't mind doing things around the house. It's the respect that matters, like they got to know they can't buy you. But if I get hired as a babysitter, it's not right to change everything all around halfway through. I got my pride, too. I like what I do, I like the *kids*. If I wanted to go clean houses, I'd go clean houses—there's a difference.

Rebecca has two children, both in school all day, as well as an extremely intense full-time career and a full-time nanny. With respect to Ronni, the babysitter, Rebecca realizes that

we're in this gray area now where we still want her but we don't really need her. Even Amy [the ten-year-old daughter] realizes it, so now she has started advocating for Ronni, telling me she looks kind of tired, that she's been working too hard. But Ronni gets it, too. She knows, and I told her, that as long as she makes herself relevant to our family, then we'll have a reason to keep her. At some point, though, it's going to be hard to justify. You just want them to morph with you, to grow and change in the same way your family does. For some people that's really hard, because they get used to a certain lifestyle and status, and then the housekeeper thing just feels like it's beneath them. But if you don't adapt, you price yourself out of the market, basically.

A quick look through the Help Wanted sections of several newspapers makes it clear that most families want to pay a single salary for that one perfect person who is willing to do it all—and who can't relate to that! One au pair in search of a live-in child-care position for her second year told me about some of the other things she had been asked to do in interviews, in addition to full-time child-care duties for children ranging from infant twins to a fourteen-year-old autistic boy. Would she paint the house while the family was on vacation in Florida? Would she give the diabetic dogs their daily injections and massage them? Would she feed and muck out the stable for the family's pony and resident goat? Would she move with the children back and forth between their divorced parents and take care of all the housework in both homes? Would she take inventory for the mother's retail business while the children were at school? Would she share a room with the baby? And do all this for four hundred dollars a week?

Had these been the choices on offer for the girl when she first arrived in this country, she might have been prepared to give it a try. Not surprisingly, having spent a year with a hardworking middle-class family, taking care only of the children and not much else (officially, au pairs are not permitted to do housework), she's no longer willing to get her hands quite that dirty. "It looks like they want a servant. It seems like the more you are supposed to do, the less they want to pay you."

Asking the nanny to paint your house, or making a donation to leukemia research to curry favor, are both probably misguided, though also understandable ways in which different families approach the financial quid pro quo between themselves and their nannies. But neither of these seem that serious when compared to the extent to which some parents become entangled in the financial affairs of their caregivers. Often it's a slippery slope that begins with a little loan here, a small advance there, usually provided on the unspoken assumption that the eventual payback—other than the money—is a small but growing pool of goodwill to be tapped at some point in the future, and in some as yet to be determined way.

Sally runs a small public relations and advertising agency with twelve employees, sort of including the nanny—but not really.

No, of course I wouldn't offer to guarantee a loan for one of my employees at the agency, are you crazy? That's way, way too personal, even if we socialize and consider each other friends. Honestly, I wouldn't feel that's ethical, like it would seriously compromise the professional relationship I have with this person. I've had people before with money issues, you know; they had loans to pay or credit card issues or whatever, but our policy has always basically been, no preferential treatment for anyone. You get paid on the first and the fifteenth of each month, there are procedures for everything else, like medical reimbursements or vacation time, and that's that.

But all right, yeah, I admit it, the nanny's different. She's actually on the agency payroll and everything, that's easier for all sorts of reasons, and that way I've been able to get her on Blue Cross. But you know, that's just a whole different kettle of fish, I mean, she's part of my family! It would be like if my little sister were in trouble and she asked me to help her out; you can't say no to that!

To be honest, I'm not really sure anymore what-all I've paid for her. I think maybe my husband has actually kept track of it somewhere. He deals with most of those kinds of details, does the accounts for both our companies. I guess I should have more of a clue, but to be honest, I've got enough on my plate as it is. And I like it that, when I deal with her, money doesn't have to come into it, you know; I just talk to her as a person, someone who's part of my family. My husband's the one who pays her, I'm the one who has the relationship. It's sort of a good cop, bad cop thing.

Jeanine has a similar story.

I know it's not a very smart thing to do, but I'd do almost anything to make her stay. We all have so much invested in this relationship, and our lives are so complicated, the thought of having to start over again with someone else is just too horrible to contemplate. I have to say, she's never asked me for anything directly, it just sort of comes out in conversations about her family, how they're always in trouble for one thing or another. Last year we gave her three thousand dollars to pay off the loan on her car. I mean, can you imagine, she was paying something like fifteen percent because her credit is so bad? So now she's paying us instead, no interest. Yeah, I suppose I am buying her loyalty in a way. And who knows if we'll ever actually get all the money back. But it's worth it.

James and Uma are owner-operators of a small, boutique design firm. They have nine people on their payroll, including their nanny of seven years and, on the days he bothers to show up, the nanny's nineteen-year-old ne'er-do-well but ever so charming son. He's theoretically in charge of cleaning up and running the mailroom, but

to be honest, if he were anyone else I'd have fired him long ago. I can't, though, because Karen [the nanny] keeps telling us that his green card is about to be approved, and if he doesn't have a steady job to show for it, it'll take another two years. It's all so complicated, this immigration thing, I really can't figure it out anymore. She knows full well that he's a total pain, but she's practically begged me to keep him on, even offered to do his work on the days he plays hooky. God knows what on earth he's really up to. It's such a mess.

That kid just has no idea how many lives he's playing with. The trouble is, my boys love Karen, and I'm really terrified that our family will just fall apart without her. So every time she asks for a little more I give in. She's worth it—he's not. But how do you separate the two? His latest plan is that he wants to join the army, and guess who's supposed to give him a reference. There's an ethical dilemma for you. What do you think I should do?

This story does not have a happy ending. Colin does enlist, but goes A.W.O.L. two days into basic training, with the result that two—"I think they were military police or something"—show up on James and Uma's doorstep looking for him. He finally calls from somewhere in Florida because (guess what) he's out of money, and Karen persuades Uma to lend her the funds to pay for his bus fare home. "Can you imagine? There she was, completely hysterical, and then *my* boys get into the act—'Please Mom, he's all alone, he just wants to come home,' for crying out loud. So—I gave her the money. Of course she promised it would be the last time, and she'd pay me back, and it wasn't his fault because 'they' picked on him. I know it was a stupid thing to do, but you know, I figured bus fare'd be cheaper than bail." At this point I'm not certain whether Karen still works for the family, or whether they got their money back, or if Colin ever did come home   there are some things I'd rather not know.

Just as much as many parents find it impossible not to get tangled up in the personal affairs of their nannies, many nannies find it is a constant struggle not to be sucked into the often far more affluent lives of their employers. There's temptation lurking around every corner, everywhere, all the time: drawers carelessly left open, money left lying around, jewelry, supplies, food, CDs, all kinds of stuff, expensive stuff—right there for the taking. Layla has worked for a "whole bunch of rich folks," and she knows temptation when she sees it.

> I'm telling you, either I'm the dumbest or the most honest person in the whole frickin' world, because the things people leave lying around you just wouldn't believe. I've never stolen a thing in my life, but I know some girls, yeah, sure, they take things. I know it's wrong, but jeez, some people are just complete idiots.

It's just not fair sometimes, you know? Okay, so imagine this: You're making maybe five hundred a week, never take cabs, shop at the dollar store, drive a ten-year-old car, you and your kids sleep three to a room in some dump that's a twenty-minute walk from the bus stop, and then, boom, there you are! It's Disney World! Refrigerator is, like, stuffed with gourmet foods, there's a TV in every room, marble everything in the kitchen, cashmere blankets on the kids' beds, and don't get me started on the fees for some of these private schools, and Gymboree and karate and violin lessons and whatnot.

And if you're the nanny, of course, most of the time you get the run of the place, maybe not the parents' bedroom, but pretty much everywhere else—you go where the kids go. I mean, you're in their home; far as the kids're concerned you're family. If you go out to do stuff, you're the grown-up with the money. I know this one girl, she takes her kids to Starbucks every morning for chocolate milk, there's a whole group of them meets up there. The mom, she just hands her twenty bucks, like almost every day, and my friend, she pretty much spends it all, every day— kids get their milk, that's three bucks, and for the rest it's lattes and muffins and whatnots, maybe a dollar change, no questions asked, another twenty the next day.

So you tell me, is that stealing? Her boss never says not to, she says, "Go take the kids out for chocolate milk," but she never says, "And go buy yourself and your friends a round of cappuccinos while you're at it." I don't know. I guess her attitude is, she didn't say not to, so it's okay, and twenty bucks for her is like, nothing. Cab rides, same thing. It's cold or raining, you got the kid, you're going five or ten blocks, you take a cab, give the driver a nice tip. But you stay late and the parents give you a couple of twenties to take a cab home—no way! Keep that money, girlfriend, take the subway. There's a lot of gray areas, you know, lots of gray.

For me, I'm like, too honest. It's not mine, I won't touch it. Too easy to get in trouble, and then nobody'll ever hire you again. But you know, there're some girls, they think they're entitled to a little extra; it's like they think, if she leaves the money lying around or doesn't ask for change back and receipts and things, they're entitled to take it. It's like it's supposed to make up for all the stuff they don't get, or maybe they think, hey, I did all that laundry yesterday, that money's mine, I deserve that money! And some of the families, too, they just don't get it. Purses, wallets left open, that's just the half of it. I've seen bank statements, credit card receipts, all sorts of stuff, just sittin' there, rubbing it in. It's just looking for trouble, if you ask me. It's almost as if sometimes the families are kind of showing off—I mean, not with how much money they got, that's pretty obvious, but like they're saying, "Look at us, we trust you so much, aren't we just wonderful." More like effing stupid, if you ask me. I mean, I guess on the one hand I do appreciate the trust, you know, and like I said, I never have taken a single thing. But on the other hand, why do you want to put anybody in a situation where she even has to think about it? Like, you wouldn't give someone who's on a diet a chocolate cake to go staring at every day, would you?

Innocent victims, had-it-coming jerks, or something in-between, every year plenty of parents find that their nanny, or someone else working in their house and with their children, has been making off with more than her agreed-upon share of the family funds. When it happens reactions seem to range from predictable outrage to sheepish embarrassment, and while there are undoubtedly some who do,

I've yet to meet anyone who has actually filed charges. One mother admitted to turning a blind eye to the pilfering that she suspected was going on because she couldn't bear to think of upsetting the family applecart, didn't know what she would say to the children, and couldn't think of a way to confront the nanny and not cause everyone tremendous embarrassment in the event the accusations turned out to be false.

It was such little things, almost all of them in situations where it could have been someone else as well—you know, a five-dollar bill I thought I'd left in a coat pocket or a twenty I always keep in a purse that I maybe use once or twice a year, gone. A pair of pearl earrings I hadn't worn in months that I could no longer find; same with a ring my grandmother had given me that was always too big, that sort of thing. First I thought it was me, you know, getting scatty, losing stuff, and no one thing was big enough to get really upset about. I guess I was just in denial, blaming myself and really wanting it to be not true. It's awful when you suspect someone who's so close to you, especially because she was just the nicest, sweetest person you can imagine. And then one day I asked my husband if he'd noticed anything, and *he* said he'd been wondering the same thing! A pair of cuff links, this little baby iPod he'd gotten as a freebie at a conference and never used, money he thought maybe I'd picked up and put in my pocket without telling him.

It was getting to be too obvious to ignore, but we still managed to ignore it for another couple of months! Even though I did start to lock things up religiously, count change, look at receipts, that sort of thing. We both had this feeling that we were at least partly responsible for not paying more attention. I mean, it's a lot asking someone to basically come and be part of your family and as good as live with you in your home, and not expect them to want some of the things you have. When she left it turned out to be for a completely different reason, but I'm much better now at keeping things separate. A couple of people called me for a reference after that, and I must admit I did say something to the extent that a few things seemed to have mysteriously disappeared while she was with us. But it's a big deal to accuse someone of being a thief, isn't it? She was really a great nanny in every other way.

Not every victim, however, is quite so ready to blame herself. One nanny used the mother's credit card information to order a number of luxuries, from the very same stores her employer would patronize, on frequent telephone or Web site shopping sprees

I guess you could say I'm the ultimate patsy. Look, I have a huge family, I love getting stuff for my kids; there's a birthday or something, like, every week, and I also work really hard. I absolutely loathe malls, so this Internet shopping thing has just been a godsend. I've always got at least a couple of Neiman Marcus boxes or whatever sitting in my hallway, I mean, I get every catalog known to man, and it's just so convenient! And I'm good about returning things too, well, *I* didn't have to, because I'd just send Angie to the UPS store to do it for me while the kids were at school or something, so it was just the perfect setup for her.

You know how I found out? So one day I come home early for whatever reason, Angie isn't there, and the doorman gives me the mail and a whole pile of boxes. So I open them, and guess what's in there—a goddamn pink rabbit vibrator! Well, I knew I hadn't ordered *that,* so the first one I go to is my oldest, she's fourteen, and say to her, Well, honey, if that's what you wanted, couldn't you at least talk to me about it? Oh, the scene, you just would not believe. Suffice it to say, it was convincing.

So I did a little research, and it turns out the order had been placed from my home phone number on a weekday when no one could have been home but Angie. Next I get the credit card company to send me copies of my bills for the last six months, and it's all there—actually, it isn't, because it only shows the name of the merchant, but all stores I buy from regularly. But you can get these itemized lists, and that's where the stuff showed up—jewelry, makeup, a down jacket, a hundred bucks here, couple of hundred bucks there, probably two thousand dollars worth of stuff, maybe more if I'd gone back further.

I did confront her, right that day. God, I was furious! It was *such* a betrayal. I didn't pay her salary that week, but she never paid me back any of the rest, just disappeared, never heard from her again. I thought about filing some sort of a claim with the credit card company, but what am I going to say? "My nanny's been buying things with my card, and it wasn't me who charged that vibrator, I swear!" I still have that thing in a box somewhere. Unfortunately, my daughter was so mortified by the whole thing that she told my husband about it, so on top of everything I ended up looking like the idiot. It's really too bad he had to find out.

The price some parents are prepared to pay to keep their children entertained, while expecting the nanny to entertain, clothe, and feed herself and her family on approximately the same amount or less, can also be a constant source of irritation and bitterness. Of course, given the huge disparity of wealth that exists in this country, a juxtaposition of the haves and have-nots in the workplace is hardly rare. But in no workplace can one ever be as vulnerable as in one's home, and rarely is one person quite so intimately and profoundly enmeshed in the life of the other as in the nanny/employer relationship. The more experienced nannies I spoke to had found a way to deal with the constant inequities, and had come to a point where they were able to take them in stride, with their dignity and self-worth intact. For the younger, and by definition more inexperienced sector of the live-in child-care contingent, however, money, or simply an overabundance of material things, is often a huge issue. Au pairs, in particular, often from extremely poor countries, come to the United States only to find themselves abruptly thrust into the midst of mall country, driving SUVs around the suburbs and bombarded from every direction by images of shiny new things and fancy gadgets that would have been completely unobtainable to them in their home countries.

Au pair agencies and more experienced host families do what they can to prepare their au pair for the inevitable culture shock, but sometimes even the best of intentions go badly awry. Jovanka is nineteen and comes from Romania. The fact that she and her family were able to save up and afford the five-hundred-dollar fee the agency requires as a deposit from the applicants before they are accepted into the program actually places her squarely in her country's upper classes. Yet the contrast between the life she is used to and that enjoyed by the family who is hosting her "on par" (hence the denomination "au pair") with themselves and their children could hardly be greater.

People in my country, they are so poor, there is so much corruption. Is impossible to get good job without connection. You have to pay for everything, everything! And is all so expensive—this five hundred dollars, for my family that is two months' wages. And look, see this toothpaste? We have this brand in my country, but only with the cheap ingredients. The companies, they make this but they don't make it good like they do here, they make it with bad ingredients, and then it cost double the price. So for me to come here, it is such a huge chance, I can save, I can study, I can make a better life for my family. So at first I come here, my little suitcase made from cardboard, all new, I'm so proud of it. And then I arrive with my [host] family, and I have this beautiful room, is bigger than room I sleep in at home with two sisters! And in the bathroom, they put all these things—the toothpaste, the shampoo, the soap, the white soft toilet paper—and when I see all this I cry like a baby. I want to put all in a box and send home to my family! We never can buy these things when I am there. Is such a small thing, but make me feel so poor.

I know they want to welcome me, to be generous, but it just make me cry. Now I get more used to this life. Now I save most of my money, and I want to stay longer, make as much as I can. I want my sister to come here, do same thing. I can send her the money. My host family, sometimes they don't understand. I am very proud person, and is hard for me not to say—look, the food you give to your dog, that chicken with the rice, in my country that is for *people!*

Jovanka's friend Ludmilla is twenty-two, by now speaking English at a rapid, lilting clip and close to the end of her au pair year. She has decided to stay on for another twelve months—not, however, on the same terms and with the same family, as permitted by a fairly new State Department regulation, but "somewhere else. I don't really care. I just want to make a lot of money. I know girls, they get five hundred, six hundred dollars a week! Maybe I find a guy and he will marry me!" Ludmilla's hard-boiled demeanor is probably the result of a year's worth of experiences such as this: "Okay, so here I am getting a hundred and forty dollars a week, and she gives me fifty dollars to pay for the kid's riding lesson—fifty dollars for half an hour to sit on the back of a stinky old pony, can you believe that? You know, I should be a horse for that kind of money."

Of course, families who can afford fifty-dollar riding lessons are far from the American norm. While no one deserves to have anyone steal from them, there is without a doubt a certain sense of glee and a she-had-it-coming attitude shared by all who hear the pink-rabbit

story (even, it should be noted, by the woman who tells it). We all like
to hear about the stupid things that rich folks do, if only so we can
congratulate ourselves that we'd never be that stupid, or thoughtless,
or mean—look no further than the huge success of *Nanny Diaries* as
a perfect example of that phenomenon: Selfish, pampered trophy wife
needs down-to-earth nanny to help her rediscover the value of love
and the meaning of motherhood. It's a good yarn and a compelling
story in large part because the mother is so clearly so clueless about
how much life for the little people actually costs. Unfortunately, this
stereotype does not only exist on the pages of Manhattan ivory tower
novels, but is alive and well, and she is thoughtless, clueless, and with
money to burn in wealthy suburbs all over the country.

Ariel was twenty-two when she started working for a family of two
lawyers and their children.

> They were ridiculously, I mean almost nauseatingly, wealthy. So
> at the beginning, they offered me five dollars an hour to look
> after their two kids, and I did that for two months, until I finally
> plucked up the courage to ask for a little bit more. I mean, I was
> totally intimidated by the mother! She was always talking about
> their previous babysitter and how wonderful she was, so that
> just made me feel like I could never do anything right, you know,
> like I was worthless.
>
> And then, all of a sudden, they started asking me to do
> more—stay another hour, do a little cleaning, cook the dinner,
> drive here and then there, and then someplace else, in *my* car.
> Not *once* did they even offer me gas money, and when I finally
> asked for it, because I literally didn't have enough to get home,
> they acted all insulted, as though they were already paying me so
> much. The last straw was when they forced me to get a cell
> phone so they could reach me during the day from work, and
> I had to pay for all the calls.

When I quit, finally, you know what they did? They actually sent me a bill for the cell phone, because there'd been some sort of penalty when they turned it off. You have to understand, these people were *rolling* in money. I mean, people want quality child care, but some of them just don't get that they have to pay for it. They want to pay someone like me the same as what they'd pay some kid to watch their pet.

Almost all experienced nannies, or those who had worked for at least two or three families by the time I heard their stories, reserved particular vitriol for nonworking mothers—read: Women wealthy enough to neither work for a living, nor to do much of their own housework or most of the feeding, dressing, playing, bathing, and general looking after required by their children. More extreme comments I noted down ranged from, "They don't want their kids; they just want help," to "I mean, lady, why don't you just put your kids in an orphanage?" I heard about some who "just bring kids into the world and then pay someone else to raise them"; a mother who "liked the dog more than she liked the kid"; and finally,"you know, some people, I swear, they think nannies don't eat."

From these and other stories it's hard not to conclude that occasionally, for some mothers, money does indeed become a substitute for all the things that are supposed to matter between mothers, their children, and their caregivers. When looked at exclusively through the great, green lens of the dollar, almost all relationships will become warped and stunted, where motives are murky and everything is for sale. In this respect it's clearly the responsibility of the employer—which in most cases this means the mother—to set a tone in her interactions with her children and with whomever she hires to help care for them, that values kindness, respect, and love far above "the going rate."

Astrud from Brazil, a very young looking fifty-eight, has been a professional nanny for almost thirty years, moving from one family to the next in one of the wealthiest counties in America. Her accent was sometimes hard to make out, but her meaning could not have been clearer.

Oooh, I tell you, I have seen everything. You cannot believe some of these houses, the butler, the staff, the driver, somebody for everything. You cannot tell the names, these are very wealthy people, some famous people, in the newspapers and everything. Some are nice families, very strict, the children have good manners. Is always because the parents, they don't forget where it comes from, what it means to work hard. Everybody's different, but is all about the character. The parents make the children; nobody can tell me it's different. I always start with the babies, I love babies. Babies don't care you're poor or rich or you have brown skin and funny accent. If I like the family I stay, two, three years; one time I stay seven, when I think they don't need me anymore. That was good family. The father working, working, always at office, some big important job he has.

But the mother, she work hard too! Four children is lot of work, she care very much, about everything, she's there for them all the time. People always say it must be easy to be so rich, it must be happy to have so much, but is bad for the kids to be spoilt. I have bad kids, I have good kids. Most important is that parents are involved with children. If I'm good nanny, I'm there to help, not to replace mother. I have jobs where mother wants me to do everything, just hand me the baby and say, here, Astrud, you change nappy, you feed at night, you take for walk, you do everything, I go to gym, I go to shopping, see you tomorrow. If you are mother like that, your children will be like that, and if you are mother like that you won't have good nanny. For little while you can keep good nanny with money, but for long time you only get to keep nanny with good relationship.

Astrud's words certainly ring true, but she does work among that tiny subset of the population that is the superrich and their offspring. By far the largest majority of nannies are employed by parents for whom the cost of full-time one-on-one child care represents a carefully budgeted, and sometimes much resented, expense. For these families the question of how to afford the nanny's salary is often tangled up in an entirely different issue, namely, a longing to spend more time with their children, or even to stay home with them altogether, instead of carrying on with an unfulfilling job in a dead-end career—if only they could afford to. Faye is a claims adjuster for an insurance company who dreams of giving up work to raise her two young daughters, and take pottery lessons and a year off to travel in Europe. Her husband, Karl, is an assistant manager at a car dealership, and a lot of his salary is based on commissions. Together they "spend most of their time either trying to sell someone something, or finding a reason to not pay their insurance claim. It can get kind of depressing." Both have long commutes from their rural home, and they have been unable to find decent, affordable day care for their daughters, particularly because one of them suffers from a fairly severe nut allergy. They desperately need both the health insurance and the income Faye's job provides. Making ends meet is a struggle—both for them and the elderly local woman who looks after the two girls in their home. Faye said:

> I can't tell you how often I come home thinking that I only work
> so we can pay Phoebe. Of course, it's not rational. I need to
> work for a whole bunch of reasons. This way at least I know the
> girls are safe, and that's really the most important thing, I'm
> grateful for that. But I also really do resent all the time she gets
> to spend with the girls—that's time I should have with them,
> while they're still young and I still have the energy! So instead,
> they have to hang out with Phoebe, who's lovely and ever so
> careful, but let's face it—not exactly me, or really a whole barrel

of laughs. I'm just kind of left holding the bag. I hold down a full-time job, I still do most of the work around the house, and I don't even get to spend any time with my kids!

Really, there are days when I think Phoebe should be paying me—I mean, she gets to do exactly what I'd do if I had a choice, with my kids, in my house, and I've got to give her half my paycheck for the privilege. Like I said, it's not rational, because she's not exactly raking it in either. But you just can't help thinking it isn't fair. I just don't understand women who hand their kids over to a sitter if they could afford to stay home with them.

When it comes to pinning down exactly how much money matters in the whole spectrum of issues that affect the ways mothers and nannies work together, what occurs to me time and again is a cooking metaphor. Whatever the currency, it's a critical ingredient to have on hand to sweeten the pot. Occasionally a small amount can go a long way, and depending on who's cooking, both too much or too little can leave a bitter aftertaste. By the same token, some recipes can't be rescued no matter how much is added, and in those rare and magical stews where the end result is better than the sum of its ingredients, money still ranks right up there with love and respect as one of the staples without which there wouldn't be a stew at all. In terms of deciding which is the best recipe, giving advice on how much is enough is a very fine line to draw: It all depends on who the players are, but balance is key. Find the sweet spot between need and ability to pay, between what's deserved and what's appropriate, between basic compensation and above-and-beyond recognition, between generosity and absurd largesse, and you'll probably be fine.

If things are not fine, and there are unmanageable fights or disagreements, money is frequently the catalyst, though not necessarily the underlying cause. This is most likely because, unlike the other staples of love and respect, it is such an obviously quantifiable, by definition measurable, thing. Certainly where child care in this country is concerned, more of it would go a long way toward making everyone involved in the child-care triangle—mothers (sorry, parents), children, and their caretakers—a great deal happier, less conflicted, and probably safer. In the end, no matter who does the counting, the fact that the cost of good, reliable, and nurturing child care is far higher than it should be is an easy conclusion to reach. Devising possible solutions and achievable benchmarks, however, would inevitably take this book into a realm where it was by definition never meant to go—namely, that of the public arena of politics and national policy. If Americans aren't comfortable with the government in their bedrooms, then they certainly loathe the idea of Uncle Sam in the nursery deciding how and by whom their children should be looked after, loved, and nurtured in those critical five years before they go off to school to be taught their ABCs. Almost without exception, every mother I know would love more help with managing the care of her children, but no one wants it with strings attached, and unfortunately that's what government subsidies of any kind often represent—as they should.

With child care perhaps more than any other issue, mothers do want the means but would rather die than give up control. With the result that everyone continues to struggle: child-care workers with borderline-poverty wages and a lack of respect for their profession; mothers with guilt and resentment over what they need and what and how they must pay for it; and in-home caretakers with the constant question of what they're really worth and how to make ends meet. Unfortunately, until the day society begins to literally value and compensate mothers for the actual work that they do, this is most likely how it will remain.

values

*t*HERE ARE PRECIOUS few things in life on which people of all shapes and sizes, colors, religions, and nationalities will agree to agree on. It's probably safe to say that one of those is a basic set of values we'd all like to teach our children: kindness, compassion, honesty, respect. That, however, is the point at which the consensus is likely to come to a sudden and dramatic halt, and where this chapter begins. The question of whose word, deed, and example count for more is the wellspring of the kind of misunderstandings and mixed messages that make the nanny/mother relationship such a minefield of emotions, and the crux of so many conflicts between the real mother and the one for hire. Is it ever reasonable to expect others to do things that we ourselves will not? What if it's the opposite, and one condition for holding on to a particular job is enforcing certain rules that violate some other, deeply held belief of ours? Is being a good mother automatically the same as being a good employer, and who gets to decide what a "good mother" is supposed to be, anyway?

Other than money issues, possibly the most common complaint I heard from nannies with respect to their employers was that, quite simply, they'd say one thing and then go right ahead and do another.

Frequently this would leave the nanny with the unpleasant task of explaining to the children why it was okay for Mom to do or say something that would get any one of them sent to their room or into a time-out. One nanny talked to me about being

> the only one who ever taught anybody anything in that family. The parents, they talk a good game, know what I mean? "Jenny, we want them to have manners, Jenny, we want them to do chores, Jenny, we don't want them spoiled." Well, hello!? So how'm I suppose to ask the kids to clean up after themselves when she's like the biggest slob you've ever seen, never makes her bed, kitchen a pigsty every frickin' morning? But it was when the little girl called me a bitch, really, that was the last straw. And then I hear the mother on the phone to one of her friends, bitch this, bitch that, like it's supposed to be some kind of joke. So now I tell the little girl, go right ahead, call anyone else bitch if you want, but you say that to me again and I'll wash your mouth out with soap. Trouble is, I don't even think she knows what it means, is just a word to her.

In the same conversation Jenny admitted to me that this was, of course, not something she'd ever say to the girl in front of the mother, and that she hadn't lasted more than a few months in that particular job. "Couldn't stand it anymore. Some people are just not nice, know what I mean?"

Among the questions I asked Jenny, and most of the other nannies I spoke to, was, what were the most important characteristics they would look for in the event the tables were turned and they had to hire a nanny. Other than the first and second no-brainers of "you've got to love kids" and "you've got to be safe and reliable," the third most commonly listed attribute was a caretaker prepared to go along with and reinforce a family's particular rules: "Do things my way," "love my baby the way I'd love her," "teach her the important things, you know, the stuff that matters, how to be safe, how to be smart, be respectful." Whether it was healthy food, no TV, no swearing, chores, or good manners, everyone agreed that priorities ought to be for the mothers and fathers to set and for her to follow.

As Jenny points out,

> It's no good if you all got a different agenda; you have to be on the same page, like if I don't know that the mom will back me up if I say no to something, I know it's not gonna work out. And kids are real smart like that. You have to have some juice, you know what I mean? It's like that nanny lady on TV. If I say no and she says yes, forget about it. They'll walk all over you. Doesn't matter how many times she says to me, "Jenny, no candy before dinner." It's what you do that counts. I actually seen her hide a piece of chocolate she was giving to Andy when she didn't hear me coming, like stick it in her own mouth and pretend it was for her. You know, that's just ridiculous, right? But I can't exactly go up to her and say, "Here, young lady, what's that you got in your mouth." I mean, she's no baby, and I'm not her mother. Might as well be that way, though, sometimes, the way she carries on.

Serena is from St. Lucia, and she has been a nanny, off and on, for fifteen years, while raising her own four children, whose ages range from thirty-one to eighteen. Her self-confidence and fierce pride in her and her children's accomplishments is immediately apparent, but she says that by now she's learned to dumb herself down in interviews.

> It seems like most people have to believe that nannies are stupid. They just can't stand it when they figure out that maybe you're just as smart as they are, that you've done something with

your life, that you're proud of what you do. So many times people would say to me, "Serena, why you want to be doing this? You're much too educated for this job." I want to ask them, "What, you want a dummy for a nanny, someone stupid, is that what you want?" It's such a double standard. You're supposed to be everything for those families; they want you to cook, they want you to clean, they want you to be their doormat, basically; but it's only okay for them to have a servant if that person isn't very smart. So I'm supposed to smile and act stupid, and then they can carry on in front of me with their little games and pretend like I don't exist. It's insulting.

Like this one family, they had two kids, both parents big moneymaking lawyers. I could tell right away from day one there was something wrong with the little boy, that he had autism maybe, Asperger's, something like that, just wasn't right. But the mother never said anything; she was in complete denial, wouldn't take him anywhere, pretended he was just normal like everybody else, maybe acting up a bit, nothing serious.

So I started reading about it, and figuring it out, and working with him. He was *so* smart, just had trouble connecting with people, you know what I mean? I used to be the one who talked to his teachers at school, take him to doctors' appointments, everything. I'm telling you, that woman was ashamed of her son. She just couldn't handle the truth. And when I started talking to her about it, she couldn't handle the fact that I'd figured it out, that he was doing better with me than he'd do with her, because I was "just" the nanny. He'd tell me that she used to scream at him, call him a dummy, push him around, all sorts of things. So yeah, just because you're rich doesn't mean you're smart or that you can love your kids like they deserve it. And just because you've got this big-time executive position doesn't mean you got better values than someone like me, who's not supposed to have an education.

Serena gives me another example:

> At the interview, this one mother I worked for, she went on and on
> and *on* about how she missed her kids all the time, and really
> wanted to spend more time with them, and how she hated to miss
> all those precious moments, and envied me being with them all
> day. So you know what she would go and do? They had this big
> house, really huge, and she'd come home from work, like sneak in
> the door, grab herself a bottle of wine, and go and hide some-
> where from her kids! Literally hide in a bathroom or something.
> I'd have to go around the house looking for her, like, "Hello, Judy,
> where are you, I got to go, kids ready for bed, where are you?"

While it's hard not to feel a twinge of sympathy for that stressed-out
working mom who'd rather spend a little one-on-one time with the
Chardonnay before facing her kids at the end of a long day, Serena's
point also comes across loud and clear—it's what you do that counts. All
highfalutin' talk and no action sends the kids the message that it's okay
to act like brats and makes discipline impossible. Not only does it get
*every*body irritated (including the children), but it takes a good nanny (or
even a mediocre one) about five minutes to see through the charade.

Serena wasn't the only one to talk about how she had learned to
read interviews for clues about "what's really going on in that family."
In her late twenties, Ella had been working with children and their
families for almost a decade.

By now she'd learned to recognize the warning signs and decode
some of the lies, as well intentioned as they may be.

> I always find it odd how so often during an interview the moth-
> ers seem to be kind of embarrassed to admit that they even need
> a nanny. I can always tell when they're putting on a front, like,
> "Oh, we're just this perfect family, and we're the most concerned

parents in the world, and we want only the very best for our children." Of course everybody wants the best for their children. But some parents don't seem to see that it's an issue for them to exploit someone else in order to do that. Some people can be incredibly demeaning, and they don't even realize it. I have this sixth sense now, you know, and if someone treats me like it would be this great privilege for me to be working for them, I won't even touch the job. But the real proof usually comes a few weeks into it, when they've got to know you and there's some kind of a crisis, like there's a tantrum or someone's late, or whatever. Nobody would ever think it's okay for the nanny to lose it, but for some reason there's nothing wrong with moms screaming and yelling. And when a kid hurts himself with the nanny it's like this big deal, but when he cuts his head open because Mom wasn't looking, it's just a little boo-boo.

But, you know, I get that. I don't even know that I'd want my own kids at this point because I know how hard it is. But you still have to respect the person who's looking after your children, respect that they're human, too, that they make mistakes, or that they might know something you don't. Ultimately, the only way a relationship is going to work—and by that I mean that it's comfortable in the long term—is if there's a mutual exchange. Until now all the mothers I've worked for have been older than me so I know I've got things to learn from them. But when they hire me they also know they're getting someone who's really a professional, who's taught kids and studied their behavior and looked at all this from an academic perspective as well as a personal one. It's really got to be like a marriage between the caregiver and the parents [though she admits that most of the time the parent she deals with is the mother]. You've got to be honest with each other, and when you have a fight you've got to be mature enough to work it out and move on.

Honesty between peers is one thing. However, the issue of honesty between mothers and caregivers (or those who interview them . . .) is evidently not nearly as straightforward as calling a spade a spade. It didn't take me long to realize that in the majority of my interviews I was, by definition, only hearing one side of the story. Separating truth from fiction was close to impossible. Nor were the facts always the point: Another thing I realized very early on in the writing of this book was that whether or not a particular story was strictly true didn't matter nearly as much as the fact that whoever was telling it clearly believed it to be so. If Serena's narrative was, in places, full of holes and even contradictions, this didn't change the fact that she had made up her mind to judge the mothers she worked for in a certain way. She was by no means the only one to cast herself as the good nanny versus the bad mother, or, just as often, the heroic, long-suffering caretaker versus the pampered, self-delusional fool of a woman. When I asked her at the end of our interview why she had agreed to talk to me and what she hoped might be the outcome, she was very clear: "I want people to know that being a nanny is a *hard* job. I want us to be appreciated. Some people just don't understand that to have a nanny that loves your kids is a godsend. What do you think would happen to all white people if all of us nannies decided to give up our jobs tomorrow?" What, indeed—hand me that bottle of Chardonnay, now!

June is a British nanny who has been working with families in the United States for sixteen years. Now married and with a son of her own, she still works close to full-time looking after other people's children but says that her "perspective on the whole mother/nanny relationship has completely changed from where it was at the beginning." She's clearly talking from both long-term as well as recently acquired, personal experience when she tells me that in the families she's worked for, "When it comes to figuring out the child care, the biggest issue is that the buck stops with the woman, even if both parents have full-time jobs. Women seem to be at this really weird time when they're expected to do everything, have careers, be mothers, be wives. And because of that they have a really hard time admitting they even need help, and that they really don't like some aspects of raising their children."

Now that she has a family of her own, with a handsome husband and a beautiful son, June also has no trouble being brutally honest about her colleagues and friends on the nanny circuit, most of whom are legal and consider themselves to be professionals just like her:

> I've really thought about this a lot. I've seen it time and time again, this complete lack of empathy from the nannies toward the women they work for. Given how hard it is to be a working mother these days, you'd really think it would be different, that you'd see women supporting each other, validating each other's choices, even if they're imperfect. But honestly, with so many of the nannies I know it's just the opposite; when they get together it's a complete free-for-all. As though it's totally acceptable, almost expected even, to put down the women they work for.
>
> It's almost a personality type, you know, the girls who choose to become nannies—on the one hand they're never done complaining about the people they work for, but on the other there's this really strong desire to be part of the woman's family, where they desperately want to be loved and appreciated and included. It's such a weird career choice, if you think about it. I mean, you're really isolated, stuck with someone else's kids, basically a kind of domestic servant. So why do it, unless what you really want is to be loved by this family? And then at the same time, behind the mothers' backs they're really contemptuous, like, "Why do you even bother to have kids if you're just going off to work." I hear that *all* the time.

Perhaps because she grew up in England, June is also not afraid to speak out about the other things that American child-care experts wouldn't dare mention in public: class, race, and looks.

> I'd say that most nannies, at least the ones I know, pretty much come from fairly traditional working-class families. Quite a few of them are grossly overweight and not exactly very successful in their personal lives. So they look at these women they work for, and they're beautiful and they're successful and they've got gorgeous children, how can they not be jealous? It's as though some of them think, You have everything I want and don't have, what could you possibly have in life to be unhappy about?
>
> I remember feeling like that sometimes. One of the first women I worked for, she was desperately unhappy, seriously depressed; all the money in the world, fantastically successful husband, but she just felt like she was a nobody, with no identity of her own. She'd talk to me for hours about her situation. So yes, it's hard sometimes not to think—God woman, why can't you be happy, you've got everything I want, at least have the grace to be grateful.

Looking at it from a working mother's perspective, gratitude is not necessarily the first feeling that springs from her gut when she thinks about her child care. According to one successful professional woman who appears to have it all, the emotion she's most likely to feel at the end of the day is that everybody wants a piece of her, and she just doesn't have anything else left to give. This is what Sheila, an interior designer has to say:

> Of course I'm lucky. If I ever had a minute to myself, I'd probably realize that and count my blessings. It's just so hard sometimes to

get your head above water and really see the big picture. The trouble is that you only ever seem to be able to realize how much you've got when you're not right in it, do you know what I mean? Between being a wife to my husband and a mother to my kids and an appreciative employer to my nanny, I feel like everyone takes me for granted, and then some. As far as the kids go, that's fine, that's normal. There'd be something seriously wrong if they didn't feel they could take my parenting and my love for them for granted. As far as the nanny goes though, that's really a different story. Yes, I do appreciate her. Boy, do I ever. And I am *really* grateful that she's just able to take over when I'm gone, and I don't have to worry about a thing. But does it ever occur to her to be grateful to me, for the simple fact that I work every day and earn the money, that I do so she can have her job? I don't think so, honestly, I don't think so.

While no one expects the mother/caretaker relationship to be a mutual admiration society, it can be extremely disturbing to realize just how much hostility is out there. Rina's first child was a spring baby, so during her maternity leave she was able to spend a lot of time in the park and "in the trenches" with the local posse of nannies and their young charges. As the weeks went by and she listened to their talk, watching them interact both with each other and the children, she became increasingly convinced that day care would be the only safe place for her son once she had to go back to work.

At first I came into the whole nanny child-care thing thinking, "This will be a member of my family. I'm going to make her love me, and then by extension she will love my child." But the reality of it, the things I overheard, were just so different. I'm the most politically correct person you can imagine, I mean, I don't just talk this stuff—I live it and I work with it every day. But what I saw among those nannies, that wasn't just indifference, it was real hostility, real disdain directed at the families they worked for.

Of course, this wasn't helped by the fact that I'm white and the vast majority of nannies I ran across were African American, so right off the bat you have a class issue, and that underlying tension between the haves and the have-nots. The crazy thing of course is that the day care I ultimately chose was every bit as expensive as a nanny—the difference being that there were lots of eyes on him, all the time. And I didn't feel that I was being held hostage by this one person and the mood she might be in, with nobody else watching her.

June agreed that

a lot of nannies just don't understand the money constraints their employers might be under. I mean, by definition she's always the one who's got more. And when you see the way some people throw money around, and then they just can't bring themselves to pay you overtime or sick pay, it's easy to get bitter. You have to have an enormously strong sense of yourself and of the value of what you do not to fall into that trap of, "it's her against me; she's just paying me off to do her dirty work because she can't be bothered." There've been lots of times where, on the one hand I would tell myself that what I do is valuable, but on the other I'd feel that what I'm doing isn't really worth anything. So you take your frustration and your confusion out on the mother, like she's to blame for the fact that you sometimes feel you're worthless, even though the work you're doing is actually really hard. It's complicated. Actually, it's all about being appreciated. That's why that annual raise is *so* important. The amount of it doesn't even matter that much, it's just hugely important to feel that your work gets recognized. And I hate to say it, but getting recognition from the fathers just doesn't mean nearly as much, even though half the time they're the ones paying you.

It's easy to see how hard, if not downright impossible, it can be to accommodate everyone's need to be appreciated. Tina is an experienced nanny who left one family

because every time Mom came home she had to make this huge deal about reestablishing her motherhood, you know, like asserting her authority. It was like, "Okay everybody, the *real* boss is here now, so forget whatever else you were doing and just listen to me." I can understand that to a certain extent, but it just totally undermined everything I was doing. It just made me wonder, you know, don't you *value* what I'm doing for you here? The dad was great, very easygoing and approachable, but getting paid was always an issue, like pulling teeth, you know? And then, when I said I was leaving, all of a sudden she just offers me a hundred dollars more per week. That's when you realize, this wasn't about having a relationship; it's just a business transaction to her.

It's like a lot of mothers, they just can't accept that maybe you have a life, too. Like this one time I was on vacation in Florida, and on my way home my flight got canceled; it was just totally not my fault. I mean, what am I supposed to do, walk? Buy another ticket for five hundred bucks? I can't afford that. So then she refuses to pay me for that first day I was supposed to be back at work, and she says, "I really needed you that day, and you weren't there for me." Like I did it on purpose to spite her or something. The woman I work for now, she's a stay-at-home mom, so that kind of situation hasn't come up again. What I think now, though, is that I should charge her extra every time she invites her friends over and they all just dump their kids with me while they go off to play tennis or whatever—I mean, my job's to look after two kids not five, for heaven's sakes.

June also tells me That's Not My Job might as well be the unofficial nanny anthem, so often has she heard her friends and colleagues complain about being asked to do things they felt were not their responsibility. She herself learned the hard way that "if you offer to do something one time, just to help out or because it was kind of on the way, then suddenly you get in trouble if you don't do it again the next time. For example, for one family I'd occasionally take the garbage to the dump, even though it definitely wasn't part of my job description. And then, when one week I didn't, there was this big scene."

The issue of whether or not there should be a contract, what exactly it should address, and how often it ought to be updated is one that comes up constantly among nannies. Yet it is also clear that there continues to be a great discrepancy between the number of people— parents and employees both—who believe a contract is essential, and those who actually have one, refer back to it, and abide by all its various terms. Most good agencies will suggest that both parties create one, and many will actually provide a boilerplate sample to start with; the International Nanny Association (www.internationalnanny association.com) has one available for purchase on their Web site that pretty much covers all the bases.

Similar to all the mixed feelings stirred up by the notion of a prenuptial agreement, many women still have a terribly hard time keeping their emotions in check in order to come up with a workable document. As Josie told me,

I tried once. I put in all the things about the hours and the money and vacations and sick days and stuff, those things we do stick to—or try to. But then I remember sitting there and starting to think of all the other things I'd expect of a nanny, and you know, it got totally out of hand, and I ended up in tears.

I mean, you can't exactly put down things like, I want you to make my children happy and to love them, and I want them to love you, but please not more than they love me. And I want them to be safe, and I want you to teach them how to be kind and how to appreciate other people and their family and all that they have in life . . . it all got to be about what kind of a mother I'd always wanted to be, and not, of course. And you really can't put that kind of thing in a contract, can you? Well, obviously not, but to be honest, those issues are way more important to me than all the nitty-gritty technical stuff.

Nanny June still thinks it's incredibly important to have a contract.

It just eliminates a huge amount of resentment if everything is spelled out, things like sick pay and vacation days and what exactly "light housekeeping" means. I really started insisting on it after this one situation where I got sick and the mother said, "If you're sick, I can't work, so why should I pay you." Or another time, when I'd booked a vacation and the *mother* got sick and she told me I couldn't go—there went my ticket and everything I'd booked and prepaid. The thing is, though, if you don't have a great relationship to start with, that's when a contract can help you end it in such a way that you don't get screwed. It isn't ever going to fix a bad situation if the chemistry isn't there to start with.

Clearly, contract or no, these stories illustrate the perspective and the empathy that June so astutely points out is often lacking when it comes to both nannies understanding "their" mothers, and vice versa. Anyone who's been forced to call off a critical meeting at their "real" job because the nanny was sick will be able to sympathize with the underlying emotion of June's employer, though not necessarily approve of the way in which she expressed it. Society continues to pay a great deal of lip service to what is perceived to be a mother's most important job. But when the reality of the lovely notion that the children come first turns into another missed meeting, neglected deadline, or colleagues left holding the bag, it also becomes clear that as a whole American employers have little sympathy or patience for child-care failures.

Ellen, mother of twins with a "very client-focused consulting job," makes no bones about her feelings regarding the whole "nannies have a life too" issue. She is down to one, from two nannies when the twins were babies.

> Look, the reason I have a nanny is that it gives me absolute freedom to do my job when and how I need to. Clients don't think it's cute when you have to cancel because your sitter didn't show up. They don't want to *hear* about that stuff—I don't want to have to tell them! I don't want that part of my life to become an issue in my work relationships, ever. And by the way, I have a lot of women clients, and I can tell you that on balance they're probably less sympathetic than the men. The women just expect other women to have that covered.
>
> So, is my job more important than hers? Absolutely, it is. It's a double standard, I guess, but let's face it—I'm a highly qualified and highly [Ellen knocks on wood] paid professional, and the reason is that I have skills my nanny doesn't have, now or ever. And I guess I'm conceited enough to say that there really isn't anything she does that I couldn't do equally as well, or probably better. I work because I love my job, I like my life, I'm proud of what I've accomplished, and because I want my kids to have all the opportunities I ever had. I do *not* work my tail off so my nanny can have a life. I don't even want to hear about what happens when she goes home. I don't care about her sleazebag

boyfriend, about her mother who's sick, or that she gets bad PMS. All I want to know is that she's there when I need her, that she's 100 percent focused on my kids, and that she follows my instructions.

Clearly Ellen is a woman who says what she thinks, does what she says, and takes no crap from anyone (except, I'm hoping, her five-year-old twin boys, whom she reports to be "real terrors, but *so* cute"). What's more, her formula appears to work, because she has happily employed the same nanny for close to four years. I suspect I'm not the only one to feel a combination of intimidation and envy at Ellen's cool confidence, and particularly at her willingness to put herself squarely at the top of the women-working-for-other-women pecking order.

What her comments also show, however, is that sometimes a successful relationship hinges almost entirely on the ability to focus and compartmentalize. Given that Ellen was described to me by an acquaintance as "incredibly passionate, one of the few really good people in this world," I can only surmise that she must be highly disciplined and selective about the information she allows to weigh in her choices and decisions.

Ellen's description of who the nanny should be and what she ought to be doing are solely based on what *Ellen* needs, and in the course of our conversation it becomes clear that, contrary to appearances, this is not because she doesn't give a damn. Ellen does indeed reveal herself to be a deeply passionate and caring individual, whose rather brutal assessment of her attitude toward her nanny is obviously as difficult for her to admit as it is for me to hear. While she paints a picture of being in complete control, I also sense that she is just a breath away from being totally overwhelmed, and is constantly struggling with how to live up to the priorities and standards she has set for herself and her children: The boys deserve the best of everything she has to give (including top-notch child care), but so do the clients and colleagues at her extremely intense job. She obviously knows full well that to also take into account her caregiver's personal circumstances, special needs, and problems could set her off on a slippery slope of compromise from which she might never recover.

Knowledge may be power to some, but it can just as easily be a harbinger of doubt and disruption in a life, like Ellen's, that genuinely has no wiggle room. It's much easier not to care about your nanny's trouble with her boyfriend and why it made her late if you can legitimately claim that you don't even know his name.

While a rigid hierarchy is essential to some, many other mothers told me that their best nannies had been women whom they considered to be peers rather than employees. Rina, who originally eschewed the services of "a babysitter" in favor of day care for her infant son, eventually found the perfect person among the staff at his day-care center. Rina could not bring herself to use the word "nanny" because

> it seems so horribly class-bound. But with Angela, we just hit it off, right from the start. One day she just sort of mentioned that she wanted to take a break and do something different for a while. So I said, how'd you like to come and work for me? It turned out that it was just the best possible situation for all of us. She came with a skill set, and this ability to love children in a way that no one else had. I felt there was a complete equality of status between us, shared values, a totally comfortable give-and-take. Classwise, the fact that she was educated, that she's American, everything. We honestly talked to each other as equals; it felt like it might feel coming home to someone you were living with. We definitely disagreed on some things, but both totally believed in a child-centered upbringing. She was genuinely gifted with children. Toward the end I know Emmett would gladly have traded her for me—he used to call her, "My 'nother mother"!

Unfortunately (and who couldn't see this coming) it was too good to last. Angela fell in love with a guy, moved away to be with him in a far-away state, and is now a single mother. Despite the fact that Rina's children are now nine and eleven, and that they've had a number of sitters since then, the experience and memory of parting with Angela clearly outweighs everything and everybody that might have followed in her wake. Rina's eyes instantly well up with tears at the mere mention of it. "We all just wept and wept. I was totally devastated, but you know, I never had the expectation that I could duplicate that experience. And I didn't. After Angela left, we had a series of sitters that were just a disaster before there was someone who I really felt was right for us."

When I had the opportunity to speak with Angela, it turned out to be one of the rare situations where, after having interviewed the mother, speaking to the nanny was comfortable and natural as well—in the way that friends introduce their friends to others. The rock-solid, child-centered values Rina had talked about were obvious in the way that Angela chose to raise her son, though this had clearly, at times, involved considerable sacrifice.

> I was really deeply committed to staying home with him for the first three years, and I just didn't want him to bond so closely with another person. I must admit, I wasn't really prepared at how hard it sometimes was just to stay home. Even though that time I stayed with Rina's family was completely wonderful. I just felt horrible guilt when I moved away. Because I did look at Em like my own child, and it felt like I was abandoning him. But as far as Rina goes, I felt truly appreciated. Even more than that, I felt honored by the fact that she recognized how I put my whole heart into it, that it wasn't just a job.

Once her son turned four, Angela was forced to go back to work for financial reasons, and perhaps somewhat ironically, the person she now relies on for child care in the after-school hours is anything but a peer: her own mother. It's unclear whether the values that drive Angela's parenting grew out of her mother's mothering, are a manifestation of a wish to do things differently, or—most likely—a little bit of both. "She's still doing the same things with him that used to bug me when I was growing up," she says. "It's a real challenge to make her respect our boundaries sometimes."

What on the surface might seem like an ideal situation for all concerned—Grandma looking after her own grandchild while Mom has peace of mind and everyone gets to stay close—is actually one of the most difficult and complicated versions of the mother/caretaker relationship anyone is likely to come across. When Grandma is also the mother-in-law, all the clichés tend to come barreling down with a vengeance. In fact, if it weren't so close to the bone, Angela's situation with her son and mother might be the perfect blueprint for a sitcom, creating just the sort of familiar, painful, absurd, and ridiculous situations and dialogues those kinds of shows thrive on. Try not to cringe when you read this:

"Mom, did Janie eat the organic spinach-and-broccoli pie I left for your dinner?"

"I'm sorry, honey, I just couldn't get her to eat a bit of it. And I must say, it was pretty tasteless. . . . You should try putting a packet of Heinz vegetable soup mix into the egg batter . . . that's always how I got you to eat your veggies."

"So, what *did* you have for dinner?"

"Oh, we ended up ordering pizza. Here's the receipt—you owe me ten bucks."

"What time did she go to bed?"

"Oh, I can't really remember, I'm sorry. We both fell asleep in front of the TV. And she should get an A on her homework assignment—we spent all afternoon on it. I wrote it all out for

her, and she copied every word. She needs to work on her pen-
manship, though. How was your day at work, darling?"

Well, yes, I admit, I made that up, but given my own mother's pro-
clivity to ply my daughters with candy, describe fries with ketchup as
"two vegetables," and send me back their adorable letters to her with
red ink and comments all over the margins, I don't think that dialogue
is particularly far-fetched. What is more, I imagine that most mothers
with small children would have no trouble whatsoever taking that
blueprint and substituting their own peculiar, personal, and infuriating (or endearing) details. Just because I raise my daughters in large
part because of the way my mother raised me, I don't want her raising
them—and God forbid I should ever have to rely on my mother-in-
law. I'm certain we would all be at each other's throats in a matter of
days, and divorce would ensue before long. I thank my lucky stars
that I've never been in a situation where either my own or my husband's mother has been the only one I've been able to afford or rely on
for child care. I love them both profoundly, have the greatest of respect for their values, and most definitely want them to be close to my
children—but please, let's stick to weekends and vacations. I'm sure
they would both agree.

Blerina is Albanian and works full-time as a receptionist in a dentist's office. She has two small children age two and five, and one of
the first things she did when her green card came through three years
ago was to sponsor and bring over her mother, who now lives with the
young family. Their bond is obviously a very strong one, as is the respect Blerina has for her aging parent and everything she's had to endure in her past life in a, "miserable, poor, and corrupt Communist
country."

Blerina tries to be diplomatic when I ask her about how her relationship to her mother has changed, in this new country, with all these
new responsibilities and a whole other generation to contend with.

I mean, she is my mother, what else can I tell you? She made me who I am today. I cannot disrespect that. But this is a new life, a new place, different rules. It's difficult for her to change. I cannot tell her when I disagree with her! It's like I would tell her that her life is worthless, that her experience doesn't count! She wants to feel useful, too, so sometimes she does much more than I ask her to, like cleaning in the house and cooking the dinner—really, it's too much, but I cannot say that because it would be like an insult.

And with the children, I can see they are still small, so for now it's okay, but already she treats my daughter so differently from my son—he has to be the little man, he has to be strong, he cannot cry. That is something I really do not want for the children, so sometimes I tell him, behind her back, your grandma is old woman, it's okay for you to cry with me. It's difficult.

There are many things I cannot tell her, not like in a direct way. It always has to be "around the corner," you know what I mean? I say, people in America do things different. I say "the teacher at school told me to do that" or "I see it on the news." I love my mother. I'm glad I can do this for her. But it's not so easy to make it work. Sometimes my husband, he get so angry with her he has to leave the house, and then he gets angry with me because I don't tell her how to do it. But I can't. Could you?

While Blerina's children are obviously well looked after and much loved, research actually shows that family day care or relative care rates more poorly than almost any other type of child care in this country. A study conducted by the Families and Work Institute in the midnineties effectively disproved the notion that children in the care of relatives receive better and more consistent nurturing than those in institutional child-care centers. Three fifths of the relatives included in the survey admitted that they were "only helping out the mothers," i.e., that they would most probably rather be doing other things, and almost two thirds of participants lived in poverty and "stressed, socially isolated" conditions. Adding to the surprise, the study revealed that children were actually more likely to be securely attached to a nonrelative caregiver, confirming the theory that for many mothers leaving their children with an aunt, grandmother, or similar relation amounts to nothing less than a worst-case scenario that they simply didn't have the means to change, and in which everyone felt trapped. In fact, more than 25 percent of the mothers included in the survey said they would use other care, if only they were able to find it, because they were so unhappy with their situations.

Meet Sinead. Now in her fifties, Sinead has, probably almost literally, been and seen it all since she first arrived in the United States from Ireland in 1962 at the age of twenty. She certainly didn't make her way here with ambitions to become a nanny, but was "simply trying to get away from Ireland. And let's face it, the work one could get at that time was mostly in domestic situations." Using "domestic" as a noun may seem quaint to us now, but the kind of work Sinead was offered in the first year or two was anything but.

> I was always working with families, in people's houses, babysitting and such. One job I had was at this country club; that was seasonal work looking after the children when the mothers came to play tennis. And then I went with the Employment Agency, they had lots of Irish on their books. None of the agencies would do that now, keep people on their books who're not legal, but in those days it wasn't much of a problem. You could still get a work permit as long as you had a sponsor.
>
> So there I was, sitting at the agency, just waiting for my turn to be interviewed, and this woman comes in, just comes over to talk to me. So she says, "I'm looking for someone to look after my children, you have a nice face, how would you like to come work for me?"

Sixteen years later Sinead finally left that job to start a family of her own with her American husband, probably at just about the time that the youngest and last of her charges was learning to drive.

Her salary, in those days, was eighty dollars per week, with Thursdays and every other Sunday off. They lived on Long Island. There were six children in all, two from the wife's first marriage, two from the husband's, and lastly, just for good measure, one set of twins, a boy and a girl, for the two of them. "I used to think of them as yours, mine, and ours," said Sinead.

I didn't cook or clean much, they had other people to do that, but I did everything for the children. They let me have full charge, all the time, took them all to the doctors, went to school meetings, organized their homework, drove them all over the state and back again. One time one of the girls got caught shoplifting, and the police officer at the station called me, not the mother; he knew I was the one to talk to. But I did tell the parents about that. The mother, she was a country club lady. She'd go shopping, play tennis, you know, your typical lady of leisure. But she never questioned me. She really wasn't that involved. We used to have a martini together every day at four. I did everything, Lord those were long days. Mothers nowadays are so much more involved. And nannies these days, they don't want the responsibility. Who can blame them? One of the girls, she herself has twins now, and one nanny for each of them!

So there I was, stuck out in the boonies with these six children, working myself ragged—it was hard to have a life. I used to drink a lot. I met my husband in a bar, actually, married him while I was still working for them. There was no sense of separation, really, you could say it was just a different era. People now, they don't want to jeopardize their privacy—that wasn't an issue when I was coming down the pike. They were too busy partying; they fought and screamed and yelled right in front of me, they didn't really care. I did threaten to quit a couple of times, just because I was tired. The only time the father yelled at me, when I was stuck out driving the kids somewhere and the parents were late going to some party, I just told him: "Go ahead, fire me." He never said anything again.

Sinead is completely believable and quite emphatic when she tells me:

> Much of the time I'd say I was closer to those children than their mother. They came to me for everything. I know they'd open up to me about things that they wouldn't discuss with their parents. Jealousy from the mother? Oh no, no, that was never an issue. I honestly don't think she cared.
>
> She loved them, don't get me wrong, they just weren't that close, and then a couple of them weren't even hers. When they were a bit older, we'd all go out drinking together, we played pool, and the parents never knew! We never told. Even after I left there, when the kids came home from school for the holidays, it was me they'd come to, to talk about things.

A bit of underage drinking at the local bar, however, clearly paled in comparison to what she told me next: "One time one of the girls got pregnant, and I took her to have an abortion. The mother still doesn't know." For once my own mother's heart sank, and I was left speechless while Sinead carried on with her story: "The girl was underage, and didn't want her mother to find out. It was all quite discreet, maybe a bit shady, but having money helped. The girl didn't seem to be any the worse for wear, got married, has a child of her own now, so it all worked out for the best."

Writing this on the day that South Dakota has officially outlawed all abortions except when the health of the mother is at risk, and one day after an article published in *The New York Times* pointed out that the requirement of parental consent has had no significant impact on the rate of abortions, I have no idea what "for the best" could possibly mean. I do know, however, that times have certainly changed. So, it turns out, has Sinead, as her story is far from finished.

Unlike her employers, Sinead stopped at two children, both daughters. She made sure that whatever jobs she had while they were small allowed her to stick close. "I did whatever I could to be working in their system. For a time I was a teacher's aide, so one way or another they were always with me. I'd work in the cafeteria, the supply office, you name it." Sinead's two daughters, Kathleen and Kara, got a decent education, and one of them joined the army right out of high school. The other didn't do so well.

She started running around with this fellow, Phillip, head over heels, barely eighteen. He was bad news, nothing but trouble. So of course she goes and gets herself pregnant, and when she tells him about the baby, first thing out of his mouth is, "Where can you get an abortion?" Actually made her get in the car and drive to a couple places he'd found in the yellow pages, seedy back alleys, neon lights, the whole nine yards. They didn't manage to do it that night, so she comes crying home to me. I must admit, I found the whole thing terribly hurtful. So I told her, this isn't the way to do this, stop and think about what you're doing. She ended up not having the abortion, though of course Philip took off like a shot; he's pretty much out of the picture.

So now we've got Patrick, he's eighteen months. Stays with me two days a week, got a sitter the other two while Kara's working at a nutritionist's office. It's hard for me, lifting him, running after him. I'm older now, don't have the energy I used to. For a while Kara was working as a nanny, had a job where she could bring Patrick along, but that didn't work out. I don't know what she's going to do. It isn't an easy life being a single mother, and I can't have her living with us forever. I don't like being stuck home like this, I need to find another job. If you know anyone who's hiring, I've got great references.

While Sinead clearly doesn't consider herself American, her children, her husband, and her life are all by now so completely rooted in this country that the Ireland that was once "home" refers more to a long-ago time in her life than an actual place. She doesn't think much of "foreign nannies," telling me quite forcefully that she feels it's simply "not fair. They should just do the right thing. If this country is good enough to work in then they should be good enough to follow the rules." At this point I bid Sinead good-bye, but am barely able to resist a crack about some rules being made to be broken. Given the whole life span of Sinead's experiences, and her interpretation of right and wrong along the way, this old cliché wouldn't even being to cover it

Ava, from the Philipines, is one of these illegal, foreign nannies who feel they have no choice but to break rules in order to do the right thing. She came to the United States via Singapore with her employer of five years and their two young sons, one of whom she had looked after from birth. On her last trip home to visit her family in the Philippines, and just before leaving for the United States, Ava decided on the spur of the moment to "adopt a baby from a woman who couldn't afford to keep her. If I didn't take the baby, I know she would have sold her." Amy Katherine wound up costing approximately two hundred dollars—make that five hundred dollars in total, for all the paperwork and lawyer's fees for Ava to officially adopt the little girl. When Ava talks about the whole process the words she actually uses are, "I bought her."

Ava is in her midthirties, and probably works harder than anyone I have ever met, holding down what seems like two and a half full-time jobs as housekeeper and nanny. She manages to find time to talk to me only because I've agreed to drive her from one of her jobs to the next, and we chat in the car. Ava had always wanted a child, though her chances of getting married as a domestic helper in Singapore were practically zero, and going back to the Philippines wasn't an option, because "back there, I'm nothing." She now proudly describes herself as a single mother and makes me pull over to show me the photo in her wallet, a mountain of pink ruffles with a tiny brown-eyed girl floating in the middle. Her daughter, whom she has been with literally for less than one week in her short life, is being raised back in the Philippines by Ava's mother and a nanny whom Ava hired before she left for the United States. I found Ava through her former employer, with whom she soon parted ways after their arrival from Singapore, principally because Ava discovered that she could make approximately three times her previous salary by basically working nonstop, except, occasionally, to go to church on Sundays. Her former employer told me she had tried to steer Ava away from the adoption, but to no avail: "I knew this was just a ploy from her mother to get more money out of her. Ava probably knew it, too, but she still went ahead—and now of course her mom and the rest of her family are milking her for all she's got, and she keeps sending them money. She can't help it, they're her family. That's what her mom did when she was young; she was a maid in Singapore, too, and she'd see her children once every two years for three weeks."

Ava has a slightly less cynical view of her situation. "All those years my mother works so hard, she deserve a rest. Now I pay her an allowance, the same as what she used to make in Singapore. She is a good mother for my baby, they are good for each other. In the Philippines a hundred dollars is a lot, it's not like here. Life is really, really hard, but what can we do? I just try not to think about it." At this point Ava starts crying, while somehow, miraculously, maintaining her megawatt smile.

"My daughter is my inspiration now. I want to pay for her education, pay for her house, I can do that—I can give her a better life. Maybe one day I can save enough money for us all to be together, my mother, me, my daughter. I am on my own, nobody ever give me anything for free, but I can do this for my family. I pray to God to keep me healthy, so I can keep working." Ava may indeed be nothing but a cash cow for her family back home, but by taking on the burden of financing her mother's retirement and saving a stranger's baby from the child brothels of Manila, she is also a humbling example of how much good can come from breaking the rules while keeping her faith. "Every month now I send home eight hundred dollars. I build a house, two bedrooms, it's perfect for my mother and my daughter. It took me ten years to pay for it, but now it's mine." Isn't it amazing what a dollar can buy!

George Bush's neocons, and any number of righteous voices in the public arena, might have us all believe that the values of good over bad and "liberal" versus God-fearing and patriotic are immutable and absolute. Throw any brand-new and innocent baby into the mix, however, and it will become immediately and painfully clear that they are not. I suspect even ultra conservatives like Ann Coulter or Pat Buchanan, who seem to think they've bypassed even Christ in their certainty as to what's right and wrong, would see their moral compass falter ever so slightly for a moment if they chose to listen to Ava's story from beginning to end. Values, it turns out, are relative, too, depending on who expresses them and whether they can afford to live by them and teach them to their children. I'd certainly rather have my children learn kindness, compassion, and industry from illegal Ava than from any number of politicians who profess themselves to be experts on the subject.

intimacy

*i*N NO AREA of her life is a woman as emotionally exposed and vulnerable as in her love for her children. To be their part-time caretaker while the mother is away means not simply knowing them but also becoming intimately familiar with the genetic, emotional, material, and familial landscape in which they are rooted. In other words, the caregiver is deeply immersed in the family, and that vast gray territory of privacy and intimacy between mother and nanny is a place where it is often impossible to draw the lines that mark the end of one place and the beginning of another. At what point does close become suffocating? Where does friendship end and exploitation begin? How much is any one person entitled to know about another, and when does that knowledge become a burden rather than a helpful tool?

One of the ways through which I have found nannies who were willing to tell me their stories has been via deliberately anonymous classified ads. I offer them a chance to "tell their side of the story" for a book project, and promise to keep their identity confidential. Some of these stories have been so hair-raising and bizarre that lately, whenever I am introduced to another mother with a nanny story to tell, I can't help but wonder—is *she* the one who . . . ?

My insistence on anonymity actually serves my purposes just as well as those of the women who have felt compelled to share their stories with me. As long as we're talking about Jane Doe from Anywheresville it's okay to listen to a stranger divulge someone else's most intimate secrets. Unfortunately, as soon as she has a name and a face, finding out that she occasionally smacks her kids or makes her babysitter pay for the yogurt she eats from her fridge, is much more than I feel comfortable knowing. Occasionally the line between feeling like a voyeur and doing legitimate research is very, very fine, and there is probably no other area in the mother/nanny relationship dialogues where it behooves me more to constantly remember: There but for the grace of God, go I. And you, and you, and you.

There is, of course, a measure of the voyeur in all of us. How else to explain the huge success of gossip rag after gossip rag, each one promising to reveal juicier and more intimate secrets than the next? I, for one, would give my eyeteeth to be a fly on the wall in Madonna's or Britney Spear's or Angelina Jolie's nursery, ready to whip out my notebook as soon as the nanny came into the room (and let's face it, of course they all have nannies) to record all nuances of their conversation. I could, of course, justify this slightly obscene curiosity by way of my professional interests—these women are celebrities, after all, and therefore, many would argue, fair game for all kinds of snooping.

I also believe, however, that there is both nothing more private or ultimately more revealing of a woman's true personality than the way in which she interacts with her children. It's every mother's soft spot, the place where she reveals herself in her truest colors, and where all her hopes and dreams and frustrations and fears come together in a tangle of exposed nerves. No wonder we are so protective of our children and their privacy, because by protecting them we also protect ourselves.

This is why, often even more so than our closest friends, relatives, or colleagues, the women whom we invite into our homes to take care of our children also gain virtually unlimited access to our minds, our hearts, and wallets, and, not infrequently, our bedrooms. They see us when we're stressed and on the verge of losing it (ever met a mother rushing home late after a crazy day at work who isn't stressed?), and when we melt in a pathetic puddle over something to do with the children. They overhear fights and private conversations; feel tension floating in the atmosphere; come across incriminating evidence for all sorts of unsavory behavior, ranging from drugs to adultery; and even sometimes look at our crumpled sheets in the morning and wonder— are they even having sex, or what? What is more, contrary to what we might like to believe, this information generally does not stay within our own four walls. I have, by now, hung out on enough playground benches to realize there really is no such thing as a secret, and that talking among themselves about each other's employers is one of the few free forms of entertainment our nannies can, and do, indulge in.

In some nanny circles I have observed there is even a degree of one-upmanship, where whoever has the tastiest little tidbit to share gets to be queen for the day. At the risk of stating the obvious, if the playground is the child-care worker's office, then their banter resembles nothing so much as a bunch of Monday morning quarterbacks congregating around the watercooler to rehash the play-by-plays of their respective teams. One particularly gregarious nanny, gently rocking a tiny blond baby girl tucked into what seemed like an armor-plated tank of a stroller, let me share in the fun once I explained what I was doing. She didn't want to give me her real name (not that I would have used it anyway), but asked me to "just call me Jane Jones, why don't you?"

Jane Jones loved babies. She loved newborns and infants especially, even though that meant having to put up with a lot of overprotective first-time mothers over the years. And this little girl's mom, let's call the baby Isabelle, oh my Lord, nutty as a fruitcake! Some of the airy-fairy stuff she made Jane Jones do, oh my Lord, you wouldn't believe. So Isabelle's mom, let's call her Diana, is thirty-one, the father's fifty-eight. Well, yeah, you know, one of *those!* His third marriage, her first, he already has three grown children just a couple of years younger than Diana.

Isabelle's dad used to be Diana's dad's best buddy, and he just went crazy when he found out they were having an affair. They didn't talk for months, but then he came to the wedding, and now they're friends again. In fact, nowadays Dad and Granddad (seeing as they're both practically retired) spend a lot of time hanging around at home watching Tiger play golf ("That Tiger is hot!"), while Diana is back at work in this big publishing company where she runs a magazine or something.

It seemed there was nothing Jane Jones didn't know about Diana, Diana's feelings, her insecurities, her crazy ideas about child rearing, and last but not least of all, all the ups and downs of her relationship with her husband, who is apparently "pretty trim for his age." Oh my Lord! Thank God I'm not Diana.

When I asked Jane Jones how she thought Diana might feel if she knew that her private life and innermost thoughts were being dissected right here on this park bench by her nanny and a complete stranger (I didn't actually put it quite like that), she was not overly concerned.

She doesn't know you from Adam, does she? It's just a bit of fun. Besides, she tells me a lot of stuff, and what I don't hear, it's clear from the way she's acting, you know, the tone in her voice, that kind of thing. I'm real good at reading people, and Diana, she's a lovely lady, real sweet, just this whole health-food stuff, organic everything, that gets on my nerves. It's just not practical. And it tastes bad! Her husband, he makes me bring him back doughnuts sometimes, those Krispy Kreme ones, because she won't let him have them.

Him and me, we've got a little thing going, if you know what I mean. I get him his doughnuts, and he doesn't tell if I let the baby go to sleep with the bottle in her mouth, I scratch your back, you scratch mine, know what I mean? I know she wants to have another baby, but the husband figures he let her have this one, so that's enough. He better be wearing those rubbers, man, because Diana, she's brooding up a storm.

As much as some caretakers don't just happen to overhear but actively relish the extraction of every scrap of gossip about their employers, others find themselves witness to things they would much rather not know. At times being the insider can be a heavy and uncomfortable burden. As one middle-aged nanny from the West Indies told me, "In my last family before this one, I knew he was cheating on her, he knew that I knew, but I guess he also kind of realized there was no way I'd ever let on, because I'd be losing my job. Or maybe he just didn't care. Anyway, if she'd have found out, she was the kind of person who'd have taken those children and left him. And I liked her, she was a good mother, she worked so hard, wasn't my place to be telling her that. It's not right, but sometimes you just have to pretend you're as dumb as a dog. They did get divorced eventually, and it got ugly really fast. I guess she must have found out about the affair. She let me go pretty quickly after that, and then they moved, so now we've lost touch."

A nanny in another family found herself in a situation where there was a lot of tension.

The air was just thick with it. I'd hear things from the kids; the mother definitely knew that I knew what was going on, constant fighting and yelling. It was pretty uncomfortable. And then her friends, they would ask me all these questions, like, "What's going on? Is she okay? How's so-and-so doing?" I always said I had no idea. You really can't exploit that position you're in, I mean, it wouldn't be fair to the kids, either.

But I definitely got to know way more about some people than even their closest friends. Like this one little boy, he would refuse to pee unless he was standing in the shower with the water running. Weird, right? So at first I'd have to do that with him, too—I bet you no one else ever knew about that.

In another family I worked for, there were two kids, an older girl and an adopted little girl. The little one used to have these violent tantrums, and the mother would just freeze, she was totally helpless. Couldn't deal with it. So in the end I used to have to step in, and she would leave. It was this strange combination where I could tell that on the one hand she was really embarrassed about her daughter and her problems and how much I knew about them, but then she wanted me to be the one to talk to the therapist because she was scared about what she might hear.

Since nannies are frequently, almost by definition, privy to some of the most painful, difficult, and personal issues a family has to deal with, they can easily find themselves on an ever more slippery slope, where good intentions to draw the line are impossible to realize. For some families dealing with crises, whether chronic or sudden and catastrophic, nannies become not only temporary guardians of the children, but also occasionally messengers of unpleasant truths, go-betweens for feuding parents and relatives, or substitutes for other relationships that may be lacking in the mother's life.

Nanny Chandra told me about one of her jobs, looking after a set of twin boys with severe learning disabilities, where she "got to be really close to the mother's mother, too." They would routinely

talk and agree about a lot of things. She was much more sensible than the mother, I think, and we used to sort of plot together how to get the mom to do something that would be better for the kids. In general, though, I try to be very conscious of these invisible boundaries in the families I work for, keep my personal views out of the parents' relationship.

It's not always easy. Especially because sometimes you become the person they want to vent to, like they want to believe you're their friend. You've got to be really careful with that. I mean, it's great to be friend*ly* with the mother if you're working for her, obviously, but if they start thinking you're their friend, I personally think that's too much. It's too close.

And I guess one thing I learned after being a teacher's aide: no physical contact with the fathers, ever. That could get creepy really quickly. Physical contact in general is a big gray area actually, even with children. Or maybe especially with children— kissing, hugging, sitting on laps, giving baths, I mean—you name it. There's a potentially sinister interpretation of everything. Better to avoid that altogether, if you can.

While Chandra was able to more or less control how deeply she would let herself be drawn into another family's drama, and actively tried to close her ears to things she really did not want to know, many others find themselves unable to resist the push-pull of their employers' lives. More than one talked to me about getting "caught in the middle" as the parents of their charges were divorcing, and another told me how, during a particularly bitter custody fight, both parents tried to use her testimony in court to their advantage. It got to the point where she was afraid to say anything to anyone for fear of giving the "wrong" evidence, while both parents were begging her to stay so as to not upset the children.

It was so stressful, I actually got sick. I had to go back and forth between their two houses, and I met with their therapists and lawyers and everything, it was just awful. Then they subpoenaed me when they couldn't agree. I mean, this mother worked really hard, she was gone all the time, definitely from seven in the morning to at least six-thirty every night. But I guess during this custody fight she must have claimed that her hours were far less, more like eight to five-thirty. When the lawyers asked me about that, what was I supposed to say? I couldn't lie.

When I went back to her after that, she acted like I'd totally betrayed her. But the truth was that the dad really was the one who got much more involved in the kids' lives. A few months before all this started, the mom actually called me one day from work, something about the kids, and then she broke into tears and told me all this stuff about how much of a jerk her husband was being, and that she didn't know what to do. I mean, this was my boss! It was awful, I had no idea what to say.

And I knew, of course, when they started sleeping in separate rooms, like six months after I started. It's impossible not to notice that kind of thing when you're living in. I finally had to leave, two and a half years later, really just for my own well-being. They offered me everything to stay—money, a car, my own apartment. I just couldn't do it. I got another call from his lawyers just a couple of weeks ago. I guess they're still fighting.

Without a doubt, across the board, one of the biggest compliments mothers I interviewed felt they could pay their nannies was to describe her as "a member of the family." This, of course, begs the question: What exactly does family mean? Clearly, other than with one's children, parents, or siblings it does not necessarily mean unconditional love. With our child-care providers it seems to be above all a realization that a person is so deeply embedded in the fabric of our lives, and has come to be such a trusted, dependable, and well-worn fixture, that without her the picture of our family would no longer be whole. By the same token, these "family" members are also fair game for much more criticism, bitching, and venting than other people such as housecleaners, handymen, or accountants, who are merely providing us with a service and getting paid for it.

Pamela has had the same caretaker, Carmela, for about eight years. Now that Pamela's children are twelve and ten and at school all day, Carmela's responsibilities have changed a great deal from the baby and toddler years, but her position in the family is as secure as ever. Said Pamela,

> There are days when I absolutely cannot stand the sight of her, but there is absolutely no way I would ever fire her. Nor would she ever leave us. We've been through too much together. And at this point, in a way, I think I know her better than she knows herself—I can recognize the pout thing she does with her mouth that means there's a big snit coming on, or the dirty looks and exaggerated sighs that means something I've asked her to do is really just too much, or that fake smile she puts on when she wants to borrow money.
>
> It's totally infuriating, but I know I'm going to put up with it for the next God knows how many years, because warts and moods and snits and all, she's part of my family. Her mother used to be mine and my sisters' nanny when I was growing up, and at this point there is nothing, literally nothing, we don't know about each other's lives.

While a description of their caretaker as "being part of our family" was frequently offered up by the mothers, interestingly enough it was almost never returned by the women who worked for them—with Carmela, begrudgingly rolling her eyes, confessing to being one of the few exceptions. This seemed to be less because the caretakers did not also feel extremely close to and loved by the children they looked after, but above all because they had families of their own, complete with sons and daughters, skeletons in the cupboard, and irritating relatives.

Bebe is from French Guyana, and has been a nanny in the United States for twelve years. Her take on the whole family thing is a great deal more cynical than one might expect, given how deeply attached she obviously is to the ten-month-old girl in her care.

> I love this child. I wouldn't love her any better if she is mine. But family? Give me a break! Look at this skin! Look at her! Look around you! Over there [she points to the other side of the playground] is the mommies. You think they come here, talk to me, have play dates together? No, no, no, that is not the way we do things. They look at me now talking to you, they wonder who you are. They wonder, why's she talking to the white woman?
>
> My lady, she is very kind. At home she tell me many things, talk about the children, her family, the husband, her work. She treats me good. I have no complaint. But out here we are *separate*. I work for her, I am not her friend. She can have her family, and I have mine, that is not the same. I am very proud woman.
>
> To me, is not a compliment if someone says I am like part of the family. It is like they say my family doesn't matter. It is like the white women say that to feel less guilty or something. Like that makes it okay, some of the other things they do, like if they say you are part of family, is not so bad that actually you are the servant. I don't want to be so close to the mother, I don't want to know about their problems, I don't want to hear it. I got problems of my own; you think she wants to hear them? I don't talk about private things with anyone. Not my business, not hers. That is the way I work.

Mianne is an editor who works from home, as does her novelist husband. They have two small daughters, one four, the other almost two, and the family has had the same nanny since before the older girl was born. Mianne, too, describes their nanny, Suri, as being "part of the family," but agrees that the reason she thinks of Suri in those terms is above all for the sake of providing continuity and stability for the children.

> They absolutely adore her. One of my greatest fears is that she will leave. The children have no grandparents around here, so Suri is like a substitute for that, she's very close to them. She's older, with grown-up children. She's been in the United States for a long time now, but her English is really pretty bad. In many ways her lack of English is a positive thing for our privacy—there are lots of things, taken out of context, that I'm sure she simply doesn't understand. Suri is very discreet—at least, I think she is. But then again, we really don't know, do we? It's what we like to believe.
>
> I certainly know there's a whole nanny subculture, where exaggeration is rife—start with one story in the morning, and hear something entirely different by the time it gets back to you in the afternoon; I've seen that happen just in our little neighborhood. I know that sometimes she will tell me terrible things about other nannies and other families, just to sort of gauge my reaction. What she really wants to know is, "What about me, am I doing okay?" I actually think that she would like to be closer to us, to somehow be even more indispensable, more part of the family. To a large extent it's a power issue—I'm here a lot, and I'm always the one to take the children to the doctor and things like that. I think she feels it's almost a snub when I turn down her offers to come along.

Among many working from home mothers like Mianne, privacy issues come up not with only their own child-care provider but also with those of other families. Here's a dilemma:

I have a friend, not a close friend, but still, someone I know. She's pregnant with twins. Suri has told me that my friend's nanny is planning on leaving, but I'm pretty sure my friend isn't even aware of this. Of course I could tell her, but if you think about it, I'd be breaking everyone's confidence. I really don't think it's up to me to get between them.

And then there's this other situation: There is a nanny in the neighborhood who I really think doesn't pay enough attention to the children, I mean, to the point that it's sometimes dangerous. I don't really know the mother, I just see her around sometimes, in passing. I really wouldn't feel comfortable saying anything directly to the nanny, because that's definitely crossing a line. But I also don't want to talk directly to the mother, because I don't want to get this reputation among the nannies in my neighborhood that I'm someone who'll rat on them.

If I did say something it would have to be anonymous, because ultimately, you can never know how much people actually *want* to know, and how much they might resent you for butting in. I've had really nice feedback from other mothers about Suri, so that's been great, but I don't actively seek it out. I just think that after four years with her, if something were wrong, I would know.

Another way for Mianne to solve her dilemma would be to anonymously post what she knows on a relatively new blog: Isawyournanny .blogspot.com. Created to "share nanny sightings or stories," this stuff makes for compulsive reading. I defy any mother who employs a nanny to scroll through the postings beginning to end and not wind up looking at her own nanny through lenses newly colored by paranoia, doubt, and fear. Some stories are positive, to be sure, but the vast majority are a catalog of all the behaviors we dread, and probably have, at one point, specifically instructed our nanny or caretaker not to engage in: feeding babies sugar-laced junk food; gabbing on the phone while a four-year-old charge swings upside down from monkey bars meant for ten-year-olds; not interfering when one child repeatedly hits another; sending a five-year-old to the toilet unaccompanied during a movie; talking to her friends about how much she hates her employers and the children. Dig deep in your imagination for a hideous scenario, and sooner or later you will find it here. Other than the fact that I've felt slightly sick every time I've gone to check out the latest postings (research!), probably the most striking fact about Isawyournanny is that this is clearly a blog created by women for women about other women. Mostly written in a conspiratorial mom-to-mom tone, the majority of well-meaning tattletales here don't even acknowledge the possibility that fathers are just as entitled to know how the nanny is treating their kid: Each anonymous posting is attrib uted to Jane Doe.

Mianne is clearly not by nature a paranoid person, and luckily thus far Suri has not given her any reason to consider such a gross invasion of privacy as a hidden nannycam or a voice-activated tape recorder. Other parents, however, are once burned and forever wary. Soledad O'Brien, news anchor at CNN and mother of four, has spoken openly about the horror of discovering that one of her nannies had hit her child, and that ever since then she and her husband rely on nannycams installed all over their house, ethics be damned. Other mothers tell me of setting up an informal spy network in their neighborhoods, actively asking storekeepers, doormen, teachers, and the staff at libraries or other places where their children hang out to report back to them. Anita, a lawyer in D.C., explains it like this:

> If she's in my home, alone with my children, it isn't a question of invading anyone's privacy. Really, I don't care about that. I do what I can—I mean, doesn't everyone? We used to have these little voice-activated tape recorders hidden all over the house. Nothing ever happened; it was perfectly fine.

But it did help me realize that our first nanny had a significant hearing problem, to the point where she was actually tech-
nically deaf. The one after that, it turned out, had this secret
mental illness. She actually wanted to come right back to work
after suffering a breakdown one weekend; just pop a few pills
and thought she'd be all better! Aaah, no thank you. The third
one was fine. I used to hear her singing to the baby and chattering away in Brazilian, but mostly she was a "go to the mall and
hang out" type of nanny; she just wasn't that good. The one we
have now we've had for five years. Far too long, if you ask me.
I've had my neighbors spy on her. I ask other people, I ask the
children, really. I'm ruthless. If there is something she does, or
says, or a place she goes or people she hangs out with while I'm
paying her to be with my kids, I feel absolutely entitled to know.
If she has a problem with that, I really couldn't care less what
she thinks. Of course, I also know that what really matters most
is that the children love her and she loves them, bottom line, so
I guess there are a whole lot of things I'm prepared to tolerate.
That does not, however, take away my right to know.

I'll tell you one thing, though, and I know I'm not the only
one who does this: I hide my purchases from her. I actually hide
the things I buy—how ridiculous is that? I don't particularly like
her, I don't much like her personality, and I'd never consider her
my friend. But I still don't want her to judge me, probably because I do completely trust her with my children. I know there's
probably something wrong with that picture, but as ridiculous as
it sounds I'll continue to put up with her, because they love her.

The notion of "the right to know" is always a tricky one, especially
when it comes to personal information that in theory, and probably in
any other profession but nannying, has absolutely no bearing on a person's ability to perform a particular job. You can be a brilliant accountant

or fantastically competent librarian despite having once been under the care of a psychologist and taken antidepressants. But looking after a colicky newborn or a five-year-old with ADHD, mixing formula with one hand while popping Prozac with the other, is probably not such a good idea. No one would question a woman's ability to be an architect, lawyer, high-school history teacher, or cook if she's five-foot-four, wears glasses, weighs upward of two hundred pounds, and suffers from asthma. But give her 8:00 A.M. to 6:00 P.M. sole charge of two-year-old twin boys whose stroller she can barely push to the playground, much less run around after them once they get there? Knowing those things about her, no mother I know would hire this nanny. Does that qualify as discrimination, or simply common sense?

And what about sexual orientation? Or, for that matter, the last time a nanny has had sex; the number of intimate adult relationships she has been in; the color of her hair (natural or dyed?); the reason she left her last position; her medical history; the type of birth control she uses; her credit rating; and whether or not she plans on having a family of her own or becoming pregnant in the near future? All of these are actual questions that various nanny-placement agencies all over this country have felt entitled to ask the women they are trying to match with families in their initial questionnaires. Not surprisingly, many of them balk at the level of detail they are expected to provide, and agonize over whether or not they should tell the truth. Choosing to provide incomplete information, or to refuse an answer on principle, is likely to raise all sorts of red flags, and women looking for nanny positions are well aware of this.

Needless to say, nannies also rarely get a chance to form a complete impression of their employers based on the same kind of information— unless they are particularly ballsy and willing to make a bad impression during an interview. As an avid lurker and sometime participant in a number of Internet chat rooms, and on bulletin boards frequented by nannies (a particularly good one is nannynetwork.com), I know that "what to tell" and "how to bring it up" are issues every experienced nanny has come up against. What they also talk about, time and time again, are the things they wished they'd known, questions they would have liked to be able to ask *before* agreeing to move into someone's house and being at their and their children's beck and call, night and day and often on weekends. Not surprisingly, the wish list included an employer's mental health history and credit ratings, as well as references from other household employees and previous nannies.

Other issues that some nannies wondered about their employers, past or present, were: What drugs had they taken or took regularly? Did they pay on time and in full? Had they ever cheated on each other? Could they keep a promise? Did they believe in God? Who did they vote for in the last presidential election? Were they in steady jobs and working for stable companies? Did they keep on top of their bills? What kind of a relationship did they have with their families? If there was a family dinner, would the parents do the dishes or just throw everything in the sink and wait for the nanny to start washing up?

This level of curiosity by an employee about the person he or she works for, and vice versa, is obviously by no means limited to child care. However, the fact that there are children involved not only makes the nanny/parent interviews infinitely more poignant, but also means that invasive questions become not only acceptable but indispensable. How else to make your mind up and choose the person to replace—you?

Legally, of course, the guidelines are very clear. While the rules vary somewhat from state to state, on the big issues they are totally consistent: Everyone is free to run a police check on their nanny; get a history of driving violations; and look up whether the social security number provided is legitimate. However, her medical and credit history, marital status, sexual orientation, and religious affiliation are off-limits, unless she gives her specific consent to disclose them to an employer. In reality, of course, those are the very issues that are always going to be at the heart of any conversation between parent employers and a potential nanny.

In the countless mother/nanny relationships that are conducted off the books and under the Citizenship and Immigration Service radar, these negotiations become an issue of faith, good (or bad) instincts, and improvisation. For the other half (or less) of nannies who pay taxes and are in this country legally, the tricky negotiation of the privacy terrain frequently falls to agencies. An owner of a small nanny-placement agency with almost twenty years of experience told me:

> This is such an emotional relationship. You try to take the emotion out of it, but you really can't. Really, what a good agency does is not very different from matchmaking—it's all about the individuals and how well they "click." We try to make it more scientific, if you will, to take the variables out by listing only the facts about someone's background, like their experience, their education, their professional affiliations, all those things. But unless there is a connection between people, none of that is really going to matter. In addition to running the background checks and checking references, what people pay me for is really my judgment, and that is always going to be based on how much I feel I know about someone.
>
> We don't ask our nanny candidates any more than we're permitted to by law, at least on the initial written application. But I would never send a nanny out to interview with a family without having interviewed her myself first, and yes—I do ask questions that will make some people uncomfortable. I've got to. And if they're uncomfortable with my asking, that in and of itself can tell me something about her. It's about character, isn't it? It's about making sure the children in her care are safe, and get

reinforcement of the kind of values the parents believe in. Of course, experienced nannies are used to this, and often they'll volunteer all sorts of information right off the bat—whether they're in a relationship, what their health is like, if they belong to a church, things like that.

Then again, some things are a lot easier to volunteer than others, if you know what I mean. I know that some of my clients could absolutely not tolerate a gay nanny, and to be honest, if I felt a nanny had withheld that information from me, I don't think I'd be able to keep her on our books. Not because I have anything against lesbians, but because, when it comes to who their children spend time with, people have a right to know.

Pat Cascio, who is president of the International Nanny Association (INA), and also the longtime proprietor of a well-regarded nanny agency in Texas, says:

What's legal is cut and dried; it's the same as in any other profession. But with the questions that people ask their nannies, what they really want is a peek into their private lives. Would you want someone who's been a drug user or has had a drinking problem looking after your children? We tell all our candidates that they should approach this work by pretending that they have a camera on them at all times. If they're not comfortable with that, then maybe they're not in the right job.

One of my nannies was shocked when the mother at her interview asked her how often she shampooed her hair. Yes, that might seem like a ridiculous question, but what is it really about? What she really wanted to know, is this someone who's clean, someone who has good personal hygiene. When you're dealing with someone's children, that's not an unreasonable thing to want to know. . . . This is unlike any other job—a defenseless child is entrusted to the care of someone brand new, and the parents want to feel confident that it is a really good person! Not a former drug addict or someone that hasn't lived an exemplary lifestyle.

As for nannycams, Ms. Cascio does not personally condone their use, but also stressed to me that

> it is a parent's right to use nannycams. It is considered illegal to record audio, though. It is the INA's and my best advice: If a parent wants to use nannycams they must respect the fact that the nanny doesn't want to be seen in an embarrassing situation— baby spits up, nanny takes off her top to launder it, and meanwhile the parents are looking at the film. The nanny was acting very silly with the child but is an otherwise shy person. . . . She would be mortified to know that the parents would be watching her dance and shake her head around later in the evening. Some very shy and sensitive people are nannies, but when they are one-on-one with a child they will let down their guard and get very playful.
>
> If a parent is going to use, or may want to use, nannycams, they really should discuss this with the nanny during the interview process. Some will be fine; others will find it intimidating and not want the job. It is the respectful thing to do. . . . It should be so parents can see how the child does during the day, not so they can catch their nanny doing the wrong thing.

Another issue in the nannycam debate that Ms. Cascio brought up is standards: Would we approve of everything we saw if we had to watch a tape of ourselves going through our day, doing all the things we do as parents? Who hasn't been guilty of putting on a video for the kids to catch a break, or trying to read a newspaper instead of watching our toddler's every step lest she should take off and dive headfirst down the stairs? Not only would constant surveillance set impossibly high standards for even the most perfect nanny (never mind imperfect mothers), but it might also unnecessarily criminalize the countless little boo-boos, testing of boundaries, and other confrontations that are part of a normal, healthy childhood.

Ms. Cascio's is clearly a voice of reason, and most parents would probably do well to follow her advice after taking other reasonable and sensible precautions. One strategy many mothers have mentioned is "dropping in unannounced," which almost no one who is concerned with privacy boundaries could possibly object to, particularly when the dropping-in is done at one's own residence. On the other hand, this approach will, occasionally but inevitably, yield the kind of information that just complicates a relationship rather than provide peace of mind. Here a cautionary tale from Gina, a journalist in New York City and the mother of a three-year-old boy:

> My new nanny was a student from Brazil, very pretty, excellent English, terrific references. I'd told her it was okay to take a shower in our place every now and again, and do her laundry in our machine, maybe once a week. She lived in student housing and told me their bathrooms and facilities were kind of disgusting. So about a month after she started I decided to drop in. This was at a time when my son often napped. I'd called but no one picked up, so I must admit I was a bit worried. Our apartment isn't that big, you basically walk right into the living room, dining room, everything room right off the elevator. I remember thinking about ringing the doorbell, but that did seem a bit weird, ringing my own doorbell when I had a key in the other hand. Well, guess what greeted me on my kitchen table? A shiny pink plastic diaphragm . . . sort of perched on top of this screaming pink lace confection underwear thing in a little heap, right

where I'd been sitting a couple of hours earlier having breakfast. I mean, totally gross. Next thing I know, she walks right in, totally stark naked and dripping from the shower, sees me, and screams, and runs right back into the bathroom.

Not, though, before I got a good full-frontal look at her: a ring in each nipple, one in the belly button, and a tattoo on her butt. I'm not sure who was more embarrassed, to tell you the truth. It was all right for her to be taking a shower of course, I didn't mind that; my son was asleep. But all the other stuff, I really did *not* need to know or see. Honestly, I am not a prude. Nudity doesn't bother me; I don't give a rat's ass about tattoos or where someone chooses to pierce themselves and for what reason. The thing is, though, sometimes you get in a compromising situation with someone and you just can't get past it. It becomes like this big white elephant in the room. I'm not sure if that was the exact reason, but she only lasted a couple of weeks after that—we just couldn't look each other in the eye anymore. It's too bad—she was a lovely girl.

While most parents take basic and sensible precautions before trusting their children alone with a stranger, others can easily cross into territory bordering on paranoia. A recent thread on a nanny bulletin board talked about an employer who had allowed her nanny and child to attend a local playgroup only after asking for the names of the other caretakers that were going to be there and running a criminal trace on each of them. Prior to that the parents had confessed to running a similar background and criminal check on the nanny's husband before allowing her and their baby to meet him at a local fast-food restaurant for lunch. Apparently these were both brand-new parents and first-time nanny employers, and one does wonder whether they will go to the same trouble before each play date for their third child and fifth nanny. While the parents might become more relaxed over the years, their ability to access personal data on the people around them, however, is guaranteed to grow ever easier—anyone with a bit of computer savvy and some basic information can easily build up an entire portfolio of facts about almost anyone they choose. Whether or not this knowledge makes for better relationships between employers and their nannies, and for happier children, or whether it is even relevant, is of course the sixty-four-million-dollar question.

It seems that for every mother out there who feels entitled to probe deeply into sensitive personal territory, there is another who would simply prefer not to know—at least, not everything. One of these is Caroline, a chiropractor and kinesiologist with two young children. Between her patients, her research, her community work, and her teaching, she has a busy and unpredictable schedule, although she religiously protects weekends as family time. Her husband is a self-employed technology consultant who often works from home, and they live in a city where housing is expensive, child care complicated, and illegal help abundantly available. Caroline thinks they've simply been unlucky with their nannies, six in all since their first child, now seven years old, was born.

> I know this probably sounds a bit unusual, but I found our first nanny literally in the street. My husband was carrying our daughter, and she just kind of approached us. I didn't really get any references, I couldn't, anyway; it was her first babysitting job. I just liked her. She was so loving with the baby. She wasn't very organized, though, and I found that she'd give me more information about herself than I really cared to know. For example, she was pretty irresponsible with her bills, and would always ask me to fix things for her. She had a four-year-old son at home in Mauritius, and I know she missed him terribly; she was often depressed about it. Actually, that was the reason she left. I guess she stayed for just over a year.

The next one was awful. We used to have this really antago-nistic relationship. I mean, it started out well but then it deteri-orated really quickly. My daughter hated her. She'd ask me, "How many more Fiona days?" I used to think it was just be-cause she didn't like my working. Fiona would stay out all the time, I think she used to take the children shopping a lot—I kept wondering why all the storekeepers in our neighborhood knew their names! After I finally fired her I went into this one store, and I discovered there was a picture of her up behind the counter, like "watch out for thief!" I can't believe she stayed with us for two years. I'm sure she must have been lying to me all the time. I did have a bad feeling about her for a while, but I should have trusted my instincts much earlier.

The successor to Fiona-the-thief was lovely but had an abusive and crazy ex-husband from whom she ultimately fled to another state. The nanny who followed her was "just odd," though Caroline couldn't put her finger on exactly why.

I did get references for her, but I still used to have this funny feeling that she hadn't really done any babysitting before. There were just so many things about her that didn't add up. Now that I think about it, I'm pretty sure there was something psychiatric going on, like maybe an abusive relationship, something. She'd forget play dates, I mean repeatedly, and ask me some really strange questions about very basic things. She was definitely holding things back. I never got to a real comfort level with her.

She ended up leaving from one day to the next, literally. Didn't give me any notice, wouldn't say good-bye to the kids, which was just cruel. She told me that she was going off to look after a sick relative, and that she was studying to be a macro-biotic cook—though I'm sure the cook thing was a big, fat lie.

I know from someone else that she went right to another job with more money. She had never complained, never asked for more money, just left.

Caroline describes herself as "very much a gut instinct kind of person. I don't *want* to be with my kids all the time, and there are times when I don't want to know all the details. As long as they're safe. And I've never really worried about them not being safe—this is a big city, but also kind of a small neighborhood. Really, there are lots of eyes on them all the time. If something were really wrong, I would know." As for her own life being an open book to her nanny, Caroline shrugs off as a given the fact that "they talk about everything, I know that. I don't get into personal things in front of anybody, but of course they can still pick up a lot. You can't really worry about that too much. What's the point?"

Although Caroline and her family obviously need the kind of full-time hands-on child care that a nanny provides, there is neither room nor need in their lives (emotionally or physically) for another family member. The nanny does an important job, but that's about as far as it goes, and it seems as though none of Caroline's nannies suffered from a great deal of separation anxiety when they left—new job, different family, but basically the same life.

Things couldn't be more different for Natalie, who has happily nannied for the same family, her fourth, for the past three years. But now, at thirty, she's reached a point where she is ready to quit nannying.

I want my weekends, I want a life, I don't want a curfew anymore, I want my own place with my own stuff. That's not to say I don't love the family I'm with now; really, I love them to death. Working for this family especially has been such a rewarding experience. I mean, you get to experience something unbelievable, where there's this child that isn't yours that you get to feel so incredibly strongly about, and you become so much part of this family, it feels almost like a relationship, where you've finding a soul mate for life, and you get to know *every*thing about each other.

What other job can you think of where you can come to work in your pajama pants, and where your boss will ask how you want your eggs for breakfast? Those are the good times, of course, but then there are the other moments, the bad days, when sometimes you realize you've gotten yourself in way too deep. They take me for granted, I take them for granted, I mean, mostly in a good way, but it's become way more than a job. I could stay there forever and just kind of tag along with their life, without ever really being an equal.

That's kind of the point where I'm at now. It feels as though I've got to get out of there now, or it'll be too late. There are lots of other nannies who've gotten really pissy with me when I told them I want to leave this family because I'm ready to start my own life. They're like, "What do you mean? You already have your own life; nannies are professionals; this is our career choice," yadda yadda yadda. Yeah, I understand where they're coming from; you've got to have boundaries and all that.

The problem with this family now is that they're almost too nice, they've never excluded me from anything, and it's beginning to feel a bit like a trap. I know they don't want me to leave; they're not expecting it. It'll be really hard to explain without coming off as though I'm rejecting them. I'm really dreading that conversation. Because it sort of feels like I'll have to tell the boys "Hey, I love you guys, but actually I don't love you enough to stick around and see you grow up." I really want to continue being friends with them, but I know quite a few nannies where, as soon as they said they were leaving, they got treated really badly, and it all went horribly wrong.

The notion of "living someone else's life" was an issue I found quite a few nannies struggling with, particularly those who were younger and still single. Like Natalie, several women I spoke to were wondering how to gracefully extract themselves from a family that was essentially smothering them with kindness. Romana had been a highly paid career nanny until she, too, quit at age thirty, before it was too late to "get to the other side" and become a mother herself. She now has two children of her own and runs a thriving, fully licensed day-care facility.

I started nannying early, when I was just eighteen, straight out of school. I've always had lovely families, so I've been very lucky, but I definitely lived in a sort of cocoon for a long time. I mean, there was always money, I never had to pay for anything; it was almost as though my employers sort of took over from where my parents had left off. I just got to hang out with the kids, which I loved, and then everything else got taken care of.

I was really naïve. But also, you know, you get used to the lifestyle—traveling; living in these gorgeous big houses while someone else pays the bills; eating out at restaurants; driving a big expensive car. God forbid, I'm not complaining; I did have a fantastic time, but real life does come as a bit of a shock after all that. I'll never forget the first time I realized that this wasn't actually my life but somebody else's. Thinking back on it, I suppose I'd gotten way, *way* too attached to one of my charges. She was two, and the mother was pregnant, and it honestly hit me like a ton of bricks when the mother fired me—I mean, she did it in the nicest possible way, and gave me great references, but I do know she went right out and hired another nanny. I was like, "What do you mean? You can't fire me, you love me, your daughter loves me, I live here." It was like a kick in the stomach. It's only when you have your own kids that you realize what that's all about.

Getting sucked too deeply into the current of another family's life is not something that happens only to nannies. Single mothers are as diverse a group as any, but it also makes sense that they in particular should occasionally be forced to rely on their nannies for a lot more than just child care. Catherine, an investment banker and divorced mother of two, makes no bones about how she feels about her nanny.

> I'd marry her if I could, just for the sake of the kids. Really, she's so much more of a parent to them than their father ever is, definitely in the day-to-day stuff. She's just as relieved and irritated as I am when he swoops in for the weekend to take them off our hands. And sends them back spoiled rotten, of course. The only thing that's a bit of a fly in the ointment is that he pays her salary, but as much as he's been a jerk about everything else, I know I don't have to worry about that. It gives him this illusion that he continues to be indispensable to our lives. She's very good at playing nice to him. But I know that if push came to shove, there's no question she'd be loyal to me.
>
> I'm dating this guy now, and I swear to God, I was more nervous about having him meet my nanny than my kids. I have a pretty good support system, but she is definitely the linchpin. We are really, really close; there's very little to do with my personal life that I don't run by her in some way. I must admit, I absolutely live in terror of the day she decides to leave.

Almost every story I heard underscored the importance of personal space—however one might choose to define it—whether it is literally a room with a lock on its door, an invisible line in the quicksand of conversation, or the sometimes subtle "stop" and "no parking" signs of body language. Caregivers debate endlessly the pros and cons of living in, and while everyone has a different notion of what type of arrangements are acceptable, on one issue almost all agree: A room that offers privacy, no matter how small, dingy, cold, ugly, or inconvenient, is *always* preferable to a larger, more lavish setup with no privacy. In general, my impression that live-out situations tend to work better for everyone involved was validated by a survey conducted in 2005 by the INA, which found that almost 50 percent of nannies who had been living in had been in their current position for less than one year. This is not to say that living in is always a bad idea or doomed to fail. Yet, this one small statistic, together with the many conversations I have had, does bear out my hunch that to be at such close quarters for so much of the time requires an inordinate amount of tact, respect, and sensitivity on both sides.

Parents are equally divided about whether the convenience of having their child-care provider live in their home is worth the loss of privacy and, let's face it, valuable real estate. Not surprisingly, this has a great deal to do with where and how a family lives: For city dwellers one common complaint was "there's simply no room!" Giving everyone their space, however small, certainly becomes a great deal harder when the living room is the playroom is the dining room—*and* the place where everyone uses the Internet, makes phone calls, and also hangs out. At least in big cities one can count on finding anonymity in a crowd and being essentially alone with millions of people around. As Caroline said, "It's ironic, isn't it? When my husband and I want some privacy we get a babysitter and go to a crowded restaurant."

One of the reasons why the notion of personal space between mothers and their nannies is so difficult to define exactly must be that anyone under the age of six generally has little or no respect for another's need for privacy. Mom/nanny is in the bathroom? Let's barge in; we have important things to talk about! All the better since you're sitting down already . . . Mom/nanny is having a conversation on the phone? Unacceptable! You should be talking to *me!* What are you talking about anyway? Is that your boyfriend? Can I tell you a secret? Yesterday Mom called Dad a jerk, Nanny, what's a jerk? Nanny, are you

poor? Nanny, did you know Grandma got sick, and she might be coming to live with us? Mom, Nanny has a fat butt and it jiggles even more
than yours; I saw it at the pool when we were getting changed . . .

Oh, mother. There is truly no end to the disingenuous ways in
which children will manage to embarrass the grown-ups around them
by simply calling a spade a spade. While in most working relationships knowledge, personal information, and skills are exchanged only
on a need-to-know basis, and in a space specifically designed for this
purpose, for mothers and nannies and their children, the opposite is
true. Heather, a single mother in her forties, put it this way:

> My *life* is her office. She probably has no idea how much space
> she takes up in my head. Never mind the fact that if she's paid
> any attention at all over the past few years she probably knows
> every little thing about me, from my tooth-brushing habits, to
> the fact that I can't stand my sister-in-law, to the color of my un-
> derwear. Nobody knows that much about me!
>
> But how can I shut her out? She's there with my daughter,
> every day, doing our laundry, making our beds, right there in the
> inner sanctum. For God's sakes, she might as well *be* me when
> I'm not here! It's a good thing I like her as much as I do. And it's
> definitely a good thing she goes home at night. Yeah, sleep. I can
> safely say that's the only shred of privacy I have left.

Just as much as there's no such thing as a recipe for the perfect relationship, there can never be a one-size-fits-all yardstick for how to
maintain a level of intimacy that everyone in the nanny-mother-child
triumvirate is comfortable with. Often it seems that in the relationships that have found a comfortable groove somewhere between the
need-to-knows, the don't-want-to-knows, and the don't-cares of child
rearing, it's an altogether different ingredient that makes it work: the
confidence to trust oneself and one's judgment, and the confidence to

trust another with something as precious, complicated, and demanding as a child. After all, if you trust her to love and keep your children while you're gone doing other things, it's probably okay for her to know the color of your underwear and who you're sleeping with. This knowledge in and of itself does not a breach of intimacy make—it's what you do with it that counts.

power

WHEN IT COMES to figuring out the dynamics of any working relationship, it is impossible to even think about the notion of power without also considering the likelihood of its abuse. Within the infinitely varied spectrum of boss versus employee, few situations present quite as many openings for power's flip side to rear its ugly head as the tug-of-love between mothers and whomever they rely upon for child care. Nannies can talk all they want about skills, professionalism, and experience, and mothers can boast until the cows come home about the terrific work environment and perks they provide and how wonderful and easy their children are, but ultimately they all admit: Being a nanny is more than a job, sometimes it's *less* than a Job, but it's always a job unlike any other.

How could it be otherwise? After all, those around whom the job is structured, namely our most wonderful, overindulged, funny, sweet, crazy devil spawns, and sweetie pies are not just the ultimate prize but also by definition innocents. Whether this definition of children as mere sheep in the herding sport of parenthood is always justified or accurate matters little. One thing the powers that be, regardless of their race, class, or culture, have thus far managed to agree upon is that children rarely call the shots, while adults almost always do—or should. When despite all these efforts the balance of power still ends up in those sticky little devil-spawn/cutie-pie fingers, Moms, Dads, and nannies: Beware!

Does power only count if a person knows she has it? Evidently not. Bettina is an illustrator who has had only one nanny since her now six-year-old daughter was born, and she readily admits that it really doesn't make sense anymore to continue employing Luisa full-time. And yet . . .

> I'm really desperate to find a way for her to stay with us. I'm *so* dependent on her. It brings up all my intimacy issues, all those relationship fears of being abandoned. I feel as though I can never relax, because I'm so afraid she might leave or find another job. It's really interesting to me that even such a positive experience as I've had with Luisa is still fraught with so much intensity. So yes, she's had a tremendous impact on my life, and on my daughter. And, by extension, on the whole family, how we all manage to function comparatively smoothly because we never have to worry about our daughter being taken care of while we're working.
>
> It's probably irrational, but I have this constant nagging fear that if she wanted to find another better, more interesting job she could do so in a minute—but that I could never, ever find someone to replace her. What do they call it, "institutional memory"? That's really what she has. So much of our family history, all this accrued knowledge, that sort of intuitive ability to pitch in where she's needed would be lost if she went away. So I do feel the balance of power is mostly on her side. I don't resent it, I just really, really don't want to lose her.

Bettina may not resent it, but other women certainly do. The power of a nanny to bring the whole house of cards crashing down by simply failing to show up is akin to a sword of Damocles dangling over some hard-won careers. "It drives me absolutely crazy, honestly it does," a creative director in an advertising agency finally admitted to me in a burst of exasperation, after first waxing poetic over her "absolutely fabulous" nanny for an hour over dinner.

> If I have to work late or do something else that's kind of unexpected, the first thing I've got to think about is, "Can I get the nanny to stay? Oh, please God, let her not have any plans tonight." You see, I have the kind of job where that ten percent of extra effort or commitment or whatever the hell you want to call it makes hundred percent of a difference to the muckety-mucks evaluating my work. They've got their minions practically salivating at the chance to work weekends, and what do I have? I have a nanny. A lovely nanny, who at six o'clock on a Friday wants nothing more than to go home, because she's exhausted from hanging with my kids all week. Well yeah, fair enough.
>
> But just think about that moment when I'm begging her to stay—that's self-loathing. Actually, there are times when, as much as I love her and everything, I loathe her even more. Look at it this way—she practically controls everything I care about: one—my children, two—my job, and three—my husband. Because if one and two aren't doing what they're supposed to, it's pretty much guaranteed that number three will *not* be a happy camper either.

There is definitely a huge discrepancy between the relatively low position on the social totem pole enjoyed by nannies and other child-care workers and the extraordinary disruption they could easily cause by simply, en masse, refusing to show up to work one day. There goes the whole damn totem pole. We all know about the chaos that ensues if, for example, the bus drivers or air traffic controllers' unions call their members out for a strike, not to mention the combination of outrage and sympathy we feel toward picketing nurses or teachers. Just imagine the havoc that would ensue without anyone left at home to look after the children: babies at the office; toddlers on the factory floor; kindergartners spilling their juice boxes all over the boardroom; and the rest of the under ten and out-of-control set spreading germs and destruction in hospitals and other grown-ups-only establishments all over the country. If this weren't such a scary thought, it might even be funny.

As well as being scary for the obvious reasons, this hypothetical scenario of unsupervised children run amok also points out how far women have come since the 1950s, and what—or who—has actually enabled them (us!) to get there. Yes, discrimination and glass ceilings are no longer as much of an issue (though they certainly still exist). Companies everywhere will judge a person by her qualifications rather than her gender, and our boyfriends, husbands, and partners are helping out a whole lot more than they used to (as much as we would like them to? Are you kidding?). Still—thank God (and thank her nicely!). There's still a ways to go, but we have already come so very far. None of this would matter much, however, if the availability of child care during working hours had not drastically increased, and the variety of choices available to working parents been broadened dramatically in the past five decades. What this really means, of course, is that even now there'd be *no* women between twenty and forty-five in the workforce at all, unless other women were available and willing to look after the next generation of worker bees (never mind clean our homes and offices, do laundry, cook, and shop . . .).

For men it has always been an accepted fact of life that regardless of their profession, in order to carry on a steady climb up the career ladder, other, lesser men would need to be stepped on. A woman's success, however, still tends to come with far more moral and emotional ambivalence, especially if she has children. To be both mother and hunter-gatherer for one's family almost always implies the presence of another woman on the homefront—for, let's be honest, how many "mannies" are there really out there? And how many nannies have ever been hired to be father substitutes? A few, perhaps, and a growing number in recent years, but they will no doubt continue to be the exception to the rule for a long time to come. What's more, when we hear of or read about a woman in the upper echelons of corporate America or politics, most of us have little questions at the back of our minds, and they are these: Does she have children? How does she manage? This is not something anyone tends to worry about when we read or hear of yet another man scaling the dizzying heights of corporate ladders.

Most women with small children and careers to manage are probably far too busy day to day to worry much about the moral underpinnings of their relationships with their (female) child-care provider—they do what works, hope for the best, and try to be decent people and good mothers without losing their marbles. Over the course of writing this book, however, I've seen far too many women struggle with a vague sense of unease and guilt, torn between what they felt they really wanted and the limits of what their actual circumstances enabled them to do. Roxanne, a successful caterer in her late thirties whose boys were six, four, and two years old, probably came closer than anyone else I interviewed to explaining these feelings.

It's so easy to get caught up in the annoying little details of what the nanny does and doesn't do. Sometimes I just have to stop and remind myself how *lucky* we really are. I mean, we make a decent living, our children are, by and large, happy and healthy and getting a good education, and thank God, thank *God* they were born in this country, where they can have genuine opportunities to do great things when they grow up.

The nanny we have now, she's in her fifties, she has grandchildren, a whole family back in Poland. Her English is beautiful, she speaks fluent French, and she's extremely well educated and smart—her father used to be a judge. I mean honestly, there is *nothing* this woman couldn't have done. And here she is, working for a middle-class family in Chicago, cleaning our house and looking after our children. And all, really, because of an accident of birth. Of course I don't want to look down on what she does—it's terribly important. But is that actually something any one of us would ever aspire to? If we could, wouldn't we choose to have our own families, make the most of our education and talents? It's her shoulders I stand on, hers and of course our mothers'. Just think how easily it could be the other way round.

Roxanne's moment of truth is poignant, but also rare. More often I found that while mothers are certainly appreciative and grateful for all that their child-care provider does for them, they also feel that nannies have a tendency to wield their power carelessly, often selfishly, and without realizing the full consequences of their actions. One situation in particular will have both sides implying that the other is abusing her power, and both end up asking bitterly, "How could she *do* this to me?" It's a familiar scenario: Mother has an incredibly important, can't-miss-it meeting at work. Nanny gets sick or is unable to come to work for another reason, like her own sick child. Mother is forced to stay home, facing recrimination and potentially a loss of income at work. Mother doesn't pay nanny for the day she missed. Nanny feels she's been treated unfairly, and the mother is furious and frustrated that at the very time she needed her most, nanny wasn't here.

Hard to say who's right or wrong, except that both have a legitimate grievance and both clearly feel they got the short end of the stick.

As one mother told me, "I'm a freelancer, okay? If I don't work, I don't get paid. And if I can't work because my sitter doesn't show up the way she is supposed to, and according to the agreement we have, why should I pay her? This isn't even about 'should' anything, it's about what I can afford. I honestly feel it's a choice *she* made that I didn't have any say in." On the other side, a nanny who had lost one job after failing to report to work one morning lamented: "She knows I have a kid, that's why she says she hire me, 'cause I'm a mother my-self. So what am I supposed to do, leave my baby when she's sick?" Sometimes, Mama is Mama and nanny is nanny and never the twain shall meet.

Another area where our child-care providers wield an inordinate amount of power is, of course, in the children's lives. Unless she works for a stay-at-home mother, or has every moment of the day mapped out by her employer, it's ultimately up to the nanny, the sitter, or the au pair to decide what everyone eats, whom they play with, and where they go. Livia admitted:

> I was really naïve about this in the beginning. Everyone in my neighborhood had nannies from the islands, and I thought—I'm not going to do that, I'm not comfortable having a black person working for me in this quasi-servant position. So we found a sitter at the local college, and I was sort of congratulating myself that I'd done the politically correct thing and all. But pretty soon I realized that our son never had any play dates, and that when they went to the park he was making sand castles all by himself when all the other preschoolers at his little classes seemed to be going from one party and play group to the next.
>
> Well, the reason was, of course, that my sitter never made friends with any other nannies—and, much as we'd like to think that color doesn't matter, never *would* be friends with any of them. Sometimes when I took him to the park myself, I swear, there would just be these waves of hostility coming in my direction. So, we switched—Ariceles is from the Dominican Republic, and she's

like the mayor of our building; she knows everybody and everything, and they have a million friends, and he gets invited to every birthday party going. Night and day, I swear.

Delia is a member of a nanny pack, and I catch her for a quick conversation one day when all her friends have gone and she is packing up. Suspicious at first, she soon warms up and tells me in no uncertain terms that her first loyalty is to her charges, but that she feels equally strongly about her friends. If she comes anywhere, I'd hazard a guess that her mom boss would probably place a distant third. "My friends and me, we got each other's back, you know. We all know each other's kids, watch out for them, hang together, stuff like that. Yeah, I go to play dates that my boss sets up for us, but we still meet up here, like once a day. If somebody needs a job, we all ask around. You need somebody? I got a couple of friends who're looking."

It goes without saying that when Delia says "looking" what she means is the search for a family with kids, and therefore most likely a mother who works and needs child care, and probably also a little bit of housekeeping. Women like Delia, who are most often illegal and get paid off the books, cannot find jobs through agencies and must therefore rely on word-of-mouth and other low-tech methods, such as scouring local bulletin boards, newspaper ads, and easily accessible forums like Craigslist. This is always a hit-or-miss proposition, as anyone who has ever composed or responded to one of these ads must know. Any informal survey of a typical day's worth of "help wanted" as well as "help available" ads will reveal that the word that seems to come up more often than any other is "loving," closely followed by its cousins "caring" and "reliable." Not surprisingly, other more practical attributes invariably on offer and in demand are both "references" and "experience," though on closer inspection the experience that's advertised can range from babysitting to waitressing, nursing, construction, housecleaning, cooking, personal assistant work, and pretty much anything in be-

tween. (Why do I know this? Because I've called a random sampling
of a couple of dozen women looking for babysitting or nanny/house-
keeper positions, and asked them about any relevant experience they
might have had.)

Oh, the reference. I can think of few other jobs where what a previous employer has to say about you carries quite as much weight, nor
where a simple matter of good or bad chemistry between people can
make quite as much difference. For a nanny, a good reference is
worth its weight in gold, not just because it opens doors and immediately sets minds at ease, but also because there seems to be an unwritten law that states that when it comes to the well-being and safety
of their children, mothers do not expect other mothers to lie or withhold facts from one another—there's just too much at stake.

But buyer, beware: Although nanny references are highly charged,
unfortunately this doesn't mean they contain fewer untruths, exagger-
ations, and plain old cover-ups than the average "would you recommend this person" conversation. One nanny with a long and obviously
checkered past happily admitted that she frequently used her own
friends as references, and more than one mother told me that unless
there had been a truly terrible transgression, they always gave their
nannies decent references. "I mean, who knows why it didn't work
out for us? Just because I didn't like the way she was with my kids
doesn't mean she wouldn't be a perfectly good nanny for someone
else. I don't want to mess up her chances of finding another job."

Aditha, a highly paid and soft-spoken Filipina nanny, who had
been with her current employer for four years, told me how one bad
reference had led to her having to endure three years of working with
"terrible families" before she regained her footing and signed up with
a reputable agency.

She tell everybody I lie, I steal, I'm lazy, I take food without
asking—it's not true! She herself tell me, "If you're hungry, help

yourself." This woman was crazy. She has five nannies in three years, and always everything is somebody else's fault, somebody smaller than her, you know what I mean? I have to give children everything they want, and when one time I say no, you cannot draw with the marker on the wall, and you must clean up, she come to shout at me—"this is my house, my children are not your cleaners!"—and next day she fire me. I find out after that she call all the agencies and says I am thief, I am lazy. But then she does same thing to girls she hire after me, so now my agency know her and don't send her people anymore.

An employee of one well-to-do nanny placement agency also confirmed to me that "some clients will never be happy with anyone we send them, but since they're the ones that pay our fee I have to continue trying to make them happy. Money and fame are always a big draw for some people. I mean, if I have a celebrity client who I know is a nightmare to work for, I'll still have girls lining up who want to interview with them. There's definitely a status thing among nannies as well, that they prefer working for people who've got money and power and influence. But to be perfectly honest, those are often the worst employers. Still, if you can later say on your resume that you worked for so-and-so, then that'll help them get the next job."

In the somewhat rarified world of mothers with help, it isn't only the help who occasionally have to fear those with more money, power, or influence than themselves. In some areas of New York City, for example, the nanny market is extraordinarily competitive, and some mothers live in fear that their most wonderful and much loved caretaker will fall prey to a better offer from another family. Take Ilva: She lives on the Upper East Side, the fictional backdrop for the (in)famous *Nanny Diaries*. She, her husband, and their two children share an apartment that's "too small and way too expensive," are vying to get their older son into a school that is "just ridiculously competitive," and both work at jobs that are "really stressful and demanding." As for her child-care situation:

> That's really competitive, too. There's so much turnover around here, you wouldn't believe. People are always kind of watching their backs, wondering what others are paying, if you're paying enough. We're up against people who can afford to go really high, so I try to make it up to Shania in other ways, like days off here and there or free tickets to things and nice birthday presents.
>
> But the truth is, she could be making a hundred, one fifty more than with us, and what's more, she's so good she probably deserves it. I'm just terrified someone will figure that out and make her a better offer. I know that some nannies, once they get their foot in the door in this neighborhood, they figure they've got it made. Why wouldn't they, if you think about it? There are parents out there who pay two hundred dollars an hour for a math tutor, what's a thousand dollars a week for a nanny?

Ilva's fear of having Shania snatched away by another family may be very real to her, but it isn't particularly realistic. Nanny heists do happen, particularly in large cities where "finding good help" is always a challenge, and full-time child care seems to be a profession more prone than many others to the "one day she just disappeared" syndrome. The other side of the power seesaw, however, can be just as fraught with fear and dependency, particularly since the firing of nannies by their mom or dad bosses is rarely a friendly transaction accompanied by weeks of notice, generous severance pay, and accrued unemployment benefits. What's more, if you are suddenly let go because of what might euphemistically be called "a personality clash," there goes your reference, and with it a critical part of your platform for finding another job. The added fact that so many nannies lack a working visa, and a strong support network in the communities where they work, presents the notion that nannies have their working-mother employers over a barrel rather differently.

The stories everyone remembers, and that make it to Dr. Phil's or Oprah's shows, and even occasionally the news, usually focus on horror nannies and (for the greatest possible tabloid appeal) dreadful things done to the children in their unsuspecting mother's absence. While I must admit to having no factual evidence or statistics to support this claim, I suspect that the occurrence of abusive behavior by parents and employers toward their nannies and other household help far exceeds the occasional suffering of children at the hands of the women who are supposed to care for them.

As Luz, the unofficial spokeswoman of a small circle of Hispanic nannies I met in the park one day, said to me:

> It's brutal sometimes. How you say? Is a jungle out there. People always try to take advantage. When you have no papers, like some of my friends, you almost get to expect that. It starts out all nice, like a little bit of housework, and a little extra babysitting, and then it gets more and more and more, and you can't say nothing because you think they fire you. It's still a good job, but in America it's like that—white people with the money have all the power. White people with papers have all the power; if they get mad at you they can say they call immigration or police, and if they don't pay you, who you're gonna go to? I have one friend, she come from Mexico when she's nineteen, had one little baby she leave with her mother, just like a kid herself. She find a job through somebody who knows somebody, like that, how everybody does. And they make it sound so nice, good family, nice lady, cute kids, but only two hundred and fifty dollars a week because she has no references. She take it because for her it's still a lot, and she want to send money home and have place to live.
>
> You know what they do? They make her sleep in the garage;

they put a lock on the fridge; they make her pay for toilet paper. Then one day she takes kitchen towel for toilet because she doesn't want to pay, and toilet flows over, big, big mess. They say it cost thousand dollars to fix it, and she has to pay. Every time I see her, I say, "Why you don't leave, you owe them nothing, you are not their dog," but she's afraid. They have one little baby same age as her son, and she loves that baby. And then sometimes she says the lady is nice, and that maybe it's her fault because she doesn't speak English so good, she probably make lots of mistakes. She just don't show up one day; I hope she goes home. Now that family, they have an au pair. I see her around sometime. Maybe one day I tell her about them. But probably she already knows!

The variations on the story of Luz's friend are literally endless, and the six or so elements common to this narrative are probably one of the murkiest parts of the immigration debate currently raging in all parts of the political spectrum. Anyone could fill in the blanks:

1. Illegal alien from _____ sneaks into United States by any means possible.
2. Illegal alien finds work doing unskilled labor such as picking fruit, raking lawns, _____, cleaning houses, or looking after American babies.
3. Illegal alien takes only cash and _____ out of the economy while putting virtually nothing back in the way of taxes.
4. Illegal alien works for less money, fewer _____, longer hours, and under conditions few self-respecting Americans would accept.
5. Illegal alien routinely ends up doing work that American families desperately need *someone* to do (i.e., child care) so they can get to *their* jobs at _____, and at a price they can

afford. (Particularly ironic since the richest country in the world provides less maternity leave, fewer maternity benefits, no guarantee of health care, and fewer child-care tax deductions or child-care benefits than practically any other developed nation.)

6. Illegal nannies work for less than minimum wage with no training or benefits, and questionable supervision. If they are mistreated, their only option is to _____.

Without getting too deeply into the polemics of the immigration debate, it's immediately obvious that this narrative often doesn't have a happy ending. In the relationship between parents and their off-the-books, illegal nannies, what appears to be merely the exercise of authority and reason in the eyes of one all too often amounts to an abuse of power by another—or occasionally even by both, as one workaholic mother and serial employer of off-the-books nannies told me: "I know for certain that every nanny I've ever had has felt I took advantage of her. In the same way, I personally think that every nanny I've ever had has probably, in some way, taken advantage of me."

In the absence of the checks and balances built into most other working relationships, the "taking advantage" territory is an easy place to slip into without awareness or even intention. After all, those who habitually take advantage of others rarely think that they're doing something untoward, and easily brush off whatever injustices they practice. Some of the oft repeated justifications I've heard from mom bosses of underpaid nannies include, "I'm giving her a job and a place to live," and its companion: "Where she comes from she'd be out on the streets." Other reasons for paying too little for too much work might run along the lines of, "She's making so much more from us than she could ever hope to back in her country," and even the rather self-congratulatory, "She's lucky to be working for us, instead of some family that would *really* abuse her."

Before we get too comfortable up there on our high horses, let's not forget that while those statements are undoubtedly self-serving, they also contain more than a grain of truth: One of the advantages of being a working mother in the world's richest country is that the buying power of every dollar we pay an illegal immigrant nanny in the United States is usually far, far greater in the place that she has left behind. In fact, this is also true for a great many au pairs who come here legally and with a temporary, though limited, work permit from areas such as Eastern and Central Europe, and certainly from South America. Their weekly stipend of approximately $140 (though with agency fees and all other costs, families pay closer to $250 per week) may seem like a poor excuse for a living wage, yet for many this represents not only the first real money they've ever earned, but also gives them an opportunity to save a few thousand dollars and return home at the end of their official year with enough saved to kick-start a real grown-up life.

Talk to any "proper" nanny however, perhaps one with several years of experience or an actual degree related to early childhood education, and you will immediately get an earful about how au pairs are *not* nannies; how at best they are glorified mothers' helpers with little experience; how their primary goal is not to work with children but merely to spend a year or more in the United States learning English; and how they give the nanny profession a bad name. To a large extent this resentment dates back to 1997 and the infamous nanny trial of British au pair Louise Woodward, who was accused of having fatally injured the baby boy in her care by shaking him violently when he refused to stop crying. In January 1998, once the trial was concluded, the International Nanny Association issued a press release that stated: "The au pair programs are dangerously misleading in their current structure," and they "should not be promoted and used as a viable full-time child-care alternative." Them's fightin' words!

Nor have attitudes changed a great deal in the past decade, if the chatter on several nanny bulletin boards on the Internet is anything to go by. The rallying cry of "We are not au pairs; we are *professionals*" comes up time and again, as does the mention of "I hate it when they introduce me as their au pair" in any list of top-ten nanny peeves. If au pairs are looked down upon by so many who are theoretically supposed to be their peers, no wonder that they also get a bum rap from many who employ them. Much of this has to do with the fact that for families who need flexible, full-time child care, an au pair is often the only affordable option. Add to this the sad truth that most everyone routinely ignores guidelines provided by the agencies stating that au pairs are *not* required to do housework (so, what's a little cleaning while the kids are at school?), and you easily get to have a full-time virtual domestic slave for a mere two hundred and fifty dollars per week.

"Au pair abuse" isn't yet a separate category of human rights violations, but judging by some of the bizarre and downright yucky stories I've heard, it certainly could be. There was the girl whose "room" was half of a damp, unheated, and windowless garage subdivided by a sheet hanging from the ceiling, and the girl who was expected to be substitute mother, housekeeper, driver, and cook for not one but two households, with five children, shuttling back and forth between one divorced parent and the other. There was also the girl who was given a fifteen-dollars-a-week allowance for food, and who had to buy her own laundry detergent, lightbulbs, and toilet paper, and pay for the cell phone that the parents forced her to carry at all times, and there was the girl whose host father refused to let her have a lock on her bathroom door, and who would routinely, accidentally on purpose, walk in on her while she was showering. Where au pairs are concerned, you could probably make up any old story and, no matter how weird or awful, it's likely to have happened somewhere to someone.

I myself have been a host mother to four of these girls, and while I'm quite certain I never abused any of them, I also know how easy it would have been to cross that line. Not to mention how tempting to sometimes explode in a shower of rage and frustration over a transgression or mistake that might have seemed perfectly harmless to a nineteen-year-old from deepest rural East Germany but that seemed more like the absolute last straw to me. Ask anyone who has persevered on the au pair route, and the litany of stories and complaints will be similar to mine: It's like having another child in the house; she cried for three months and then went home; her boyfriend came to stay and never left; she'd sit at the table and expect me to serve her dinner just like her mother at home; she forgot that here we drive on the other side of the road (oops); she wanted to buy the cheapest gas so she filled up my car with diesel; she cleaned the baby's bottom with Lysol; she thought international calls were free and racked up a five-hundred-dollar phone bill talking to her family in Serbia; she left the baby in his stroller under a tree while she went shopping because in her country that's what they do . . . stop me, please, before I scream. Of course it's also true that approximately one time out of three you get lucky and find an au pair who turns out to be a friend for life, who is truly gifted with children and devoted to looking after them, and who will always refer to you as her "other family" and invite you to her wedding. Perhaps these happy endings make the rest of the drama worthwhile, but for anyone without a bottomless well of patience, and who isn't fully prepared for the hit-and-miss aspect of the au pair to family matching process, I would not recommend it.

In the United States the pros and cons of au pairs versus nannies, babysitters versus day care, and illegal versus on-the-books are well documented, and anyone willing to do a bit of research will be able to find out the pitfalls and advantages of each option as well as what's legal and what isn't. The system or rather multiple parallel systems that exist to provide child care for working parents may be far from perfect, but at least there is a sense that the worst transgressions will be punished, and that because ours is an open and generally just society, people may be able to get away with bad stuff for a while, but sooner or later they'll either be stopped or some kind of justice will prevail.

Unfortunately, in many other countries of the world the women who provide child care (usually lumped in with all the other duties comprising domestic help) have far less to rely upon when it comes to getting fair compensation and humane treatment. It's a fairly simple formula, and one that predictably follows the money: A poor country, rich in nothing but corruption and manpower, will ship its only asset to other, wealthier countries in dire need of cheap labor. According to the ancient rules of poor versus rich, one man's trifle is still another man's treasure, and so the exploitation of one by the other not only becomes desirable, it becomes law, and deeply embedded in the social fabric. The economies of poor Southeast Asian countries rely so heavily on the revenue generated by the laborers they send to work for their oil- and technology-rich neighbors that the money they send home can be those countries' single largest source of foreign currency—not only keeping hundreds of thousands of families fed and clothed, but also literally keeping their countries afloat: In the Philippines, remittances from foreign workers make up 10 percent of the *entire* economy. In the larger scheme of things, to be sure, the phenomenon of guest workers is only a very small part of the puzzle, but in its own way it still provides a glimpse of what happens when worlds collide and some people are free to exploit others, not just because they want to, but simply because they can.

I confess that I myself have done my part to fund and perpetuate this system, and I also know for a fact that any efforts to abolish it would *not* be met with a warm welcome in the countries from which most of the domestic workers hail. From 1994 to 2001 my family and I lived in Hong Kong where, just like literally millions of local Chinese and expat families, we employed what was locally known as an amah, or a woman from Southeast Asia, in most cases from the Philippines. She lived with us, in a tiny room next to the kitchen, a standard feature in all apartments in our neighborhood, and hundreds of thousands of other homes all over the former British colony. She was not permitted to drive (this would have deprived many Hong Kong Chinese of perfectly good and higher paying jobs), but other than that she was available and required to do our bidding in any other activity that could even remotely be described as "domestic," which naturally included babysitting. The amahs were in Hong Kong courtesy of a specific domestic worker visa issued at two-year intervals, which was the length of time of the average contract they were required to sign with their employers. While their behavior was strictly supervised and circumscribed by Hong Kong law, the same was certainly not true of their employers: If an amah failed to find another employer within two weeks of finishing one contract, they would automatically be required to return home. The same was true if they got pregnant, or if they got into any kind of trouble with the law. They were required to work six days a week, usually with Sundays off, but there was no limit to the number of hours they could be asked to be on-duty—for most amahs, their workday started when they woke up and did not finish until the last member of their employer's family was asleep.

In return, the employers were required to pay them HK$3,850 per calendar month (approximately US$485 at the fixed exchange rate of HK$7.8), to provide two weeks' vacation and a ticket to return home once a year, as well as room and board. In many cases (as in ours) this meant a small room of their own and a share of the same food the family was consuming, but for just as many others it meant either sleeping on the floor in the kitchen of an overcrowded family apartment or sharing a bunk bed with one or more of the family's children, and eating only leftovers. Given the parameters of the relationship I just described, it's easy to see that the potential for abuse was and is enormous, and that all the power has been, and always will rest, in the hands of the employer.

And yet . . . $485 a month to a poor family in a rural province in the Philippines is a fortune, then and now. To their relatives back home, whom they frequently support, feed, clothe, and send to school with a large chunk of their monthly salary, the amahs are the ones who have made it, who've been able to get out of a world where choices are few and poverty is constant and practically inescapable. In other countries with similar foreign domestic worker programs, such as Singapore, Dubai, and Saudi Arabia, the imported help earns even less, and their working conditions are frequently even more draconian—at least in Hong Kong they receive health insurance (though rudimentary), have the opportunity to report their grievances to the authorities and a government appointed watch dog, and are supposed to receive a severance payment at the end of their contract equal to one month's salary for every year they work for a particular employer.

What's more, Hong Kong citizens are generally a law-abiding lot, and since Tiananmen Square and the colony's return to China and its heavyhanded rule in 1997, general awareness of the importance of human rights issues has increased. Still, no one is in a hurry to send the amahs home, least of all the amahs themselves or their left-behind relatives who benefit from their work and largesse. Obviously, if the amahs were ever permitted to put forth a wish list they would ask for more money, improved working conditions, and laws to protect them that are not only enforceable but enforced. At this point, though, most of them are resigned to the status quo in that they realize that ultimately everyone gets something they want and need, and if you come from a poor country with a million girls queuing up to take your place, you don't exactly have a whole lot of bargaining power. In terms of counting the cost to those families and children left behind by the amahs, who's to say that a mother should never abandon her children when her only alternative is to raise them in poverty in a country that is deeply and systemically corrupt, with no prospects whatsoever? Just like Roxanne said, occasionally it behooves all of us working mothers to remember: It's their shoulders we stand on.

My own family's much-loved amah Abela told me the story of one of her friends whose family "generously" allowed her to stay and work with them throughout her pregnancy. They "permitted" her to give birth in Hong Kong, but she then had to send her newborn son home to the Philippines without her at just two weeks' old or risk losing her visa status, work permit, and job. It was obviously indescribably hard, a heartbreaking outrage that would be practically impossible to fathom for mothers in this country, but there was still never any question that Abela's friend would comply.

> It's like a cycle—somebody from one family go to another country like Singapore or Hong Kong to work, they make money, they send home their children, and then when the children grow up they do the same for their parents. The money is a lot, but you know the price? This is what we always say: The price for a better life and independence is that your husband or your boyfriend go run around with other women or marry somebody else, and your children have bad time because you're not there to teach them; they take drugs, they get in trouble.
>
> Some people, they pay their family everything, and then nobody at home have any reason to find job, to save money for himself. I always just give my family a little bit. I pay for two of my nieces to go to college, but I only pay the tuition—the rest they have to earn alone. It's like they say, you have to teach them how to catch a fish, not just to give the fish. I want them to be responsible, to make their own life.
>
> It's all right to go if you are young and single, but it's terrible when you have family. And if I want to become really rich, you know what I do? I go back home and I get into politics. So you invest maybe hundred thousand dollar, get some job in the government, and you get back two hundred thousand—this is how it works in my country. Everything is corrupt. Money is power,

money is what connects everybody, family, employer, government. When you're rich you have power, your children have
good life—but most of us, we're still poor.

Filipinas all over the world, in Western Europe, North America,
and Arab countries, have a reputation for being good with children—
loving, kind, patient, and loyal. For this reason quite a few of the
mothers I interviewed told me that at some point, particularly when
their children were infants, they were convinced that what they needed
was a Filipina nanny. When I asked Abela how and why she thought
her fellow Filipinas had come to have this reputation, she shrugged
her shoulders and laughed. "In my country, we do everything for our
children. And if we can't do it for our own kids, we do it for the other
kids. I know so many of my friends, they stay with horrible employers
because they love the kids. You ask me about power—when the employer have all the power, all the control over your life, to love the children is one thing that make it okay."

Nannies in America (not at all the same thing, as we know by now,
as "American nannies" with passports and visas) only rarely experience this same level of powerlessness, but of course this doesn't
mean they don't also occasionally resent the way their employers play
with their lives. Judging by many of my interviews, as well as by nanny
chatter on the Internet, probably the area where they feel most
abused (and powerless to do much about it) is time: Employers who
are chronically late; who give them a five-minute warning for a delay
of several hours; who assume the nanny must be available at all times
and at little or even no notice; and who feel that asking her to cancel
plans in order that they may do as they please is no big deal and part
of the job description. Thea's lament pretty much sums it up:

> I can't just get up and leave the children, can I? I mean, what
> am I supposed to say when she calls me at five to seven and says,

"Is it okay if I come home in an hour; this meeting ran late," or whatever? What I should do is just leave, but you can't do that. I've tried talking to her about it, especially when I've told her like days and weeks in advance that I had plans, like something I really needed to be at. She just says it isn't her fault either, that sometimes there's just nothing she can do about it. What the hell! It's always somebody else's fault, right? But I'm the one who gets screwed.

It is indeed ironic that when an employer breaks a promise and lets the nanny's precious free time trickle away in late meetings or just by dawdling, he or she is essentially relying on the fact that a nanny will never break rule number one: Never Let Children Out of Your Sight, Ever. To compromise this in any way whatsoever will always be considered by far the worse violation when compared with an hour or two of unexpected overtime or a missed train. Case in point: One nanny was fired by the mother after she left the children with the doorman of the family's apartment building because the mother was running more than an hour late. Why couldn't she wait? She had promised to attend her own daughter's high-school graduation. Another: A Nanny booked a nonrefundable flight for her vacation, but missed it because her mom boss was delayed for two hours in a hideous traffic jam. Nanny presented MB with the bill for the lost ticket; MB was outraged and fired the nanny. "She just totally overstepped the line on that one," said the mother. "How can you say it was my fault her ticket was nonrefundable? And it certainly wasn't my fault that there was an accident on the way home." Fault or no fault, nanny still got screwed on all counts, with her ticket down the drain and her job up the spout. It's hard to argue, however, that at some level Mom and the kids didn't also get screwed as well.

Where the use and abuse of power between mothers and nannies is concerned, the moral of these stories is unfortunately not always immediately obvious. In a perfect world we'd have Mom neatly shelved in one place, Nanny in another, and everyone would know their places, do their jobs to the best of their abilities, and be fairly compensated. But add the children, mix them all up like a well-shuffled deck of cards, and you might as well be playing poker. If there is any advice that is worth giving, I believe it's this: Never use the fact that someone else loves your children against them, even indirectly. Be aware that love has a tendency to distort the truth, and that a decision made in anger or fear should probably be postponed until a calmer time, when you've had a chance to walk a little way in the other person's shoes. And finally: Always be kind, try not to be cheap, attempt to be fair, and for God's sakes don't be late.

fathers

ISIT ANY PARK on any weekend day and you will encounter them in heartwarming multitudes: fathers playing with their children, pushing swings and strollers. Fathers handing out snacks, kicking and throwing balls, spotting the monkey bars, tying shoelaces, applying sunscreen or expertly strapping babies and toddlers of various sizes into Baby Bjorns, backpacks, and strollers. To see them take on whatever needs to be done of the schlepping, playing, and cleaning up seems utterly routine, and it's obvious to anyone willing to take a closer look that they're truly and deeply passionate about wanting to spend time with their families in all their messy glory. Watch them, and you will see: These are not the loving but largely hands-off fathers we grew up with in the sixties and seventies. These guys know their kids and are profoundly connected to them. They're not afraid to get dirty; this is for real. Oh, why can't life be a playground, and every day a weekend?

I've yet to meet a parent, male or female, who has told me that coparenting is a bad idea, and I'm sure I never will. In fact, the vast majority of fathers I've talked to, either about this book or their children and families in general, seem to think they're pretty good at the coparenting and sharing responsibility thing, at least as far as the demands of their professional lives allow. They might not have their children's daily schedules memorized down to the last detail, or have changed *exactly* their half share of stinky diapers, but ultimately that's the small stuff. On the big things they are right there, always. They might still leave the nitty-gritty of arranging birthday parties and play dates to the mom, but they will faithfully attend every parent-teacher conference; check homework; chaperone field trips; get under the covers and tell stories; protect their kids from every bad thing out there when they're little; and cheer them on every step of the way from the sidelines when they're bigger. Of course there are still millions of kids in America whose fathers—and mothers, for that matter—engage in less than stellar parenting for all sorts of reasons. What's more, the sad truth remains that more than 90 percent of one-parent families continue to be headed up by women, and that those who are delinquent in paying their share of child support are almost 100 percent men. Still, the bottom line can't be denied: Screwed-up families always have and always will exist, but this generation of fathers is more closely bonded and deeply involved with more aspects of their children's lives than any other before it. On the whole it's a considerable improvement on the "Mother knows best" model of the sixties and seventies, and there is no going back—thank God.

If that paragraph sounds like a disclaimer, that's because it is. Now that we've paid homage to fathers as loving parents, let's take a closer look at what those guys are actually contributing to the arrangement, supervision, and management of their families' child care. Not only that, but how much has the modern dad's version of himself as equal partner and coparent established itself as the new normal among those who are supposed to be our generation's child-care gurus? Well, sorry, Dads, we appreciate the effort, really we do, but you have a long way to go. Seems there is a bit of a conspiracy afoot to make sure the title of primary caregiver remains firmly in Mom's department. This is not a conspiracy theory, and we have scientific proof: A study published in 2005 in the journal *Psychology of Men and Masculinity* concludes that while fathers and mothers have been shown to be equally competent in responding to an infant's needs, the "experts" overwhelmingly continue to address themselves to mothers. The authors of the article, entitled "Popular Child-Rearing Books: Where Is Daddy?" found numerous instances in the randomly selected child-rearing manuals included in their study where the text would use the word "parent" in a gender-neutral way as an opening gambit. Before long, however, the tone of the writing would change to use examples that were obviously addressed to mothers. We might live in an age where deliberately bland and politically correct language often leaves one wondering who exactly the author is talking about. Still, I doubt many fathers would seriously take up suggested stress management techniques from child-rearing experts that include "going to a spa, getting one's nails done, or talking with a girl-friend."

Overall, the rest of the evidence cited in the article proves equally as damning: In all the books and 56,379 paragraphs included in the study, there was simply no mention at all of fathers in any passages concerning children's medical needs, health, and nutrition. Even more shocking, only *two sentences* explicitly referenced fathers and day-care concerns. It's hardly surprising the authors came away with the conclusion that across-the-board a mother's role with her child is still generally considered to be "obligatory and primary." The father's role, by contrast, by and large continues to be depicted as merely "voluntary and negotiable," regardless of how often Dad coaches Little League or leaves work early to relieve the nanny. That is not all. Not only do "experts" continue to subliminally give fathers the message that they can choose whether or not to step up to the parental plate (no choice for Mom, sorry), but on top of that, many mothers apparently fall into a behavior pattern called "maternal gatekeeping." I'm experiencing déjà vu all over again as I write this, because a maternal gatekeeper is one of those moms who deliberately keeps Dad at arm's length so she can get on with organizing the kids' lives according to her own liking. Faced with a wife who is convinced she knows better, and child-care manuals that recommend parents get themselves to the hairdresser for a bit of peace and quiet, what's a father to do? Take everyone to the playground on weekends, that's what.

So there it is, the chicken-and-egg question of mothers, fathers, and their child care: Why is it that the dads generally have so much less to do with hiring and supervising their children's nanny, or whatever other forms of child care a family uses? Is it because they truly feel it's not their responsibility, or because the gatekeepers and experts among us actually conspire to make them believe they couldn't do it properly even if they tried? One mother, Kristen, with "a totally loving and completely involved" husband for a coparent, made it clear that there is no one answer, and certainly no blame to be placed squarely upon anyone's shoulders.

Okay, so I guess we're a fairly traditional family, even if that's kind of rare these days. All new traditions, I suppose. Is that an oxymoron? We both work, we both earn about the same, and now that Dana and Tom are out of the tiny baby age we're more or less out of the woods with the sleepless nights and everything. So yeah, we have a nanny, and we both interviewed her and everything and agreed that she was the one. But we're pretty new to all this, and of course she's only supposed to work so many hours, while we're working. I mean, that's normal, right? And she's supposed to get some sort of guidance, like a schedule, and phone numbers for emergencies, and what to do about discipline and naps. It's only been three months, but I'm still totally conflicted about how to handle this. Like, if she has a question on any stupid little thing, she automatically calls me. And then, you know, I figure it out. Go home if I have to, calm her down, make arrangements, whatever. But actually I've been furious that she just always assumes I'm the one who's responsible.

So the next time—last week, actually—she calls Mark [Kristen's husband] instead, when Dana fell and got this goose egg on her head. So he dealt with it, in the same way I would have done, I guess—ice it, keep an eye on her—and I come home and know nothing about it. I completely flipped! I was actually screaming at them both—how could you not tell me? I mean, Dana was totally fine, but I just felt like everyone had betrayed me, and this was some sort of proof that I'm a crappy mother. Now, I do know for sure that Mark would *not* have felt the same way if the tables were turned. He'd have just kissed Dana and said, "Poor sweetheart, wow, that's some bump," and gone off and played Lego with her or something.

According to the scientists who study human behavior, and who believe in data and logic, "obligatory and primary" and "voluntary and negotiable" couldn't possibly be grouped under the same job description. For mothers like Kristen and fathers like Mark, however, logic really doesn't come into it—they want it all, and God help the nanny who stands between them.

While my methods in the writing of this book were hardly scientific, and my choice of interviewees fairly random, there was still a remarkable consistency in my conversations with men. Above all, they were short. Most of the time they were to the point. Once I'd explained the topic, a typical exchange might go along the lines of "Oh, how interesting." (pause) "You should talk to my wife." A scheduled, sit-down conversation rarely proceeded to the sitting down part, and mostly we would end up talking about the kids after just a few minutes of going down the checklist of my questions.

Jared, thirty-six, father to Marie and John and living with their mother, Sue, told me this: "Jealous of the nanny? Never even crossed my mind. I know Sue gets uncomfortable sometimes with how close they all are, and I'm constantly having to tell her that she's not the terrible mother she thinks she is. Far as I'm concerned, they're happy, I'm happy." Martin, thirty-nine and with three daughters, made it just as clear that he thought my question was slightly ridiculous: "Hey, when the little one decides to crawl into the nanny's bed in the middle of the night rather than ours, great!" Other responses ranged from "no," to "never" to "of *course* I'm jealous of her boyfriend, because she is a babe. Just kidding" (please excuse me while I gag).

The other consistencies I noted were more subtle but far more interesting, probably because, as my husband pointed out when looking over my notes, it "sounds like we all lie about the same things." Among one particular group of ten fathers who all answered a brief e-mail questionnaire I'd sent them, everyone claimed to have a decent basic knowledge of the children's and the nanny's daily routine. When I tried to confirm this with the wives/mothers, the responses ranged from, "Yeah, kind of," to "Are you kidding? He doesn't have a clue. At least not unless I tell him." Similarly, my question as to how much they were aware of and worried about the nanny's feelings and moods was mostly met with earnest assurances of "I always try to be helpful," "We worry about her a lot," and "I care about her a great deal." The "buts . . ." that followed these statements, however, probably came closer to telling the real story, such as, "For the most part, I was informed by my wife or children," and "I consider her to be an employee, not a family member. I only get involved with her relationships if they affect our family, and then I can come down on them pretty hard." Because, after all, most of these guys did realize that "the incremental quality of life we enjoy because of her working for us is enormous."

Only one of the ten admitted to ever talking about the nanny to his guy friends, and then definitely "not daily or even weekly. But the

subject does come up regularly in conversation with my male friends—
mostly in the context of discussing my wife's work status and satisfaction with working." For the others the answer was a straight "never,"
because "frankly, it is a conversation that would never come up in the
normal course of 'guy talk,'" or "seldom. And only whenever somebody
is desperate, but even then, guys do not take any advice. . . . So we
don't waste time on topics like that, and rather focus on drinking beer."

As for the number of times any of these men (all known to me personally to be loving, concerned, and involved fathers) would call to
check on the nanny during any given day: actually, never. They might
"talk to her if I accidentally get her instead of the children," but other
than that it was pretty much out of sight, out of mind. On this, not surprisingly, the mothers of their children all agreed, mostly while making
sure I also knew that they, of course, called regularly or at least once or
twice a day.

I will not do all these wonderful fathers the injustice of lumping
them together in the "voluntary and negotiable" parent category. What
has become clear in many follow-up conversations is that in their own
minds they certainly don't feel as though they have much of a choice,
nor room to negotiate when it comes to pitching in with child care.
Nor, on balance, do they really resent it—to the contrary, spending
time with their children is something they genuinely cherish and a
central part of who they are. They don't see themselves as "voluntary"
caretakers, or even primary, obligatory ones, but simply as fathers.
"What do you want out of my life? They're my kids! Of course I'm responsible. I'd give my left arm to protect them, and do what I can to
make sure they're happy," said one otherwise monosyllabic dad after I
continued pestering him with questions. So enough already of voluntary versus obligatory, or whatever else the experts choose to call it.
Moms, dads, nannies—we all just want everyone to be happy, especially the children. Now that we're all agreed on that, let me count on
one hand the number of fathers who actually see themselves as the

primary employer of the nanny, or who are otherwise the principal organizer and manager of their family's child-care arrangements.

From CEOs with full-time, high-income professional wives, to regular working Joes married to women with full-time, part-time, or no jobs at all, the consensus was overwhelming:

"My wife has the primary relationship with the nanny."

"I don't assign tasks to the nanny—not my role."

"Everyone knows who is in charge. She's the one who deals with them daily."

"I don't really know what she does every day. My wife is the primary employer."

"My wife definitely takes on the vast majority of the work and worry of the hiring process. She is totally attuned to their schedule—I just know the basic contours."

"My wife is the one who has a close working relationship with her. My involvement, as in managing the process? Zero."

"I don't really know the boundaries too well; my wife is the one who has established the rules of the game."

"In terms of hiring the nanny, I'm just tangentially involved. I might do the interview with my wife, but the final decision is hers."

"I come in only at the tail end of the selection process, more as a formal blessing and to provide support. If my wife feels comfortable, I'm normally okay with it."

"I help my wife weigh the pros and cons, but she makes the final decision."

"Of course I was consulted, but she was certainly in overall charge."

"My general view is, if my wife likes the nanny, then I like the nanny."

"My wife fires them. Not a surprise—she fires everyone. She is
faster to the holster than I am, by far. I'll suggest coaching
and development and different management techniques,
and she looks at me like I'm an idiot, and cans them."

Not surprisingly, most nannies' view of which parent tends to be
the primary employer is similar, but the fathers in my sample would
probably be relieved to know that their involvement, however dispro-
portionate to the mother's, is almost always hugely appreciated. Marilynne has worked for six families, and is currently onto her twelfth
newborn. She has even worked for a time for a single divorced father
with full custody of his two children:

The interview is always a dead giveaway, isn't it? I don't think I'd
work for anyone anymore where the father wasn't involved, at
least to the point of wanting to meet me before I started. Used
to be that I'd just get to meet the mum, and then maybe the dad
at the end, but the last few years that's really changed. It's kind
of natural, though, that you'd be dealing more with the mother,
I mean, for starters, she's another woman!

I've had all sorts, really. I don't think you can generalize, because each family is different. But there's not been many dads
who've really gotten into the nitty-gritty of things with me, except for that one time where there was a divorce. He was fantastic. But he'd have had to be, wouldn't he? Considering how it's
still so unusual for dads to get custody.

Another thing Marilynne went on to point out is that the quality of
the relationship between a man and his wife is just as important as
how they treat the children—any nanny who has ever been caught in
the cross fire of marital spats will tell you that.

What I like about my job now is, they're just a really nice, happy family—you can tell the dad really cares about the children. He really wants to make sure his wife's happy and has got all her ducks in a row. Because she does have the bigger job in terms of both working and then having to stay on top of the children as well, doesn't she? I think he appreciates that it makes his life easier, too. He's much more formal with me than the mum, if you know what I mean. But he obviously respects that I've got a job to do, and I really appreciate that. Let me tell you, there're still lots of dads who think a nanny's just a babysitter, no better than a cleaning lady. That really does tick me off.

Most of the men I interviewed would probably be loath to admit that they engage in any kind of gender role stereotyping. Yet almost all of them do. They (and their wives) might consider themselves to be the most fervent feminists, doing their manly best to raise strong daughters who won't, if their daddies have anything to do with it, be denied a single opportunity in life. These fathers are also smart and pragmatic enough to know that unless their wives are happy and comfortable with their family's child-care arrangements, dire consequences will ensue for all. Phillip is a technology consultant, father of three girls, and married to Adrienne, a psychologist. He has the most politically correct vocabulary and demeanor of almost anyone I have ever met, and his wife would kill him if she ever suspected for a second that he was faking it.

Much as I hate to say this, there probably is some deeply embedded sexism in the way I approach the distribution of child-care responsibilities in our household. My feelings about our nanny do, largely, relate to how well Adrienne is getting on with her. All our lives are just incomparably better when that relationship is running smoothly. Because the nanny, when all is going well, that is, gives Adrienne peace of mind, so Adrienne can give me peace of mind.

It's true that this other woman does sort of become an extension of the woman already in your life—I think men just don't feel the connection in the same way. Maybe that's why my wife is always so much more eager to make sure the nanny is happy. Also, for whatever reason, I've always been the money guy: paymaster, accountant, dealing with social security. And that automatically creates a different dynamic as well.

On the whole, though, I know for sure I'm not the only one among my men friends who resents the amount we have to pay the nanny, particularly given what she actually does. And I don't mean the child care, that is absolutely fine, it's the other stuff, the housekeeping and cleaning and cooking. I just don't see why that shouldn't be a natural part of her responsibilities, as an employee of our family. But there again, Adrienne is the one who sweats the complexities of who does what. And it's not just that I think she is better at it, I think she needs to feel that she's the one in control, for her own peace of mind.

Although Phillip is the self-described "money guy," I really did not discover a pattern in terms of whether the mother or father was more likely to be paymaster and keeper of the books. Here, too, it seems that while traditional roles might play a part, the real issue is control. One way or another, almost all mothers seem to have a need to control and shape their children's lives, particularly while they're not around themselves. Sometimes this includes paying the nanny and sometimes it does not; sometimes it's deliberate, at others just the way the cookie crumbles. Lorraine, for one, admits that her husband holds the purse strings in their family: "It's stupid, but David's just better with numbers than me. I have enough on my plate, so that's his role. I actually think he kind of likes it, because it's proof that he has *some* kind of role to play. For everything else the nanny and I just work things out between us; I pretty much never consult him."

For Mikaela the opposite is true:

> Oh no, I'm the one who pays her. She's really my employee, after all. I wouldn't hand that responsibility to my husband anymore than I'd expect him to deal with the salaries of the people who work at my office. Besides, it makes our relationship more professional—I don't want a nanny who's my best friend. I know, I know, they're *our* children, and she works for both of us. But in practice I don't really consult him very much. There are other things he pays for, like the car and our vacations, and I don't really ask him about those, either. Of course I'd take it seriously if he had some major objection, but most of the time he just lets me get on with it, and then he totally does his share on weekends and the rest of the time. He can't stand it when she's around the kids at the same time he is. If he's the first one home, that's it, she's gone. When I get back, I always check in with her for a while, find out how the day went.

Whether fathers regard their nannies principally as employees of the family or think of them more as coparents, jealousy vis-à-vis their attachment to the children seems to have gone out the window right alongside the guilt. I can easily think of several dozen examples of mothers obsessing repeatedly and in many creative ways over exactly where to draw the line between the nanny's child-care duties and other domestic chores, but would be hard-pressed to come up with more than one or two from the male "head of households." Baby takes a nap every day from eleven to one? Got two hours between dropping off one kid and picking up the other? What the heck is wrong with asking her to do the laundry in the meantime? As we know by now, nannies and mothers tend to be rather sensitive when it comes to making assumptions about domestic responsibilities, and can tell you exactly what might be wrong with asking Nanny to pick up and wash a family's dirty underwear. Fathers, apparently, cannot.

Frank, forty-three, father of two and married to "a career girl," is surely not alone when he confesses to being slightly confused and rather irritated by the whole thing: "I just don't get it, I really don't. I wouldn't dare anymore to ask our nanny to do anything that isn't strictly related to the kids, because my wife just jumps down my throat. She wants her to be completely focused on the kids and their needs—even when the kids are out of the house, and even now that our youngest has started preschool. So go figure—this is apparently more than my male chauvinist mind can comprehend. I know it's definitely more than my marriage is worth, though, to question her judgment in these things. All I know is that instead of one we now have three people working for us, and apparently they're all specialists. So there's the child-care specialist and there's the household specialist, and there's the woman who walks the dog. Oh, and don't forget the weekend babysitter—I mean, God forbid we should have all these people working for us and actually be able to go out on a Saturday." When I told Frank that women like his wife are only doing what comes naturally, and are, in fact, known by the experts as gatekeepers, he laughed and said, "I can see you know what you're talking about." Yes, indeed I do. Gatekeepers of the world, unite!

In the working couples I interviewed almost all fathers did say that quite often they were the ones rushing home to relieve the nanny, but on balance they felt extremely resentful about having to do so. Not because they felt that this should be the mother's responsibility, but because "I expect the nanny to have flexibility." Cooper, fairly new to his role of nanny employer, with a young wife and six-month-old baby girl, lamented that "this is really not working out the way I thought it would. Our lives already changed so dramatically when Poppy was born, and I naïvely thought having a nanny was supposed to make things easier. Instead it feels like now we're constantly molding our schedules not just around the baby but the nanny as well. With all the hassles we've had with her either showing up late or just point-blank refusing to do certain things, or ever work weekends, I'm just tempted to go with day care instead. Then maybe we could afford a babysitter to actually go out sometimes. My wife won't hear of it, though, because she wants Poppy to have that one-on-one care. It's something she feels a lot more passionately about than I do, so I don't want to push it."

Michael, who happens to wander in to listen during my conversation with his wife, turned out to be the ultimate cynic. Both he and his wife, Zelda, work from home, and are in constant, mutual proximity with their nanny and each other during any given working day. The extent to which their appreciation of Maria's role in their family differed surprised even them.

> ZELDA: "She helps me with everything. She's very steady, very mature. She actually does a lot of things better than me, finding stuff, fixing, organizing."
>
> MICHAEL: "Oh please. Maria simply does what she wants to do. I can think of a number of things she's supposed to be responsible for but never does. Like walk the dog? Make dinner? And she's extremely moody."
>
> ZELDA: "What she earns is a big chunk of my salary, but it's really not much for a person to live on. I don't resent it."
>
> MICHAEL: "Oh, she's definitely overpaid. The money's just a necessary evil—really, these nannies have us over a barrel, don't they?"
>
> ZELDA: "I think it's completely natural for me to give her things, especially if we no longer need them. I always pay her full salary, even if she's worked a few hours less in a week. It all comes out in the wash."

MICHAEL: "I've told Zelda to stop giving her things all the time. It's too much. I think it happens all too easily for people's expectations to change, and they start to take advantage."

The definition of "taking advantage" turns out to be a particularly touchy subject. When Zelda tells me she thinks it was completely inappropriate for a neighbor to ask her (illegal) nanny to paint the garden fence, Michael chips in with, "Well, you could say she was doing her a favor by finding her some work to do." Another moment when all of us actually gasp is when Michael talks about having spoken to the nanny's "previous owner" before he and Zelda decided to employ her. Even though he quickly corrects himself, I'm not certain whether Zelda makes things better or worse for her husband when she goes on to assure me that "Maria does listen to Michael more than me, but that's probably because he says less." There's just no way to get this cat back into the bag.

Michael does get full marks on the self-proclaimed curmudgeon scale, but from a nanny's perspective, too much happy maternal meddling is not necessarily a good thing either. Sharonne was building sand castles with her two-year-old charge, and she interrupted our conversation twice to take a phone call from the child's mother on her cell phone. "She gets so emotional about everything, like I'm supposed to write a report about what we did every minute of the day, and if Fraser seemed happy or not or whatever. She's always talking to me about making sure he's 'engaged,' like some activities are engaging and some aren't engaging, and I'm supposed to know the difference. I feel like her shrink sometimes, you know? With him [Dad], I just tell him, these are my hours, he pays me, and I'm outta there. God, if only the mother could be like that."

I certainly don't want to reinforce the old stereotypes of emotional females doing battle with their rational male counterparts, especially where their mutual offspring is concerned. There are just as many cold and distant mothers dishing out the discipline as there are warm and fuzzy dads handing out the love. And unlike the previously mentioned "experts," the mainstream media seems to have actually caught up with reality in that department, from movies and TV series to glossy celebrity gossip and serious op-ed pieces. Yes, fathers get plenty emotional about their children. They do not, however, tend to get particularly emotional about their child care. Or if they do, it's usually more about frustration with logistics or "worrying about the wacko nannies" than doubts and regrets about another adult forming a deep bond with their children in their formative years.

In this department au pairs prove to be particularly exasperating. Mostly on the young and immature side, often with little child-care experience and limited language skills, these foreign girls have a tendency to drive even the most patient of fathers up the proverbial wall. Dave and his wife have been doing the au pair thing for more than ten years now, and inasmuch as this is possible, have the whole process down to a science. This includes a ten-page "Welcome to our Family" handbook that each au pair is presented with on arrival and is expected to memorize by the end of week one. They've mixed and matched with more girls than either of them care to remember, and as a result of "the annual au pair fender bender," their car insurance premiums are "higher than anyone else's on this planet." If there's one thing Dave knows for sure, it's that he will be better prepared for the trials of parenting teenagers than any of his friends, because he's been through it so many times already.

> The whole big-sister thing does sometimes work out, in theory, but what you've got to realize is, in actuality you end up with another teenager in your house. Oh God, the stories I could tell you. Do you really want to know? Coming home drunk, getting into accidents, hiding a boyfriend under the bed—yes, literally. The crying; the bizarre things they cook.

That's the harmless stuff. There's no getting away from the fact that you have a responsibility toward these girls, though, and much as I've sometimes wanted to, I can't just say, "You're fired." The good ones never stay long enough. With the others it's just like having another kid to be responsible for. I mean, how many people do you know who really knew what they were doing at eighteen? I think in my next life I should be a high-school career counselor. It just makes me feel old.

Old and weary for some, horny for others. It won't come as much of a surprise that none of the fathers I interviewed would admit to ever having lusted after one of their nannies or au pairs, and it's even possible that none of them ever have. Yet anecdotal evidence to the contrary is aplenty: from Jude Law to the Kennedys, and for many ordinary and far less attractive men in between, fantasies about shagging the female help seem to be a common theme. While many fathers like Dave take extra care to never get into anything even remotely resembling a compromising situation with the young women living under their roofs, others just can't seem to help themselves. Charlotte is a local area coordinator for a large au pair agency who has anywhere between a dozen to forty girls (and a few boys) under her wing at any one time. Not only has she heard her fair share of sordid stories, but she has sheltered a few runaways under her own roof, and even shown up personally to rescue others from the unwelcome advances of host fathers. These families immediately get expelled from the program, and one can only imagine what excuses Charlotte must on occasion come up with when trying to explain to a desperate host mother exactly why she won't be sending her another au pair in rematch. "These girls are so vulnerable. It's a horrible experience to have to go through, especially from someone who is supposed to be more like a father figure to them. I would never say that the girls are partly responsible or to blame—these men really should know better."

Clearly, many don't and the circumstances of au-pair'dom seem to be particularly conducive to making some guys lose their heads: An attractive young woman comes to live in your house, to look after your young children who are exhausting and impossibly demanding. Your house is small, money is tight, and sex with your wife has become a distant memory since the arrival of the children. But this young woman looks up to you! She asks you for advice! She wants to please you! It's been four years since you last touched a breast not grotesquely engorged or dripping with breast-milk—what harm would it really do to stumble accidentally-on-purpose into the bathroom while the au pair was undressing for her shower? Or to brush up against her a little closer than necessary in the hallway, or to take a smile at dinner as an invitation to steal into her room and attempt to climb into her bed at night? The justifications are easy to imagine, the ramifications much harder, particularly in terms of the pain and humiliation they are bound to cause for everyone involved.

For the man you love to start acting out his sexual fantasies with the (usually younger) woman who is supposed to take care of your children must be the most bitter kind of betrayal, not to mention how it feels for the one who is at the receiving end of the unwanted attention. Mila from Poland is a dark-haired, big-bosomed beauty who has had to move families twice because her host fathers just couldn't keep their hands to themselves. "It's just disgusting. You feel sorry for them. Is like they think they have a right to touch you or something, and with the mother right there, she does nothing! Now I lock my door every time, I wear big sweater. Is really sad for these families."

As proof for just how sad, one need look no further than the now-blighted career of actor Jude Law, who famously had sex with his kids' nanny while his new and gorgeous fiancée was off filming a movie. In the words of Helen Fielding's chronically childless heroine Bridget Jones all that's really left to say is "Oh dear. Really wanted a little baby to love. Though not, obviously, weekend nanny to shag ex-husband, if had ex-husband . . ." Husband or ex, baby or no, it seems that shagging the nanny is an unforgivable sin universally reviled by all. So just in case you have a choice, Dave'll give you one piece of advice for free: "The more homely looking, the better."

According to fathers, what are the factors (other than looks) that make for a good nanny? The answers to this question were surprisingly varied, long, and thoughtful, and not a single one implied that no special skills would be needed because "it's only babysitting and anyone can do it." Final proof, in case we still want it, that fathers care every bit as much as mothers what type of person is spending time alone with their children. While the moms' wish list could almost always be boiled down to "loving, warm, and safe," with a few optional extras, my dad interviewees displayed a lot more creativity and pragmatism, and expressed it in efficient shorthand to boot.

> "Perfect nanny is respected and liked by children. Knows to teach through doing, and is a good example. Should think like a family member and pro at same time."
>
> "A caring nature, patience, intelligence, and an ability to impose discipline and provide privacy to family when needed."
>
> "Someone who truly cares, whom you can trust completely, and who works really hard, with a good attitude."
>
> "Maturity and a strong relationship with the children."
>
> "A: loves the kids and puts them above all else; b: organized and can cope on her own; c: emotionally stable."
>
> "Spending quality time with the child: playing, talking, listening, interacting; also, knowing to recede into the background when the parents are around."
>
> "Reliability; engagement in the responsibilities of the position; pleasant disposition; attention to detail and safety."
>
> And finally: "Experience, good attitude, faith." Amen!

With the exception of "entrepreneurial" and a $250,000 salary, Donald Trump himself could not have offered a better overall description of a winning apprentice. Just as Anne Crittenden said in the title of her book, *If You've Raised Kids, You Can Manage Anything.*

Because reality so often falls short of the wish list, I also asked a few fathers how they would prioritize. In and of themselves the answers were not surprising, but once again the vocabulary was, especially since looking after children is so often such an inherently messy affair:

As one father put it,

> I would sum it up as hygiene. The basics you need to have covered before you can walk out the door in the morning; you have to trust the nanny to keep the children safe and moderately entertained. Anything over and above that is nice but not strictly necessary.
>
> For me, it's also the point where the real value-added comes in: I like to have a nanny who'll pitch in and is flexible, and someone I can talk to as equals rather than conducting every conversation through my wife and children. If the relationship is going to last, those elements have to be there, but we've had both short term and long term. Sometimes you need to put up with bare-bones hygiene to give you the space to look for someone who's a better fit.

Above all, as Ronald put it, "the one thing doomed to failure is approaching this type of work expecting the world owes you a living, and treating it as just a job." The only surprising thing, given the long list of skills and job qualifications fathers looked for in their nanny, was that this did not generally correlate to a willingness to pay higher wages. This then is perhaps the last vestige of the old gender stereotypes we're all working so hard to get rid of.

the other
women

maggie: the first
corrupt bargain

W
HEN MY HUSBAND and I married in our early twenties little did we know that moving to New York City to start our first "real" jobs and living together in our first grown-up apartment was not just the beginning of a fantastic adventure, but also the beginning of the proverbial end. Now in our midforties we are not, by any means, old (that is, unless you ask our children), but thinking back to those fabulous prebaby days, Oscar Wilde's wistful notion that "youth is wasted on the young" seems more true than ever. We might have been free of work and child-care hassles once, and it must have been fun for a while, but we definitely didn't appreciate it nearly enough while it lasted, and it definitely didn't last nearly long enough.

Leaving the Big Apple for a European adventure as a carefree couple of yuppies and returning as a family of three would be a rude awakening for anyone, and it certainly was for us. The time was the midnineties, and because we clearly needed more space we immediately got sucked into the complicated business of selling one apartment in order to buy and renovate another. I was also pregnant with baby number two and continuing to drum up as much freelance work as I could find. Clearly more child care was needed.

How did people handle finding a babysitter in New York? We turned to more experienced friends, followed by our initiation into the New York Caribbean nanny mafia. Rather than messing with ads or expensive agencies, we were told that by far the best thing to do would be to get the word out through one or two particularly well-connected nannies. We did, and soon we were fielding phone calls from all over the Bronx, Brooklyn, and Harlem.

After a highly unscientific interview process (hand her the baby and see what happens), I selected Maggie. She was large, Jamaican, and sported impeccably painted bright red fingernails. I hired her simply because I liked her, and because my insufferably energetic toddler went straight to sleep draped over her ample shoulder— something she had never done for me. The clincher (an important fact for Virgo neat freaks like myself): Maggie and I shared exactly the same birthday, same day, same year. As for the rest, different planets would just about begin to cover it.

Together she and I became a part of what Barbara Ehrenreich calls "the global heart transplant," in her book *Global Woman: Nannies, Maids, and Sex Workers in the New Economy.* Maggie's son Jackson, a rebellious fourteen-year-old, was in Jamaica, and my daughter was with Maggie, while I was someplace else writing catalogue copy and press releases, thinking about bathroom fixtures and whether this time I might have a boy. The money Maggie made supported Jackson and her mother, with whom he lived; eventually Maggie hoped to bring them both over to live with her and her new husband.

To forestall a feminist guilt attack I paid her generously, showered her with hand-me-downs to send to her family, and tried my best to be friends. Despite my good intentions, little did I know that the "presents" I was giving her—all perfectly nice things that I no longer wanted after the move—were little short of an insult to this very proud woman, who certainly didn't want my castoffs. All she really wanted was for me to get out of her hair so that she could get on with the job and make her own arrangements for play dates with other children and their nannies—her friends.

Anyone who has ever lived in New York for any length of time, with or without children, will have seen evidence of the ubiquitous Caribbean nanny circuit. In other cities, depending on geographic proximity and tradition, it might be predominantly Latinas or Filipinas—whatever their nationality, the difference in class and race between the women who push the strollers and the white children sitting in them is immediately evident.

The nannies walk up and down the avenues, wait outside preschools at pick-up time, and hang around the park benches near the playgrounds to chew the fat. I was very explicit with Maggie when I hired her that I didn't want her to talk about us, and what went on in our home, with anybody. She nodded sincerely and assured me that of course she wouldn't do such a thing. I, of course, was young and dumb enough to believe her. I probably would have done the same in her position—what, after all, is more fun to gossip about than (sometimes literally) your employer's dirty underwear? Added to their visa status, green-card applications, and stories from home was the latest ridiculous, thigh-slapping-funny rule that little Dick and Jane's mother has dreamed up to torture both children and nanny.

Since that time, as I felt this book taking shape in my mind, I've had quite a few conversations with Maggie, now working as a nurse's aide and no longer beholden to me or my family in any way. When George Bernard Shaw talked about Americans and Englishmen being "separated by a common language," little did he know that one day his words could be applied just as accurately to New York City mothers and their nannies. Same words, different meaning, then and now: Just ask what exactly either one means by "a little light housekeeping," "discipline," or "nutritious food."

Slowly but surely Maggie and I worked out a tentative equilibrium, with the understanding that I might make suggestions, but she made the rules: with whom my toddler had play dates (the children of her friends); when she ate, bathed, and napped; and which activities fit into her schedule. In truth I was far more intimidated by Maggie than she was by me, and her arrival signaled the first of many corrupt bargains that I've struck between me, my conscience, and my love for my children where their nannies were concerned. Maggie might have scared the daylights out of me, but that was just fine as long as I was able to believe that she truly loved my daughter and would throw herself in front of a truck to save her life.

And this I believed she would. With her own son inaccessible to her in Jamaica, on whom else should she lavish all that desperate longing, love, and affection? My perfectly adorable, freckle-faced daughter, and half a year later her brand-new baby sister, were entirely enveloped in Maggie's big, warm love, from their strawberry-blond heads right down to their sweet, pink toes. I needed help, she needed work, and we all needed each other. It just goes to show that a lot of love and a little bit of cash can go a long, long way. Sadly, as far as Jackson was concerned, only the cash made it all the way down to Jamaica.

Whatever the twisted logic, our arrangement worked, including the little "light housekeeping" Maggie did without my asking by cleaning the children's room and doing their laundry and dishes. I had heard enough horror stories from friends and acquaintances to know that upsetting the applecart just wasn't worth it. Serial-nanny mommies were a miserable breed, and I did not want to be one of them.

One year later, ever the pragmatist, my husband pointed out that the money we paid Maggie was almost exactly equal to what I made with the few freelance projects and assignments I'd managed to cobble together. After a family conference it was decided that my plans to attend business school at Columbia should be postponed (indefinitely, as it turned out), and that we would all move to Hong Kong to take up a great opportunity my husband's company had offered him. As the main breadwinner the decision was clearly his to make and mine to agree to—after all, what better time in his life as a professional and our life as a family, with tiny, rootless children, to move around the world, all expenses paid?

In what he and I believed to be an entirely benign and well-meaning gesture, we "offered" Maggie to my brother and his wife, who had just had a baby boy and lived in a cool loft in SoHo. It turned out that the relationship between Maggie and their family lasted far longer than ours, and that luckily it was a good fit—yet it was only years later that I found out how common, demeaning, and infuriating to the nannies this sort of farming out actually is. The receiving end of good intentions isn't always a pleasant place to be.

amanda: upsetting
the applecart

Two weeks before we left for Hong Kong, with our life's possessions already in boxes and halfway across the world, twenty-one-year-old Amanda, Mandy for short, arrived from England to be our nanny. We had found her through a fancy London agency and, unlike Maggie, she was a "trained professional."

Home of Mary Poppins and *Upstairs, Downstairs*, Britain continues to be the only Western country where nannies can receive two years of official training at various nanny academies. The best of the schools award their graduates a bona fide degree, and the accompanying certificate, bearing the Queen's own seal. This credential assures the prospective parent employers of the nanny's ability to prepare nutritious meals, organize creative and stimulating activities, perform CPR and other lifesaving procedures, discipline unruly children when necessary, and perform all other tasks critical to the smooth running of a nursery.

Mandy was a jolly, rather pretty, almost middle-class white girl from a small town a few hours north of London. She had ambitions to travel the world and eventually meet Mr. Right, get married, stop working, have children of her own, and live in a semidetached faux Victorian house in a genteel British suburb. There had been plenty before her who had followed the same path, the very picture of blue-collar professionalism and upward mobility in a society that was still as class-bound as it had ever been.

For my husband and me somehow the notion of moving to Hong Kong with a "British nanny" was a great deal less terrifying than showing up there with no one to help us settle in and take care of the toddler and the baby. In reality, the notion of bringing Maggie, or someone like her, with us was, quite frankly, completely absurd—pretty much akin to throwing a baby into the lion's den. From previous visits to Hong Kong and China in the late eighties, my husband and I knew that few people will discriminate more openly and unapologetically against people who look different from them than the vast majority of Chinese. Less than a decade later, with a few, all-important exceptions, the local Hong Kong people among whom we lived and worked tolerated *gweilos* (white people) like us only because we had money and usually brought with us the possibility of greater business success and material prosperity. At that time this was a far more important concern to the average Hong Kong citizen than human rights or racial equality, even after Tiananmen Square. As a rather large, African Caribbean woman, Maggie probably would have attracted both crowds, open ridicule, and scorn. Certainly no one would have known how to deal with or address her, and her status in the Confucian pecking order would have been even lower than Hong Kong's approximately 250,000 Filipina maids. They, at least, were Asian!

At first, Mandy was lovely. She took over the care of the children with the ease of the professional she so clearly was, and immediately instituted her own set of rules by which they seemed to thrive. Unlike Maggie's rather musical lilt, Mandy's language was crisp and direct, brooking no misunderstandings and setting very clear limits. These included how the children, her proper little charges, were expected to behave, how much I was permitted to interfere in her domain as a "full-time, sole-charge" nanny, and exactly what she was prepared to do and what was clearly outside the realm of her responsibilities. The latter included any type of housework whatsoever, with the sole exception of preparing the children's meals.

Not surprisingly, in the absence of a household staff of cook and maids, all of this jolly good Mary Poppins stuff soon began to grate on me. While my husband was putting in twelve-hour days trying to establish himself in this foreign place, I did every bit of the cooking, cleaning, shopping, and laundry, and Mandy was out playing with the children; at least so it seemed. On more than one occasion she expressed surprise that I hadn't yet employed a Filipina amah for all the housework—wasn't this what all expatriate families did? Even though she couldn't really be faulted for asking the question, there was still something about it that rubbed me entirely the wrong way. First, it seemed to imply that my unique and incomparably wonderful family was really no different from any other that fit the general expat mold. How could she not see that we were special, unusual, comparable to no one? Second, she seemed to be hinting (subtlety was not her strong suit) that had she known that she would be expected to pitch in with the household chores, she probably wouldn't have taken the job. The fact that she might have had a point (or two . . .) was not a mitigating factor. I didn't like her and she was to blame.

Most irritating, while Mandy was busy assuming that she and I should act like friends, I was alternating between just plain dislike and feeling like her maid and butler. Chitchatting in the kitchen over cups of tea (which I washed, never she), Mandy loved sharing gossip about other mothers in our little compound of apartments, to which I listened with reluctant fascination. Gossip about her also reached my hungry ears, and to this I listened with far less reluctance. Several neighbors told me that when she went out with the children, almost everyone mistook her for their mother and treated her accordingly, a fact that she rarely bothered to correct and clearly enjoyed. Adding fuel to the fire, I took this as an extraordinary and glaring violation of the rules on the circuit of toddler life: mothers and children among other mothers and children simply do not conduct themselves in the same way when one in their midst is not the Real Thing. The unwritten laws of the nursery clearly state that play dates can be arranged only when the adults present to supervise (coffee or cup of tea in hand) are either *all* mothers or *all* nannies. To pass oneself off as Mama when one is not is akin to the worst kind of espionage and betrayal.

Outwardly, we continued to be civil and friendly, but inwardly my resentment grew as I felt her taking over my life and our home. For the first few months, the process of moving, unpacking, figuring the place out, and just settling in turned out to be so time-consuming that the notion of making a change in our child-care arrangements was simply inconceivable. While she went to the beach or the playground with the children, I worked to set up house, unpack boxes, lease a car, sort out health insurance, figure out the supermarket, set up bank accounts, have the phone connected, and all the other countless, menial, and time-consuming tasks associated with learning to live in a new country at the same time as trying to find a job.

Meanwhile, her presence seemed to spread to the point where it felt as though she had taken up residence in every room, closet, cupboard, and corner of my existence. While by Hong Kong standards our apartment was positively palatial, coming from a brownstone loft in New York the place seemed small, poky, and increasingly claustrophobic. Mandy was everywhere. At the table when we had dinner, in the living room at night when my husband and I wanted to talk, and all over the bathroom that she rather begrudgingly had to share with the children. My husband made no bones about the fact that he hated her, which put me in the absurd position of having to defend her or play down the fact that I probably hated her even more.

A month or so later I started to work again, as a writer and account director in a local PR agency, and made feeble excuses about how much the children loved her and how much trouble it would be to find someone new. Once again, I worked hard at convincing myself that what I felt didn't really matter, as long as I could be sure the affection between her and the children was deep and genuine. Yet more and more often we would find ourselves retreating to the bedroom and speaking in whispers so she wouldn't hear. "You've got to get rid of her, please, I can't stand this any longer!" my husband would implore me in the morning as we kissed good-bye and both went off to work. Clearly, firing the nanny is a dirty job, and Mama's got to do it.

It may no longer be a colony, but at that time Hong Kong was certainly still an expatriate paradise, teeming with husbands on fat, perk-rich packages. Their upper-middle-class wives played a lot of tennis, drove the children back and forth to private schools, play dates, and activities, and thus made friends with the other wives and families. We, too, followed this pattern (though we were clearly still as unique, special, and different as we had ever been . . .). The only exception was that Mandy was doing the driving rather than I, and the other mommies with whom I might have become friends were instantly suspicious and generally annoyed with me for having a life and a job outside of our compound, thus disproving the widely held belief that expat wives don't work.

So there we were, barely five months into our Asian adventure, with practically no social life, a nanny we hated, and both of us work-ing our tails off. Something had to give, and not surprisingly it was Mandy. The sad truth was that in large part I had started working as soon as I did to get away from her, and of course do something to pay her fairly substantial salary, which once again ate up a disproportion-ately large part of mine.

The turning point came when both my husband and I realized that contrary to what we had been telling ourselves, we saw real evidence (finally!) that she clearly favored one of our daughters over the other. Yet still I didn't find the courage to confront her with all the reasons why I could simply no longer bear to have her under my roof, and made up another reason for sending her back to England: We wanted our children to learn German, my mother tongue, and the language spoken at the international school they would eventually go to. We were going to find a German nanny, and Mandy would have to go home, very sorry, but that's the way it was.

In the end it turned ugly, as these things inevitably do when you don't tell the truth. I gave her a less than glowing reference, and made no bones about the fact that she might have taken decent care of the children, but had totally blown it when it came to us, the parents, and especially me, the mother. This obviously stymied her chances at an-other glamorous international posting and she was furious. On two days' notice she threw a monumental hissy fit, declared her honor sul-lied, and left in a flurry of suitcases, tears, and recriminations.

Later, she wrote me (no mention of my husband) one of the ugli-est letters I've ever received. In it she told me in no uncertain terms that I was a bad mother, a bitch and a coward who had used and abused her, and that because of me she would now not get the job she really deserved. All this because I didn't have the courage to face up to the fact that I was really a sneaky, snobbish, upper-class toff who felt threatened by competent, working-class people like her who might not have lots of money and education. But (nyah nyah nyah nyaaaah nyah!) wasn't it obvious that she could clearly do my job—looking after my children—far better than I could myself?

Ouch. One for Mandy, zero for Mama. Time to change tactics. Maybe the German nanny thing really was a good idea! No centuries-old class system in Germany to fall foul of, *richtig?*

Besides the relief I felt at our collective Mandy liberation, I had to admit to myself that she was right about one thing: I did think I was better than her. I still do, and always will, even if that means Mandy was probably right when she called me a sneaky snob. The biggest mistake I made was not to trust my gut from the start and admit that there has to be more to a good nanny than just competence and nice references: If I don't like her after one week, I will never like her, and my children, bless their expansive little hearts and trusting souls, will jolly well have to put up with whomever I tell them to.

irma and abela: everyone's doing it

RATHER PREDICTABLY, toward the end of the Mandy debacle I finally caved and hired a Filipina amah, a sweet and very soft-spoken single woman in her forties by the name of Irma. As we launched the search for a German-speaking nanny, for the next few months Irma and I rather frantically shared the task of looking after the children during the part of the day they were not in the local version of day care. The latter was actually a Montessori-type arrangement set up by someone with questionable qualifications in a rabbit-warren-like apartment close to ours. But the adult-to-child ratio was amazing—lots of cheap labor in a place like Hong Kong! And "they" do love children.

They: Other Filipinas just a step above Irma in the local hierarchy, all of them working at far less than what would be considered minimum wage in the United States. The amah's salary is actually an official rate set by the Hong Kong government, which pragmatically legislates that every Hong Kong Chinese family is entitled to the cheapest possible full-time domestic help.

With the rapid growth of the former colony's economy and wealth in the post–World War II years, came the familiar notion that this type of work was beneath the average Hong Kong citizen. Nothing could have been more natural than to hand it off to women hailing from poorer Southeast Asian nations like Thailand, the Philippines, or Indonesia—how else to become an economic superpower? Never mind democracy; the rules of the market are the rules of life.

In accordance with her contract, issued and ratified by a special government agency, we paid Irma the officially stipulated monthly wage of approximately five hundred dollars a month. We always added some cash on the side, but were certainly not obliged to. In return she was at our disposal for twelve hours a day, six days a week of "domestic help," and was given her own room and bathroom, literally the size of a closet off the kitchen—a standard feature in millions of Hong Kong apartments.

I was mortified to show it to her, but she appeared thrilled. At her previous job, with a Chinese family, she had had to sleep on the floor in the pantry, which she admitted to me with a shy little giggle and shrug as though this arrangement were her fault. The prospect of a room of her own, although it looked out over the air shaft and had previously been home to our luggage and spare boxes, was evidently a big step up in the world.

I was working too hard at juggling everything to torture myself about the contradictions inherent in my domestic arrangement. Instead, I equivocated: After all, the kids were happy and everyone's doing it. And where would Irma be if she weren't working for me? Either unemployed and poor back in the Philippines, or, God forbid, still working for that Chinese family and sleeping on the floor. Would that not be infinitely worse?

At least with us she had a proper bed and could eat all she wanted from our overstuffed American refrigerator. She had no children of her own, but the money she sent back home every month paid for a decent education for at least half a dozen nieces and nephews. Occasionally it bought expensive medicines for other relatives, or paid for a bribe to get one of her clan a job, a driver's license, or another type of leg up in an economy that is both deeply corrupt and highly dependent on the foreign currency supplied by the hard labor of its citizens working as virtual domestic slaves in wealthier countries.

As for Hong Kong's expats, many of them otherwise compassionate and politically correct Americans, no one could quite believe their luck at having all this cheap domestic help at their fingertips. At first each of them (us?) went through a stage of worrying about becoming complicit in the exploitation of the amahs, but in the end everyone succumbed— my husband and myself included. It was simply too good to resist and, after all, bound to be merely a brief and temporary phase of our lives before we all returned home and would have to start doing all the work ourselves again. Or else, pay someone a proper salary to do it.

The trials and tribulations of having amahs frequently came up during dinner party conversations. The absurd phrase that inevitably put the genie back into the bottle was that "an amah here makes as much money as a brain surgeon in the Philippines!" This was usually followed by a story about how someone's amah had been mistreated by her previous Chinese employer, and how grateful she was to have found such a nice, Western family. Weren't they all lucky to be working for us! Ah, the hypocrisy. But there was also undeniable truth in everything that was said. The money Irma made was indeed critical to her family's survival back home, and I know for certain that she earned significantly more and had a far better life with us than she had had in her previous job. What exactly were we guilty of? What should I have done differently?

Either way, someone got screwed, and nothing I could do would ever change the system. So I chose to go along with it, treat Irma as kindly and fairly as possible, and console myself with the fact that at least she hadn't left her own children behind in the Philippines, as so many other amahs were forced to do. Small consolation, as it later turned out, since Irma would have loved to have children and a family of her own but was unable to conceive. There clearly was no good answer other than to get on with life, not abuse one's power, and think about it as little as possible.

I did, and my career continued to thrive. I moved to a great job managing corporate communications and regional marketing for a major Asian property consulting firm. Now after taxes I made enough money to pay for the new nanny, her minute apartment, her overtime, Irma's salary (no overtime), and my taxi fares to and from work. There was even a bit left over for upgrading and dry cleaning my work wardrobe, and buying presents to placate the children when they complained that I wasn't home as much as other mommies.

In the company where I worked white working mothers were somewhat of an anomaly. Most of my colleagues immediately assumed that I didn't need the money, knowing, as they did, that my husband worked for a large American company and was sure to be on a generous package. As a result they paid me the least they could get away with, particularly given the fact that I refused to work a half day on Saturdays, as most people in Hong Kong still do. That fact alone probably reduced what I earned by a third, and of course signaled to the management that while I might have been very good at my job I wasn't really serious about Making It. This was another dilemma to which there clearly was no good answer other than to keep doing a job that I enjoyed and think about it as little as possible.

Life certainly kept going: Baby number three was born, and went straight into the nanny's welcoming arms, swaddled in the sheets that Irma washed and ironed every day. The other expat wives with children still looked at me with a combination of envy and resentment, but by now I'd made enough good friends not to care anymore. Six months later I still loved my job, but pumping breast milk in the toilet was beginning to feel ridiculous and sad. What is more, the rest of my coworkers—almost without exception Hong Kong Chinese working five and a half days every week—also resented me for the special treatment I appeared to be getting as a white *tai-tai,* or literally, "spoiled wife."

Standard maternity leave in Hong Kong is ten unpaid weeks, including a mandatory three weeks' prior to one's due date. There is no guarantee that the same job will be available once the leave is complete, and in fact a demotion in both responsibility and pay is considered almost standard. The notion that a woman might lose her job entirely as a result of having a baby was something everyone simply took for granted. Bonding? Breast feeding? Getting up in the night to feed your own child and rock her back to sleep? Aiyaah, you Americans are so sentimental. Have the amah take the bunk bed in the children's room so you can sleep through the night. What's she there for, after all?

Soon after my third daughter turned two, I decided to quit, rent myself a little office, and start freelancing instead, naturally with my old company as my first client. Without a steady salary our nanny once again made more money than I, but I justified this by how much fun I was finally having in my fledgling career as a journalist, not to mention the flexibility it offered me to spend more time with my daughters. I tried not to think too much about the cost of the nanny's apartment. My husband could bloody well pay the amah's salary. It wasn't as if he hadn't also come to take for granted all the things she did for us. She didn't earn that much anyway!

After Irma had been with us for four years it became clear that at some point we would have to leave Hong Kong. At that time the rules stated that we would be able to take an amah with us only if she had worked for us for a minimum of one year. For Irma, the thought of moving to the United States or England—so cold, so foreign, and so far away—was more than she was willing to bear, and so we parted ways. When I gave her a check that was the equivalent of four months of her salary, a payment actually required under Hong Kong law, she burst into tears. It appeared that her previous employer had never bothered to comply with this pesky little rule and, having no recourse to any sort of legal representation, she had been forced to simply let it go.

In Irma's place we found Abela, young, ambitious, and just dying to get out of Hong Kong. I knew that bringing her with us wouldn't be easy, but I was determined to try, both for her and for us. By the summer of 2001, what was supposed to be a stint of two years in Hong Kong had turned into more than three times that long, and was finally ended by the proverbial seven-year itch.

My husband and I both knew that in terms of leaving our artificial, expat paradise for "home" it had to be now or never. All of our acquaintances who had stayed to live and work in Asia beyond seven or eight years had found it impossible to leave. We had strayed dangerously close to that line, seduced by the exotic ease and opulence of our life as privileged outsiders in a foreign land, but ultimately realized that neither we, nor our children, could ever truly belong there.

Once a decision was made the juggernaut of international corporate transfers went into action, and on my thirty-eighth birthday we arrived in the States: My husband, the patriarch king, his harem of wife, daughters one, two, three, and two-month-old baby daughter number four tucked into the hand luggage, followed by the housekeeper. Having been nomads for so many years, my husband and I thought that we would finally strike roots, while Abela happily tagged along on our coattails, attracted by the bright lure of a future in America. There were many other attractions, of course: a great public school system for our children; relatives around the corner; a place to ride bikes that wasn't the roof of a multistory parking lot; and the proverbial white picket fence around our beautiful garden. We would get an SUV and a dog, and Abela would plant a vegetable garden and get married, pretty much in that order. Just two weeks later we watched in speechless horror with everyone else as the towers fell, and counted ourselves lucky to be alive.

For Abela, coming to the United States was a dream come true— the great and shining reward for five years of constant domestic drudgery (plus the last two years with us), and the ultimate escape from the poverty of her rural upbringing. She set out to marry and have children of her own, and did indeed find an American husband within six months. Since after 9/11 no one in her family stood a chance of getting a U.S. tourist visa, my husband stepped in as father of the bride at her wedding. Needless to say, I cried.

Almost four years later she continues to work for us, but for double her previous salary and less than half of the hours. After enduring her third New England winter, she desperately misses home and longs to start a family of her own. As for me, I pray that she finally gets the baby she so desperately wants, and secretly regret that this will probably mean she will leave us. My husband's pragmatic "we'll get someone else" simply does not begin to address the bottomless well of feelings I have for this woman. She, who has held my babies, cleaned up after them and me, and on countless mornings taken a screaming child out of my arms with a reassuring "just go" when I was desperate to get—well, here. To the office and my research; to the library, with my laptop. To write, about this strange and tortured relationship I have with the women who look after my children while I "work." What her feelings are for me, I can only begin to fathom. Without a doubt there is a good measure of gratitude, respect, and real affection, but I am also certain there are many times when she grits her teeth and does as I ask, simply because I am the boss. I'm sure she talks about me with her husband and friends, and regardless of how well we get along during her days, I'm sure the stories are not always friendly. After all, she is literally doing my dirty work. For that, if nothing else, I am just grateful she's there.

cecilia: how much for that baby?

ONCE MANDY HAD LEFT, we turned to the surprisingly difficult task of finding a German-speaking nanny. After placing ads in several German newspapers and recruiting various relatives to screen out unsuitable candidates among the dozens of semiretired cooks and housekeepers who responded, we settled on Cilla, short for Cecilia: twenty-four, recently unemployed from a factory town in the Rhineland, with good references and one previous nanny job for a German family in England under her belt. The fact that she "wanted to see the world" and "quickly made friends wherever she went" probably should have set my alarm bells ringing, but unfortunately she must have been wearing her flaming red long hair in a demure chignon, as well as a bulky turtleneck and dumpy snow boots, when my older sister interviewed her on a snowy day in December.

In Hong Kong's tropical climate Cilla no longer had any reason to conceal her breasts, which were large, gorgeous, usually braless, and extremely jiggly due to the girlish spring in her step. She took excellent care of the children during the day, and was really very good at making up all sorts of games to force them to speak German. They, of course, loved her jiggly boobs and pawed them with abandon—a sight that stopped many a sexually repressed Chinese man in his tracks in the streets, and caused at least one fender bender.

Much to his amusement, my husband enjoyed a newfound respect among the men in our neighborhood, nudge, nudge, wink, wink. As for me, I liked Cilla very much, despite the fact that my subtle suggestions to perhaps wear less suggestive clothing from time to time fell on deaf ears. She was irrepressibly cheerful, didn't mind pitching in, and was a fearless and competent driver—an invaluable skill in the urban canyons of Hong Kong. What is more, she took the children to all sorts of exciting local places that prim and proper Mandy wouldn't have touched with a barge pole, and could wind even the most grumpy and recalcitrant Chinese official, doorman, or parking lot attendant around her little you-know-what.

Unfortunately, her craving for excitement didn't end with finding new adventures for her and the children to try in daylight hours. Within the first week she was out almost nightly, making friends wherever she went and getting free drinks at the *gweilo*-scene bars and clubs. These were populated mostly by young, attractive (or not) white guys hanging out with exquisitely beautiful Chinese women. Often they couldn't understand much of what the men were saying, because much of the time English was a second language for both. To put it politely, body language counted for a lot more than conversation, as did the promise of exotic sex and alcohol—a heady combination.

This *gweilo* scene was at the heart of Hong Kong's thriving population of aspiring small-time entrepreneurs and dreamers from all over the world trying to make their fortunes in China. During the day they would work crazy hours, dreaming up countless schemes and setting up little companies, each with the unspoken motto of "If I could only sell *one* toothbrush to every Chinese . . ." And then at night they partied—with Cilla.

It took only two months for her to fall in love, and two more for her to get pregnant. The father was a dashing marble-tile sales rep whose Catholic upbringing Italian style clearly encouraged sex before marriage, but not necessarily marriage itself. Confronted by Cilla, who was thrilled at the prospect of being pregnant and wanted to get married, he denounced her as a whore, declared that it was all a trick to ensnare him, and made it very clear that if she chose to have the baby it would be the end of their relationship. She did, and it was.

Unfortunately, at this point I was also pregnant again, just a couple of months ahead of Cilla, working full-time and completely unprepared to deal with the debilitating morning sickness and quite heartbreaking dilemma of my nanny. She would have to leave, that much was clear to both of us, because the only people willing to support her and the only place where she and her baby would have health insurance was with her parents back in Germany.

On top of that, she was pretty much broke. She had come to us with no savings, and had routinely spent the all the money we paid her, usually in cash—it isn't for nothing that Hong Kong is known as a shopper's paradise. Following Massimo's rejection, she was obviously heartbroken and could barely muster the energy to get out of bed, much less do the demanding job of looking after my five- and three-year-old daughters. Meanwhile, I had no choice but to head to work every day, trying vainly not to overdo it for the sake of my own growing belly.

So for the first but not the last time, I was forced to ask myself the question: what's a baby worth? Mine, conceived in love and marriage, and Cilla's, conceived in a moment of passion with no thought for the future. At birth they would be practically indistinguishable, wrinkled little bundles of sinew, flesh, and bone, and the deep blue eyes with which all newborns first look upon the world and the exhausted faces of their mothers.

I was sure Cilla would be a wonderful mother, but how daunting the thought of what was before her, the things she'd have to do just to get by. Not for her the luxury of a nanny, or the choice of career versus family, staying home or not. In the end I paid for Cilla's ticket home, and gave her a suitcase full of baby stuff and a check equivalent to four months of her salary—more or less the same amount of time that she had been with us.

For the first few years I heard nothing from her except a brief announcement of the birth of her son, Lorenzo—return address care of her parents. Since then I have written her a couple of references and know that she is married, has a second son, and is living somewhere in Bavaria. I can only hope that nursing her two children didn't ruin the best feature of her anatomy, as it had mine (times four), and that her husband is a kind man.

valery: the real mary poppins

FOLLOWING THE CILLA DEBACLE, once again my husband and I turned to the "professionals." For a huge fee another discreet London agency screened out unsuitable applicants and ultimately found Valery, complete with prerequisite diploma, references, and experience with "families abroad." This time we decided to take no chances, and to interview her in person during our summer vacation. Finally, we got lucky: Like Mandy, Valery had a good, strong northern English accent, but came without the accompanying chip on her shoulder. She stayed for the next five years.

I wax nostalgic, but those really were the best years. In many ways I still think about my life in terms of before Valery and after. Certainly there were times when we bickered, but mostly we really were friends who truly appreciated the insights each other had about the people we both loved most: the children, of course.

Other factors that oiled the wheels of our relationship was our shared addiction to Malteser chocolates and Wensleydale cheese and a very silly fondness for Monty Python jokes. We also both enjoyed rolling our eyes at each other behind my husband's back as he occasionally tried but failed to pack a proper diaper bag or identify the children's favorite stuffed animals by name. Poor man—faced with Valery and me, I think no father in the world could *ever* have packed a diaper bag to our complete satisfaction.

Despite my husband's shortcomings on the child-transportation-logistics side, he and Valery had a great friendship of their own, completely separate from mine. It didn't have all that much to do with the children, and the fact was that they simply enjoyed each other's company and would talk about all sorts of things. Yes, I do boast when I say that Valery is still our friend, our youngest daughter's godmother, and a frequent and always welcome visitor in our home.

She is also a legend among our friends. I think all of them would have gladly stolen her away if they weren't certain that my husband and I would have had them publicly flogged, humiliated, and forever excommunicated from the circle of good and decent people in the world. For working mothers, nanny theft is the one unforgivable sin, every bit as bad as snatching bread from the hands of a starving child.

While we were still in Hong Kong I never knew—nor asked—how Valery felt about the fact that she, quite obviously, was paid approximately three times as much as Irma, and later Abela. Within the little corporation that was our household, the hierarchy and order of command was clear: I was the chairman of the board, who would take over in the evenings and on weekends, and make most executive decisions. Valery was the acting CEO, Irma the secretary, and the children the go-fers and minions.

If there had to be a title for my husband, I suppose it would have to be king, since the extent to which he was actually aware, much less involved in, all the down-and-dirty details of our domestic arrangements was pretty much zero. What's more, he had to travel frequently all over Asia and, in order to do justice to his extremely stressful and lucrative job he needed to be 100 percent certain that no constraints would ever be placed on his schedule.

Together Valery and I made sure of that. With her I felt for the first and only time that I had found a true partner in all the work, time, effort, and love that it takes to raise happy children and make a family grow up together. Where Mandy had simply rubbed me the wrong way with her assumption that she should be my equal, Valery never assumed but simply was. Not, quite emphatically, in the sense that she was or wanted to be a substitute mother, but simply in the sense that she took over where I left off. Because she had such a natural and commonsense confidence in herself and her relationship to the children, I was able to trust her completely and was no doubt a better mother to them because of it. Not to mention the fact that she was—and still is—extremely smart, very funny, and altogether incredibly capable. She is, of course, a Virgo just like me.

Although Valery is clearly an uncommonly good nanny and altogether wonderful person, there are also a number of important lessons in the success of our relationship. I do not consider myself an expert, but at least by now I have a pretty good idea of what works for me. Start with a no-brainer: I've got to like her and she's got to like me. I treat her as a professional, because that's what she is. I try not to be chummy and end up belittling what she does by asking, "So what will you do when you get a *real* job?" I made that mistake only once.

Money is important: I pay her as much as I can possibly afford. I never, ever undermine her in front of the children. I try really hard to come home when I say I will. I try never to make her change plans she's already made. I grit my teeth and try to have the humility to know that sometimes she knows better. I have the confidence to know that no child has ever loved his or her nanny better than his or her mother. I try to never forget that she works for me, and that no matter how much we like to paint a rosy picture of all being one happy family, we are not—she has her own family, and as much as she may love my children, they are not hers. Finally, I trust the references I get from other mothers only as far as I trust and like those other mothers. Sometimes that isn't very much. And otherwise, just like everyone else, I somehow muddle through.

In the end, our return to the States and my (reluctant) settling into quasi-suburban nonworking motherhood and complete financial dependence on my husband spelled the demise of our working relationship. Both Valery and I are really city creatures at heart, and being cooped up together in this big old house in small-town New England would have been a recipe for disaster. She was used to running the show, having her own place to live, and heading to all sorts of exotic destinations for fun and games after work. There's not much of that around here. Ultimately we both agreed that in order for us to remain friends she would have to leave, although when she did all of us were devastated. Luckily, she didn't move far.

The same agency that had found her for us sent her to work for a superwealthy, highly dysfunctional family in New York City who paid her an obscene amount of money to make sure they never had to spend any time with their two young children. We, of course, loved to hear the gossip about her nutty employer, and smugly congratulated ourselves for bringing our children up "properly"—unlike some! We even believed her when she swore that she was doing it only for the money, and until she had saved up enough to buy a house of her own.

Two years later she's almost there, but has moved to superwealthy dysfunctional family number two in England—sadly, no more juicy gossip, as she has signed a confidentiality agreement. What's the fun in that!? When we do talk or write she promises to tell all just as soon as she's finished working for them and paid off all the loans on a tiny little house close to her parents. I can't wait.

peggy, angelika, nora, and agnes: parade of ingenues

IN THE MEANTIME WE are onto au pair number four. Missing Asia, I started my own business importing pearls from China and designing jewelry that I sell to other "unemployed" women like me, in-between various writing and research projects. My husband was mortified when I explained that I basically follow the Tupperware-party model, made popular by housewives in the 1950s. His col-leagues' wives and my friends and neighbors are clearly not plagued by the same reservations, as they come to my sales and load up on pearls while we gossip.

For months I avoided telling my sisters and my mother what I had been doing, in addition of course to managing my family and all the other boring paperwork and bill paying. In truth I'm loath to admit where my fantastic education, fluency in three languages, and impres-sive résumé has taken me. Still, I seem to have a talent for this kind of thing, and the jewelry is a great success. Needless to say, once again all the money I make goes toward Abela and the au pair—still, this much, at least, I manage to pay for, as well as freeing up the time to write.

The first au pair was Peggy from Dresden. Plump, stoic, and awk-ward at first, she was twenty-three years old and didn't want to spend the rest of her life wasting away in the insurance agency where she'd worked since she was eighteen. The first two months were horrible. I compared her, unfairly, to Valery with every silly mistake she made, and she thought I was imperious, cold, and impossible to please. But somehow we persevered (must be the German in both of us), and I realized that no one could ever match up to Valery. Peggy found her groove with the children, made friends in the neigborhood, and be-came a model of the positive au-pair experience.

Considering that of the thirty-eight girls with whom she arrived more than half went home or changed families not long after they ar-rived, this was quite an achievement on both our parts. For me it was the realization that having an au pair involved learning a whole new vocabulary, and playing a role that I really wasn't prepared for or par-ticularly thrilled with. The "host mothers," as we are called, are often just that—hosts to a bewildered, parasitic, utterly dependent, foreign, and generally homesick teenager whom we have to feed, teach English, and explain American customs.

The au pair agencies' rosy promise of competent, pretty European girls bringing the flair of their own culture into our homes while taking wonderful care of our children rarely translates. The only thing that saved Peggy and me was that I was able to dig deep into the German part of my brain and find ways to understand and put into context her off-putting Teutonic behavior. Trying to put myself in her shoes, I realized that had the culture shock been reversed I would have fled this brave new world and returned to the familiarity of small-town East Germany in less than a day. Then, of course, there was the old "can't upset the applecart" problem, the children who were still missing Valery, and me determined to make it work rather than go through the whole painful process of looking again.

Not so very different from the amahs in Hong Kong, au pairs come to the States under the auspices of a U.S. government program of "cultural exchange." For many this turns into nightmarish situations with truly exploitative families or alternatively, it becomes a way for them to enter the country legally and simply stay. Officially considered a "visiting student," should an au pair violate the terms of her visa and overstay by even a short period of time, there is a good chance that she will never be allowed into this country again.

The agency rule book states that they must be paid just under $140 per week, usually cash in hand, plus be given their own room, food, etc., and fairly rudimentary health insurance. In total we pay approximately $250 per week, including the agency fees, and in return get forty-five hours a week of child care, plus a little "light housekeeping." Thanks to Abela's regular visits this isn't much of an issue between us. However, as any live-in child-care worker knows, the definition of "light housekeeping" is just about the most elastic and problematic term in the lexicon of domestic work. It is rarely light, and once you

start on the slippery slope of cleaning up after the children, it becomes harder and harder to know where to draw the line.

The cruel joke about au pairs is, of course, that by the time they
really know how to do their job it's time for them to leave—courtesy
of a twelve-month limit on their J-1 visas imposed by the U.S. government. Contrary to all expectations, this limit was recently extended to
twenty-four months, but the change came too late for Peggy and her
successor, Angelika, or Gella for short.

Gella had just turned twenty when she arrived on our doorstep in
the middle of winter, wearing a tiny T-shirt and a confused, deer-in-
the-headlights look on her face. Gella had grown up on a farm in a
middle-of-nowhere village in Germany, and wanted to avoid the fate
of many of her friends and contemporaries: small-town life, unemployment, boredom, alcohol, and drugs (and that's just the parents). A
classic case of "if only I could be anywhere but here for a year . . . ,"
she spent her entire first month being miserable, pining for home
and eating pints of chocolate-chunk Häagen Dazs in front of the
tiny TV in her tiny room. But, like Peggy, with the combination of
my mothering and other au pairs coaxing her out of her shell, she
grew up at least five years in ten short months. Also like Peggy, she
was lovely with the children, though more like an older sister than a
responsible adult. By the time her year was up and she had to go
home, she would have given anything to be able to stay with us, her
"other family." But leave she must, and after a week of tearful good-
byes I wearily prepared myself and the children for the arrival of the
next ingenue, Nora from Warsaw.

While the annual changeover does get easier, no one ever looks
forward to this time, another month of constant explanations of
everything, of speaking slowly, of trying to sense what is required to
make the new girl feel less awkward and to lessen the tremendous
wallop of the East/West or North/South culture shock. That I should

be the one to explain the "meaning of life in America" seems a cruel joke at best, but I have gotten surprisingly good at it. I have even developed a tour of our town, and a script of sorts: I point out strip malls and explain the mechanics of car pooling and the meaning of Halloween, the Super Bowl, and Thanksgiving, what's a PTA, an SUV, the YMCA, and UJC, and manage to draw a rudimentary diagram of a baseball diamond, complete with pitcher's mound. Unfortunately, the rules of American football are still a mystery to me, but so far no one seems to mind.

As I go over the bedtime routine for each child, the silly names for their blankies, and which cartoon character denotes whose toothbrush or lunchbox, it's hard not to be struck by the randomness and occasional absurdity of the routines we take for granted. But these are the rules that enable my family to run along the tracks of our lives, and so they must be learned, over and over again.

With Nora we hit the au pair jackpot. She was funny, self-confident, independent, a good driver, and a quick study. I could share a glass of wine with her at the end of a long day, but also knew that she would drink responsibly, and that she had a large and supportive circle of friends with whom she went off to have exactly the sort of adventures that au pairs are supposed to have: getting on a Greyhound bus to visit Niagara Falls; heading to D.C. and Boston for a weekend; and sharing a seedy motel room in Miami so that she and her best friend could spend a week on an American beach. For ten months we cruised—I took on more and more work, the children were happy at school, the days were long, busy, and complicated. I smugly brushed off the dreadful thought of her leaving with the knowledge that she was clearly so happy with us she couldn't possibly refuse the offer of staying a second year—an opportunity, after all, that Gella would have given her eyeteeth for.

Day one, month eleven, we sit down to have "the talk." The au pair agency had been pressing me for an answer as to whether or not we had "matched" with another girl to replace Nora, and I happily continued to put them off until the very last moment, confident she would accept my irresistible and very generous offer: basically, same everything, except for an extra hundred bucks a week. My little business was doing well; I could afford it. She said no.

Turns out there had been a worm in the apple for a while. As is so often the case, the prospect of money, a *lot* more money, made Nora greedy and me stupid. A friend in D.C. had found her a job with the family next door—two kids (not four, for heaven's sakes); no weekends; room and board; a car and cell phone; all for $475 a week cash in hand. So thanks for the ride, but she'd be leaving in three weeks. I was furious, though mostly at myself for being so dumb, and Nora's last month was spent in a desperate search of the au pair agency's Web site and many late-night phone calls to various Eastern European countries for someone to replace her. Agnes from Romania looked like she had a lovely smile, a fondness for folk dancing, years of experience babysitting younger cousins and neighbors, and a burning desire to come to Ahmayrika to improve her Eenglieesh. I was charmed by her accent (beeg meestake), studied her photograph for hours on end as though it might come to life and talk to me, and finally we took the plunge and made a match.

We were all getting better at this, but there's no denying that the story was getting old. When Agnes arrived it was a disaster right from the get-go. Like a fish out of water, she could not stop crying for "mai cawntree" and I found myself mysteriously devoid of any sympathy whatsoever. The trouble was, Agnes had a hero complex. Used to being adored (her parents and boyfriend called every day, sometimes twice, and everybody wept), she was confused and deeply hurt when all I could muster in response to her tragic Slavic suffering was irritation and impatience. But she tried so hard! She did everything I required! But she asked ten times, every time, whether everything she did was to my complete satisfaction! But it was so hard for her, so terribly hard to be away from her cawntree! Everyone in my family thought I was acting like a total witch, except for daughter number two, who agreed with me that Agnes was just about the single most annoying person she had ever met in the entire eleven years of her whole entire life.

Longing for Valery I headed to the library, looking for support, humor, distraction, advice, anything at all—and found none. Instead I realized, for the umpteenth time, that to find an American nanny—or even just someone with a green card—to do the same work for the same amount of money would be akin to discovering the holy grail. In the same week that Agnes crashed our car (backward, into a large tree—she was so deeply ashamed and afraid of bringing disgrace to her family, I ended up apologizing to her), I realized I had two options: Either Agnes had to go, or I had to pull myself together and turn all this into a book.

Agnes stayed.

However wonderful or strained my relationship with any nanny or au pair of mine has ever been, this much I know of myself: I expect her to do her job in a certain way, though I also expect her to look at it as more than a job. I expect standards of her which I am not always willing to enforce myself, and I can do this because I am the mother, and she is not. Show me one mother who has never been guilty of this double standard, and I'll eat my daughter's blankie. And show me another mother who has never obsessed about her relationship with her nanny, au pair, or sitter, or felt used, guilty, resigned, intimidated, furious, jealous, betrayed, or deeply grateful, sometimes all at once, and I will eat this book. If you find her and introduce her to me, I will agree never to hire another woman to look after my children for as long as they all live under our roof. In the meantime, I think I had better start looking for au pair number five.

Jessika Auerbach was born in Germany, but grew up primarily in England. She studied at the Fondation Nationale des Sciences Politiques and the Sorbonne in Paris and at Oxford University, and since that time has lived and worked as an editor and writer in New York, Connecticut, the Netherlands, and Hong Kong. Her four daughters were born on three different continents, and she and her husband remain happily in touch with almost all of the nineteen nannies, au pairs, and part-time babysitters who have provided them with child care over the years. She currently lives with her family in Singapore, where she is working on her next book.